THE SOHO DON

THE SOHO DON

GANGLAND'S GREATEST UNTOLD STORY

MICHAEL CONNOR

MAINSTREAM
PUBLISHING

EDINBURGH AND LONDON

First published in Great Britain in 2002 by
MAINSTREAM PUBLISHING COMPANY (EDINBURGH) LTD
7 Albany Street
Edinburgh EH1 3UG

ISBN 1 84018 781 6

This edition, 2003
Reprinted, 2004

A catalogue record for this book is available from the British Library

Typeset in Trixie and Van Dijck
Printed and bound in Great Britain by
Antony Rowe Ltd, Chippenham, Wiltshire

To Paula,
for all her help, encouragement and enthusiasm in what
proved to be a major project
and to
Laurence

Was there ever a Soho don? . . .

The hardmen of the London manors and Soho did have their don. Billy Howard had the respect and obedience of the underworld. Importantly he had an in with the police. He settled grievances and had a hand in everything. He even leaned on the Krays for a percentage of their club earnings . . .

His story is the great untold story of the underworld.

Elephant Boys by Brian McDonald
Mainstream Publishing

CONTENTS

PREFACE

Without Fear or Favour

Research into the story of the life of Billy Howard began in the 1970s, when I became interested in the shooting of Alfredo 'Italian Tony' Zomparelli at the Golden Goose Amusement Arcade, in London's Soho.

Michael Howard had not seen his father for many years and towards the end of Billy Howard's life, Michael and Bill shared a flat on the seafront of the south coast seaside town of Margate. During that period they would sit in a corner of The Cottage public house, a favourite haunt, and in beach deckchairs, during which time Bill talked at great length, and with candour, about his life as a villain at the top of the criminal underworld.

For many years, it has been difficult to pull together the complex strings of Billy Howard's existence. Many people have now died, leaving the way clear to disclose facts that, during their lifetimes, would have been inappropriate. But it would be wrong to say this book has been written with the good wishes of both the criminal world and the celebrities on whose lives Billy Howard had a commanding effect. Many seem to feel some things remain best unsaid. Phone calls have been made and subsequently doors have been firmly closed.

Despite this, the book has been written with many of the day-to-day events recreated, conversations reconstructed and events played out. Information has been obtained, cross-referenced and, where possible, verified by one of the people present at the time.

The conversations between Michael Howard and his father have had a strong bearing on the book. Of the early years, Michael's mother, Vera, was able to provide a great deal of background, and Bill's wife, Jan, was a source of information for the middle years. Billy Howard tried to avoid publicity. Unlike the Krays he considered it bad for business, so press cuttings have been of use, albeit to a lesser extent. However, it should always be remembered that people involved in crime, be they villains or a corrupt police force, seek to bury the truth, while other members of the criminal scene seek to paint the picture with their own colours to enhance their egos or to dispel their own failings.

In *The Soho Don* I have sought to show the truth without fear or favour, both the highs and the lows. That is my right. I expect there to be many dissenters.

CHAPTER ONE

Find Billy Howard

'That's the old cow, down there,' the man sitting in the front seat growled, partly to the driver and partly to the two men sitting behind him. He pointed with a hand-rolled cigarette at the moving image of a middle-aged woman, walking in and out of pools of light some 20 yards ahead, the fur collar of an astrakhan coat pulled up around her face. ''ave her legs off,' he added at almost the same time as sniffing snot back up his nostrils and coughing.

'Drive down and round the corner,' a voice from the back mumbled, also coughing on the cigarette smoke that filled the car, windows closed to retain warmth.

The black car cruised past the woman and some 50 yards further on turned the corner. Deep shadow covered the pavement. The driver brought the vehicle quietly to a halt and the four dark-suited men got out. Their scarred faces and broken features gave their smart, expensively suited appearance an incongruent air. Menacing. It was cold, colder than it had been in London. The driver would have preferred to have remained in the car, mounted the pavement and done her legs, as the front-seat passenger had suggested, but they had been told to scare her, put the shits up her. No more.

As Elizabeth Lawrence drew level, one of the men pulled her around the corner by her shoulder and pushed her, almost casually, into the arms of one of the others. The smell of cheap perfume and body odour caught his nostrils. Gently he pushed her back again, glad to have the salt air return. They were playing with her. The four men formed a circle. She was piggy in the middle.

'What d'ya want?' she asked in a faltering voice, sweat having broken out on her face despite the chill wind.

'We're Billy Howard's boys, see. And we've got a message for ya,' one of them answered, in a clearly menacing tone.

It was nearing midnight on this wintry November night and the streets were empty and damp. The sound of her heels echoed around the buildings. All the windows were in darkness, except for a few on the upper floors of the townhouses towards the top of the street. It seemed unlikely that any sound would attract attention. The men felt safe. The woman did not.

'I don't know Billy Howard,' she told them, the tone of her voice pleading the case that they had stopped the wrong person.

'I know, love, but he knows you,' another of the group said, giving her a shove, only this time harder.

'He told us to tell you not ta say anything against his friends in court,' one of them told her, speaking slowly. His voice trembled, but not from any fear. The icy chill had penetrated his thin jacket and his shirt provided no protection.

The driver took a razor from his pocket, opened it and put the cold flat side of the stainless-steel blade against her wet cheek. It flashed in the light. When pressed, it cut into the skin formed by layers of cheap make-up. Harder, it would have sliced flesh. 'You'd better do as 'e says, 'cause if ya don't Billy Howard's going to come down 'ere himself and he'll cut ya tongue out and chop you up.'

One of them chuckled and pushed her again across the circle. This time nobody caught her. She fell against the wall and stumbled, her foot twisting off her tall-heeled shoe. The four men walked back over to the car, got in and, appreciating the shelter, drove off.

It was this incident Gerald Howard QC reported to the court the following day.

* * *

Counsel for the prosecution, Mr Gerald Howard QC, part of the four-strong team headed by the Solicitor General, Sir Harry Hylton-Forster QC, rose and gravely addressed the Bench. The shuffling of chairs and the whispered background chat stopped. His demeanour, the solemn set of his face and slow deliberation of his voice immediately captured the attention of his audience. For the next few moments he knew he held the entire court within his power. It was an advantage he intended to play to the hilt. The Bench, the defence and the public waited and weighed each word. A high priest addressing the minions, the tone of his statement could have made innocent men tremble.

'Last night a woman witness for the prosecution in this case, Mrs Elizabeth Lawrence, who has not yet been called, was threatened by persons who said they were Billy Howard's boys.' He stopped, glanced around him, allowing the drama to build. 'They said that she would be cut up with a razor if she gave evidence.' There was an audible silence from the public gallery, preceded by a collective intake of breath. He waited, held the moment and then continued. 'It is right that I should make it plain that there is no evidence to connect any of the accused with this. But you may think it right and proper to warn Billy Howard's boys not to interfere with witnesses.'

This dramatic intervention, made towards the end of the third day of the Brighton Police Conspiracy Hearing, brought proceedings to an abrupt halt. Gerald Howard had timed his statement well. It left the magistrates with a powerful image before retiring that day. An image that could only cast the defendants in a bad light, regardless of the caveat with which he had ended his statement.

Had anyone been close enough to the dock to scrutinise the faces of the defendants, it might just have been possible to detect the merest hint of a smile on two of their faces, but before a second glance could have been focused to confirm the fact, it would have been too late. The sternness had returned and each bowed their head and began scribbling notes in the books they carried with them. Notes they would want to discuss with their solicitors. Lies, unfair submissions, possible grounds for appeals if eventually things went badly.

The importance of the case was clearly established by the presence of the Solicitor General who, apart from being a barrister in his own right, was normally both a Member of Parliament and a member of the Government. His main duties ordinarily would be to assist the Attorney General, the principal legal adviser to the Crown (the Government), who was often required to give legal advice to the House of Commons involving complex constitutional and international points of law; an office generally bound up in legal affairs of State. It was rare for any member of this office to be sent to a provincial court to lead a Crown prosecution in a committal hearing.

Mr Howard Vokins, Chairman of the Bench, immediately directed that detectives from Scotland Yard's Flying Squad be ordered to find the mystery men who had threatened Mrs Lawrence and the man who had given them their orders. The direction from the bench echoed out.

'Find Billy Howard.'

★ ★ ★

Music weaved gently through the smoky atmosphere, cigar and roll-up smoke mingling agreeably side by side. The pianist's fingers allowed the notes of Cole Porter's 'Night and Day' to linger above the background industry of a West End club. Chairs fidgeted. Champagne corks popped. Service doors swung and boofed. Glamorous hostesses seated at the other end of the club chatted in whispers or giggles, bubbling or bored. Their table guests were an assortment of dark-suited, well-heeled City gents seeking excitement and illicit pleasure before returning to Park Lane hotels or leafy Surrey suburbs, and home. This was Billy Howard's world, one of the places where he felt comfortable and secure. In control.

It was late afternoon, but in the windowless, Moorish-designed Spanish Garden Club, tucked away in a narrow cobbled mews of London's fashionable Mayfair, day could be night and the night could be dangerous. Mayfair, then as now, was the haunt of old money and the nouveau riche. Property prices outstripped all other areas in the capital, probably the whole of the UK. Restaurants charged over the odds to maintain exclusivity and casinos fixed their stares clearly on the high-rollers. It was a world where only disposable income and celebrity status were acknowledged.

The crime reporter of the *Daily Sketch*, Michael Pilley, a seasoned campaigner in the routine of the capital's underworld, sat opposite Billy Howard, the man often referred to as 'The Laughing Boy of the London Nightclubs'. Pencil in hand, the *Sketch* reporter wrote down the flippant replies to the questions everyone wanted answered. The copy would make tomorrow's front pages and that would be good for Pilley, but he knew Billy Howard of old. The truth behind the Brighton Police Conspiracy Hearing would not be found in the columns of any of the nationals. Would probably not be found at all. But press interest was not in the truth – it had little concern for right and wrong – the overriding factor was good copy. Good copy filed before deadline, of course.

'You didn't send your boys to threaten Mrs Betty Lawrence at midnight, two nights ago, down in Brighton, and have them tell her that she would be sliced up if she gave evidence?'

Howard sipped his triple gin and tonic, studied the slice of lemon and the fizz of the clear liquid, then, after a moment of glancing up to the heavens, or perhaps it was the crystal chandeliers that threw light on the club but not much else, looked back at Pilley.

'I don't have any boys,' Howard said in a serious tone, barely camouflaging the faint smile on his lips.

The reporter switched his gaze from Howard to the group of burly men hanging around the bar a few feet away from where they were sitting.

'Well, apart from those boys,' Howard added, having caught Pilley's drift. He allowed his grin to break through as he circled his free arm in the direction of the group.

Pilley laboured on, between gulps of his second drink. He would probably be offered a third, he thought, if he was lucky or didn't probe too deep. It was about boundaries – always knowing them and not stepping outside.

'So you're not the "West End Chopper Man" whom detectives are keeping a special watch for on the roads into Brighton and at the railway stations? And you're not the Billy Howard that The Sweeney have been told to scour Soho and Mayfair for?'

Howard paused, appearing to give full consideration to the question.

'I think it's a bleeding liberty,' Ed, a small, thin-faced man in his early 40s, chimed in from the edge of the group at the bar. Pulling a roll of notes from his trouser pocket, he added, 'There's a pony.' He repeated the phrase on several occasions over the next 20 minutes, each time flashing the bundle of cash.

Another of Billy Howard's boys, Bugsie, dressed in pressed trousers and a white open-necked shirt, seemed not to want to be outdone in his support.

'I've only got three months to live but I'll say this before I go, Billy's a gentleman.'

Billy Howard's bodyguard, a dark-haired, thick-set man wearing glasses, picked up a paper from the bar and slapped it loudly with the back of his hand. 'It's diabolical what they're saying about him. Billy's a great man. He'd help anyone. If you said you didn't have enough to eat in the house, he'd plonk a tenner on your plate.'

Ed, determined to have the last word, added, 'He's the Guv'nor. He's tough, but he's got a heart of gold.'

The accolades were interrupted by Michael Brown, another crime reporter, entering the club. Seeing the group at the bar and recognising both Howard and Pilley, he walked over. Howard, standing slightly less than six foot tall in his heeled black suede shoes, got up, brushed the creases out of his grey checked jacket and grey flannel trousers with an automatic action, and laughed loudly at the sharks beginning to circle. Brown readily accepted the offer of a drink and showed Howard a copy of the early edition of the evening paper. He had hoped to find Howard alone, without other members of the press being present. Pilley was equally disappointed. Quotes obtained now would be shared. The front page linked Howard's name with the Brighton Case. It accused him of attempting to pervert the course of justice by using the threat of violence, namely a slash from an open razor, against witnesses who had said they were prepared to give evidence.

'I'm a peaceful man. I didn't threaten anyone. I live for my wife and children. No one from Scotland Yard has been to see me. They know where I am. My conscience is clear.' Billy Howard replied to Pilley's previous and yet unanswered questions. He spoke in the form of a statement, with a string of defensive sentences, enunciated clearly and with apparent sincerity.

Earlier, a statement from CID had confirmed that they knew Billy Howard, a 40-year-old man who was an infamous figure in London's West End. They added that raids had already been made on the homes of several notorious violent criminals thought to be members of the gang that accosted Mrs Lawrence on her late-night walk home. They also made it known that another female witness, the mother of two young children, had been threatened by the same gang a few nights earlier. The spokesman also confirmed that all the homes of witnesses in the 'Brighton Case' were being guarded as a further precaution.

Both Pilley and Brown were aware of the CID statement and it was equally clear to them that neither Billy Howard nor any of his boys were among those whose homes had been raided. It was no secret as to Howard's whereabouts. The reporters, their editors and half of London's nightclub and casino management would have been able to supply the police with the necessary information, without feeling they had given away a confidence or grassed anyone up. Members of the force were also not uncommon faces at the Spanish Garden Club, sometimes looking in with the hope of picking up a bit of gossip, but usually more interested in wetting their whistle at someone else's expense. The two reporters knew the lack of police activity around Howard, in itself, brought into question the integrity of those at Scotland Yard directing the investigation. When the Chairman of the Bench at the Brighton Hearing, a case warranting the presence of one of the most senior members of the Bar, instructs the police to arrest Billy Howard, and he is allowed to go openly about his business with apparent immunity, the question must be asked. Why? They also knew it was a question neither of their editors was prepared to ask in a wider forum. Crime desks, if they are to have any hope of operating efficiently, of obtaining scoops, being in at the kill, need the trust and favour of both the police and the criminal fraternity. They need the ability to mix freely in both circles – circles that often seemed indistinguishable from each other.

'I know nothing about this business, this woman my boys are supposed to have threatened. It's all tripe. I don't know anybody down there. I'm not interested in the case. Ask the boys, they'll tell you.'

'The Guv'nor hasn't been in Brighton for months. There's a pony,' Eddie spoke up, again taking the £25 from his pocket.

Laughing, Howard declared, 'Not for at least a month have I been in Brighton.' It was spoken with a touch of theatre.

Another of his boys went behind the bar and poured a round of drinks without ringing the cost on the till. Howard took his fresh triple gin and tonic and placed it on the table. Nobody was drinking singles.

'I've got a newspaper pitch at the Kennington Oval, £15 a week and hard work at that.' Howard looked steely-eyed across at Brown. Momentarily he dropped his grin, then continued, 'I know nothing. See? I don't want to know anything. And I'm honest. So just be careful what you say.'

Deep down Howard knew that some publicity was good, it allowed the press to do his work for him. To keep him in business. It reduced the need for actual violence. If people were told they should be afraid, they would be afraid. However, if the press coverage was directed too strongly at his illegal activities or headlined for too long, all the insurance provided by corrupt officials would not prevent the establishment coming after him.

Everyone present knew the newspaper pitch to which Billy Howard was referring. It stood on a windswept corner, sheltered from the rain by a tiled entrance awning, just outside the Oval Underground Station in south London, a short walk from the world-famous cricket ground. Although £15 was well above the average weekly wage at that time, it would stretch the imagination that this pitch or that amount of money a week could come close to supporting triple gins and tonics, even occasionally, in a Mayfair club, particularly for a working man with a wife and four children to support.

The next morning Billy Howard and Michael Pilley, as predicted, made the headlines. Solicitors acting for Howard wasted no time in speaking to the editor and the following day the *Daily Sketch* carried this retraction:

THE SPANISH GARDEN CLUB

It has been suggested to us that a statement in yesterday's *Daily Sketch* has been read as meaning that the Spanish Garden Club, Mayfair, is owned by Billy Howard to whom reference was made in proceedings at Brighton. Mr Howard is not the proprietor of the club, although he is a member of it.

The lease on the property and the licence were held by Peggy, a girlfriend of Howard's. There was nothing on paper that could connect Howard to the club. By 1957, at the age of 40, Howard had a string of convictions gained during his teenage years that had resulted in spells in borstal and a number of convictions for illegal gambling which, although not custodial, would have prevented his holding a liquor licence. Any acknowledgement that Howard had financial or operational control of the Spanish Garden Club could have caused the closure of this lucrative business, which was not only a source of ready money but also provided contacts amongst the hostesses' clientele, many of whom were in positions capable of being exploited. The use of other people, especially girlfriends, to front businesses was a situation Howard had favoured in the past and was to be repeated on numerous occasions over the following years.

Soho now entertains members of the media, the theatre, the gay community, and that has changed little over the years. Like all places it has had its trends and periods of depression. During the 1990s, it saw a particular surge in fashionable coffee shops, gourmet restaurants and lively bars, with the odd porn shop maintaining a presence. During the 1970s, a profusion of seedy sex shops had dominated, having ousted many of the celebrity-led clubs, restaurants and epicurean shops of the 1950s and '60s. That is not to say one style of trading completely wiped out the other at any time. No. They have always traded side by side, but on occasions Soho has evoked particular images with the general public, images that have been equated with the dominating influences at that particular time.

Recently Brighton has been referred to as the new Soho – Soho by the Sea. This is probably the case, but it should not be considered a recent phenomenon. Brighton and Soho have, for the best part of a century, enjoyed an affinity. Nobody would be surprised when wandering through the quaint and cobbled Brighton lanes if they bumped into someone they had stopped to chat with in Soho's Wardour Street, a few days earlier. There were also the close criminal links.

* * *

November 1957 brought ten years of major police corruption in the popular British seaside resort into public focus. It did not bring it to an end. Dubbed by some newspapers 'The Brighton Case' and others 'The Brighton Affair', the hearing took place before the Chairman of the Bench, Mr Howard Vokins, at Brighton Town Hall. The charges read out echoed around the high ceilings; the tone, the sound and the language galvanised everyone's attention and left them in no doubt where everyone stood. Those charged were the 57-year-old Chief Constable of Brighton, Charles Field William Ridge, of Bavant Road, Brighton; Detective Inspector John Richard Hammersley, aged 39, second-in-command of Brighton CID, of Glenrise, Withdean; Detective Sergeant Trevor Ernest Heath, aged 36, of Bramble Rise, Withdean; Anthony John Lyons, aged 62, a licensee, of Marine Gate, Black Rock, Brighton; and Samuel Bellson, aged 42, a commission agent, of The Drive, Hove.

The charges the defendants had been brought before the court to answer were that the police officers did, between 1 January 1948 and 18 October 1957, conspire together and with other persons unknown, corruptly to solicit and obtain rewards for showing or promising favours contrary to their duty and to defeat the course of public justice. The other defendants' charges related to bribery and attempting to obtain favours in relation to affairs of the Crown. All were serious charges that went to the heart of the justice system: providing immunity for villains in their criminal activities and large amounts of illegal cash paid directly into the pockets of corrupt police officers. A cancer.

The charges were brought following a three-month investigation by a team of detectives, headed by Detective Superintendent Ian Forbes-Leith, of Scotland Yard. The investigation began after a known felon walked into Scotland Yard and made a complaint against the Brighton police officers now standing in the dock. All three were named in the original complaint. The investigating squad failed to bring any other police officers before the court. The inference was that Brighton police corruption was wholly restricted to those in the dock, and that no other officers were actively involved in corrupt practices or were beneficiaries of the illegal funds.

On Monday, 25 November 1957, the hearing began. It was a freezing day with a chill wind blowing off a rough grey sea. The pebble beach was pounded by thundering waves and there was heavy spray soaking the deserted promenade. From 7 a.m., cold, wet, determined people queued around the block outside Brighton Town Hall, waiting to be admitted to the public gallery. The queue comprised many local people simply wishing to see the defendants, to hear at first hand the stories of corruption that had been circulating the town since the arrest of the town's senior police officer. Others were shadowy figures with a personal interest, having previously fallen foul of the blackmail, extortion and threats that were alleged by the Crown to be part of the daily routine of those accused.

Towards the middle of the long line, a woman with a cold, pinched face, seeking protection behind the fashionable fur collar of her long camel coat, stood alone. Sent each day, she joined the queue to listen and observe. Those who were not members of the press may well have taken her for a reporter and in many respects that is exactly what she was. But none of the information she noted down would be used to fill column inches. She was there to note which witnesses would take the sensible course when taking the stand; to observe who would step back from the statements they had earlier made to the Scotland Yard detectives in return for immunity from prosecution, as they admitted their own involvement in the web of deception alleged to have been weaved by the accused. She was there to report back.

Four hours after the queue had first started to form, Sir Harry Hylton-Foster, who had been collected from the railway station at 10 a.m. in a chauffeur-driven car, opened for the prosecution with a bold warning. 'People in a conspiracy trial are often people who break the law to prevent the impact of justice. Much of the evidence the Crown will be calling upon will come from people generally described as shady sources, not from the best people. Generally speaking they are people of a criminal past. People who are in a conspiracy are those who do not want publicity. They may wish to arrange that police action be prevented and that they should be tipped off – that is the phrase I think – if police action is contemplated. Therefore, it would be unwise, I submit, for anyone to form any conclusion about this case until the matter has been fully tried out before a jury. I expect to be calling more than 60 witnesses and the case will probably last for some 14 days.'

It was not until 10.40 a.m. that the 50 people waiting to gain entry to the public gallery had been admitted. Others had stood around the foyer of the Town Hall, eager to see the accused arrive to answer their bail. Commander George Hatherill, Deputy Head of London CID, who had been responsible for the London end of the investigation, slipped virtually unnoticed into the court. Chief Constable Ridge, the most senior of the accused and now suspended on two-thirds pay, mingled with members of the press congregated on the front steps. They chatted and shook hands congenially. Ridge was a confident man, confident in his position and confident in his manner. And this was his manor. He controlled it, he had been promoted through the ranks and he knew everyone. Power sat easily on his shoulders. He did not display the demeanour of a man possibly about to face a long prison sentence.

On the first day of the hearing, much of the early part was taken up with the usual formalities and legal submissions. Evidence was then introduced against Detective Inspector John Hammersley who was accused of using police intelligence to help a man by the name of Barnard, a private detective who had been a member of the local police force. In August 1953, Barnard experienced difficulty in locating the whereabouts of Samuel Bellson, also in the dock, so that a civil writ could be served on him. Barnard approached Detective Sergeant Trevor Heath who successfully assisted Barnard in his search.

Bellson was a known villain. Born in London's East End, he had served a prison sentence during the Second World War and, shortly after it had ended, moved to Brighton where, with the backing of Jack 'Spot' Comer, a powerful East End gangster, he built up an impressive chain of gaming clubs and nightclubs. Soon after, Hammersley approached Barnard and told him that he would have to pay for the service he had received from Heath and that it was a service that could be made available in the future on a similar financial basis.

The following day, the court heard the catalogue of offences alleged to have been committed by those in the dock over a ten-year period.

Alan Bennett, witness for the prosecution, a tall man of military stance, sported a handlebar moustache and spoke out with an upper-class accent. He remained in the box for more than three hours, during which time he gave evidence against Heath, whom he said had blackmailed him on the instruction of Chief Constable Charles Ridge.

On the first occasion, he informed the court, £40 had changed hands. Asked to explain why he had paid the money, he told the court Heath had informed him that Wenche Bennett, his wife, had been arrested in the company of a known felon, Alan Walker, and that she could be in a lot of trouble. It subsequently transpired that, at the time the money was paid over, she had already been released from custody. Later, Bennett was tipped off by Heath that a man called Walker alleged £1,000 had been taken from his bedroom at the Astor Hotel in Brighton. Bennett held the lease on a drinking club located at the Astor Hotel and, although denying any connection with the theft, he alleged that, after a visit to the crime scene by a detective from Lowestoft, Heath had demanded 'his whack of the grand'. Bennett was not asked to estimate the amount of money Heath expected as his share of the stolen cash, nor was he asked to comment on the arrival of the Lowestoft detective on the scene. Bennett continued, saying that later Heath had told him he was wanted by police in Leeds. Bennett said he had told Heath that he had not been in Leeds for 20 years, so there must be some mistake. He gave Heath £20 and that was the last he had heard of the matter.

The next contact had been a few weeks later. Heath pushed Bennett into buying a ring from him, which Heath said was to assist in the purchase of a second-hand car. Heath had explained that he needed the cash from the ring as a deposit. Bennett gave him £70, which was the amount Heath had said was the value of the ring. But later he had the ring valued, Bennett told the court, at £20. The prosecution laboured each allegation in an attempt to show the persistent nature of the corrupt practices.

Next Bennett told the court that Heath stopped him in a busy street as he was about to get into his car, a Rolls Royce. Heath had said, 'You seem to be doing well, I can't say things are going so well for me.' Heath then said that Bennett was wanted for a £6,000 jewellery robbery in Bournemouth. Bennett was taken to see Hammersley, who advised him that they would handle it the same as they had handled the Leeds enquiry. On hearing this Bennett said that he screwed up some £5 notes and threw them on the floor. Hammersley had not asked for the money, but had thanked him.

Not long after that Bennett said Heath phoned him at his flat in London, and said that he was now wanted on a warrant for a screwing in Folkestone and that he should come to Brighton, but not in his own car, as the police in Bournemouth and Folkestone had his registration number. An arrangement was made to meet that evening in the Bodega, a licensed premises in Ship Street. Bennett did not keep the appointment. Instead he went to Scotland Yard, where he spoke to a detective in the Fraud Squad, Detective Sergeant Fredrick Powell, who, the prosecution informed the court, would be called as a witness on the tenth day. The day following Bennett's failure to attend the meeting at the Bodega, Heath telephoned Bennett to ask why the appointment had been broken. On being told of the visit to Scotland Yard, Heath angrily said that the cozzers at the Yard didn't always know what was going on in cases outside London.

Bosley, the solicitor for Ridge, then cross-examined Bennett. Bosley put it to Bennett that he was one of the men the Solicitor General had referred to as a person of bad character. Bennett agreed, but retorted that at least he was not a blackmailer in the way that Bosley's client was. As the questioning progressed, Bennett also agreed that he had on occasions used the names Brown, Ferguson and Poyner, but denied using Montgomery and Holt. He also admitted a string of stealing offences and to posing as an RAF pilot, but refuted having been guilty of unlawful wounding. At this point Bosley held firm, putting the question again. Bennett finally agreed that he had been to prison for six months in 1947, but that the charge of unlawful wounding had been reduced to common assault. Why had he not been open about all of these matters, Bosley enquired?

'I've paid money for years to keep my past quiet, old boy. I didn't want it all to be thrown away. Ridge is no better than me, just that he has never been caught.'

That all but completed the defence cross-examination of Bennett. Solicitors for the other defendants did put questions to Bennett, but gained little that had not already been established. Bosley's effort to discredit the witness had been seriously undermined by the prosecution's opening remarks concerning the status and past behaviour of the witnesses the court could expect to encounter.

The next witness was called. She approached the box shakily, but with a clear determination to have her say. She was the owner of the Astor Hotel, the property that housed the Astor Club and the centre of much of the illegal dealings that provided the background to the case. Dressed from head to foot in black, with a black feather adorning her pillbox hat, the white-haired, heavily built woman stepped into the witness-box and took the oath. She gave her name as Mrs Blanche Josephine Cherryman, of the Royal Hotel, Brighton, formerly the Astor Hotel. Standing before the court as a prosecution witness, she confirmed that she had personal knowledge of the club that operated in the hotel as she had on occasions worked there as an unpaid receptionist. 'It never closed before 1.30 a.m. There were always fights and trouble with women and everyone spoke of it as a bad club,' she said, with a strong note of disapproval in her voice.

At that time, most licensed premises were required by law to finish serving drinks at 10.30 p.m., or 11 p.m. at the weekend. A licensee could apply for a supper licence if a meal was being served, thereby gaining an extra hour. After further questioning she said, 'I went to the police to complain about what was going on there, but nothing happened. After some time had passed, I returned to the police station and spoke to Mr Charles Ridge. I told him I did not know who I could trust in CID.'

'What did you tell Ridge about the club?' Mr Maxwell Turner, for the prosecution, asked.

'I can't say exactly, I told him what was going on in the Astor Club, how it was being run, the late hours and the drunkenness that was going on there. I also told him that one night I received a telephone call from someone who gave his name as Charlie. He said to close the club early that night.'

'What was Ridge's reaction?'

'He said that he would look into it.'

'Did he look into it?'

'I don't know, but if he did, nothing came of it.'

Mrs Cherryman was not asked if she thought the person giving the telephone warning and using the name Charlie could actually have been Charles Ridge.

A lawyer for the defence then asked the witness if Mr Bennett owed her any money. She replied that he did and agreed with the figure put to her in the sum of £2,000. Asked if the money was outstanding rent on the club, she agreed that it was. The implication was that it was not that she disliked the club because of its bad reputation, but because she was substantially out of pocket and would have liked to have seen Bennett out of it. After a short cross-examination, which failed to make any gains on behalf of the defence, Mrs Cherryman was allowed to stand down.

Earlier, when questioning Mrs Wenche Bennett, the attractive Norwegian wife of Alan Bennett, Turner had asked her if the club was ever raided by the police during the time her husband owned it.

'No. No, never,' she replied. When cross-examined by Bosley, for Ridge, she agreed that she had seen criminals using the club, but that she did not know the place was often referred to as 'The Bucket of Blood', because of the amount of blood spilled in fights on the premises. Wenche Bennett had then been allowed to stand down.

After stating her name as Mrs Mary Mason, and giving her address as

Montpellier Road, Brighton, the ninth witness was questioned by Gerald Howard on behalf of the Crown.

'After the Astor Club closed down, you reopened it in January 1956,' he said. 'Is that correct?'

Having confirmed this to be the case, the Chairman of the Bench allowed the witness to sit to give the rest of her evidence. She went on to say that she understood the previous owner had given money to the police and it was a practice that Tony Lyons, the licensee of Sherry's Bar on Brighton's seafront, thought she should continue. The previous owner had also given Lyons £20 a week to bring in customers and to spend in the club.

'Did you ever pay money to the police?'

'No. I didn't pay any money to anybody. Never.'

'Were you ever raided by the police?'

'Yes. In August of this year,' Mrs Mason replied. The inference was, as previous witnesses had testified, that money was habitually given to the police via at least one of the police defendants and that this had allowed the club to trade after hours. When the practice ceased, the club was raided, even when it was not trading outside the legal licensing hours.

As the case continued the number of spectators grew and the revelations were the talk of the public bars of Brighton and behind the discreet net-curtains of suburban Hove. There was only one other topic of conversation. Teddy Boy gangs, some 30-strong, were roaming Brighton and Hove coffee bars. Their pleasure was violence and brutality. Two coffee bars received particular attention during the weeks of the hearing, The Espresso Lounge in North Street, Brighton, and The Hideaway in Hove, where chairs were thrown through plate-glass windows, tables were overturned and crockery smashed. The owner of one coffee bar retired and employed a manager, whilst another employed a bodyguard. But it was the trial that had really caught the town's attention.

* * *

As the days progressed, the tenth witness, Mr Harry Waterman, of London, gave evidence. When asked for his address and telephone number he mumbled something, then being asked to speak up, he requested that he be allowed to write them down as he did not want them to be reported in the press for fear of receiving threats. A piece of paper was provided and the details, written in a shaky hand, were passed to the Bench. This was not the first time in the case that witnesses had requested this facility, and the longer the case continued, the more nervous the witnesses appeared.

Waterman confirmed the details in his written statement, but with little conviction, specifying that he had come to Brighton to work in the Astor Club, as he was a friend of Bennett, the owner. Although at that time, he said,

Bennett was regularly using the name Brown. On one instance he had seen Bennett put cash into a rolled up newspaper. He then accompanied Bennett to Sherry's Bar, where Bennett gave the paper to a man. Asked if he knew the man in question, he replied that he did not, but was able to identify him as the man in the dock. He pointed directly at Charles Ridge. Heads turned to follow the direction of the outstretched arm. Ridge stayed steady, staring directly back at his accuser without the slightest sign of emotion. As attention returned to the witness-box, Ridge lowered his head and wrote a short note in his ledger. On another occasion, Waterman said, Bennett put a wad of notes into an envelope and later handed the envelope to Heath. Solicitors for Ridge and Heath both denied their clients had received money in the manner suggested by Waterman and put it to him that he was lying. He restated the event previously outlined and shortly after finished giving his evidence.

* * *

On the fourth day, Thursday, 28 November, a woman serving 15 months in prison for procuring an abortion was brought to the court to give evidence. Sobbing and sipping from a glass of water, Mrs Alice Brabiner said, in a quiet voice, that over a period of time she had given Detective Sergeant Heath £68, in the hope of obtaining a lighter sentence. She said that she had done this because he had told her she could get a sentence as high as 14 years for what she had done. Having been requested to speak up, she placed her hands on the edge of the box and gripped, her knuckles white as she described how she had been to a flat in Vernon Terrace, Brighton, where she had performed an abortion on a young girl, using a syringe. Later Heath had told her to hand over the syringe. She did not know why he had asked for it, but she had given it to him. She was asked if she thought he was offering to destroy the evidence. She replied that she did not know.

Abortion was illegal in the UK at this time; terminations carried out by the National Health Service, or at private clinics, were against the law. Money could procure the services of a qualified medical practitioner prepared to carry out the operation in clean, sterile surroundings. It was expensive, and doctors prepared to work in this area risked being struck off and facing a lengthy prison sentence. Or there were the back-street abortionists. Men and women, with no medical experience and less compassion, for a few pounds would carry out the service in squalid surroundings, in dingy flats, on what was in effect the kitchen table. No sterile instruments, no antiseptic and no after care, usually just a great deal of fear and pain. Finished, the scared, sobbing young woman would immediately be escorted onto the pavement and told to keep her mouth shut. No one wanted to be caught with a patient on the premises. Severe bleeding and infection often required immediate hospitalisation. Questioning by the police would then be inevitable, and girls regularly died from loss of blood or blood poisoning.

The following day, Ernest Waite, a greengrocer and butcher, gave his evidence. 'I was the golliwog,' he told the court. Standing in the witness-box, looking little like a greengrocer, the thickset, dark-haired man sported a bright blue waistcoat and a red bow-tie and answered the questions in a defiant voice. 'A friend of Hammersley's knew a firm of thieves in London. I was their golliwog, handling large quantities of stolen goods on two separate occasions.'

Asked if anyone else knew of this arrangement, Waite replied that he was the only person in Brighton who knew what was going on, apart from the police. A roar of laughter echoed around the public gallery, causing the Chairman of the Bench to warn those involved that any further behaviour of the sort would leave him no alternative but to clear the public from the court. When questioned about the origin of the goods, Waite said that he only handled goods that had been stolen outside London.

'Were any of the defendants in this case aware of your arrangement?' Mr Gerald Howard asked.

'I discussed it with both Hammersley and Heath.'

'Did you give any money to any of the defendants?'

'I gave Hammersley more than £200 and Heath £50. But they all had meat as well. Heath and Hammersley would come into my shop on a Saturday, order £3 worth of meat, give me ten shillings and wait for the change. Ridge usually went to a pet food shop on a Friday evening, in Marine Gardens, owned by a man named Matheson. The shop used to take a lot of my stolen meat. Ridge would always take a joint or two from there.'

'You say you used the shop for illegal meat, so the joints were part of that illegal meat?' Gerald Howard sought to clarify.

'Yes, sir.'

'Did he pay for the meat?'

'No, sir.'

'Now leaving that aside for the moment, there is the matter of the stolen cigarettes. Can you tell us about that?' Gerald Howard asked.

'I had arranged it with Hammersley, 15,000 cigarettes and 40lb of tobacco, which were stolen and again I was the golliwog that had to get rid of them. Shortly before the goods arrived, I told Hammersley that a man named Richardson was bringing them down. He said, "Oh my God. I can't have him around. I must go and see Richardson right away and tell him to burn the lot." But I don't think he was able to find him.'

'Why do you think he wanted Richardson to burn them. They must have been worth a great deal of money.'

'I did not know at the time. But later it was obvious that he knew Scotland Yard was on the trail of Richardson.'

'What happened later?'

'Detectives from Scotland Yard and the Railway Police raided my shop and my home. The cigarettes and tobacco were seized and I was taken to the local police station, where Heath took a statement.'

'Did Heath say anything to you?'

'When the other officers left the room, he told me to cut my statement short. He said to carry on for a while when they got back and then to finish it.'

'Is that what you did?'

'More or less.'

After being in the witness-box for more than two hours, Waite was cross-examined by Mr Bosley, acting for Ridge.

'Are you an undischarged bankrupt?' Bosley asked.

'You should know, you were once my solicitor,' Waite replied.

This gained him another roar of laughter from the gallery and a comment from the Bench, shortly after which he was allowed to stand down.

* * *

Flames belched from the rear ground-floor windows and smoke filled the upper rooms of the Castle Club, on Castle Street, Brighton. The roar of the fire, fanned by powerful winds blowing along the Channel, quickly took hold. An elderly woman trapped on the second floor screamed and cried for help, before turning back into the heat of the burning building. It was the early hours of Friday, 6 December 1957, the final day of the committal proceedings of the 'Brighton Affair'.

'I will not be intimidated,' William Page, the proprietor of the club and well-known local bookmaker, told a group of reporters.

Earlier in the week, Page had given evidence in the conspiracy hearing on behalf of the prosecution.

Firemen arrived at the blaze shortly after 6 a.m., by which time the whole of the ground floor had been gutted. They immediately smashed through a top-floor window, working from a turntable ladder, and quickly brought the woman, now unconscious, out to a waiting ambulance, which rushed her to hospital. A spokesman later issued a statement saying she was lucky to be alive.

After the fire had been brought under control, and while smoking, waterlogged furniture was being pulled out on to the street and piled high on the pavement, Mr Calvert, the Chief Fire Officer, refused to speculate on the cause of the blaze.

Later the same day, the proceedings at Brighton Town Hall came to an end. In excess of 100 witnesses had stood in the box to give evidence for and against the five accused. Hundreds of people, mostly men, had queued for hours every day to be allowed into the public gallery, to hear how people trusted to maintain law and order in their town had been profiting from corruption at the town's expense. After a spree lasting almost a decade, they had been charged and finally brought before the courts to answer to their peers. The closing legal arguments put forward were not greatly concerned with whether the five had a case to answer, but concentrated on where that case should be held. The Prosecution favoured the high-profile Old Bailey, whereas the Defence sought to retreat to Sussex Crown Court, Lewes. After deliberation, the Chairman of the magistrates was not moved by the Defence's arguments and stated that a date should be set for the case to be held at the Bailey.

Some say 'The Brighton Affair' is a prime example of the methods used by 'The Laughing Boy of London Nightclubs'. Combining a personal charisma and the threat of violence and intimidation, attempts to pervert the course of justice and closely fostered connections with corrupt members of the police force were his stock in trade. Billy Howard was considered by many to be the Don of Soho, a mediator, a settler of grievances, a power broker and the Don of Dons.

CHAPTER TWO

Growing Pains

'Miss Young. Get down from there and go to my office.' The female voice was clear and commanding.

Vera Young recognised it immediately, without having to turn her head skywards to see the face staring from a top-floor window of the large brick building. Billy Howard ran off into the crowd of screaming boys that churned around the playground, pushing, shoving, laughing, demanding, playing and sulking. Lost amongst matching school uniforms and little red faces, breath cold like smoke from a sly fag exhaled before them.

Vera lowered herself from the top of the high wall that divided the girls of Kennington Road School, London SE11, from the boys. Although the school was mixed, as was not unusual in the 1920s, the sexes were separated in lessons and the playground, and both had different entrances. Touching her feet on the ground and scuffing her hands and knees on the brickwork, she joined the female version of the scene on the other side. Pushing her way through the unruly crowd, she opened the school door by its polished brass handle and climbed each stair slowly, not wanting to arrive at the top. Timidly she tapped the door, hoping there would be no reply. Her small fist hardly made a sound on the painted wood, but it was loud enough to gain a response.

'Come in.'

Vera turned the handle gingerly and eased open the door. She took the least number of steps possible to bring herself into the room with sufficient space to allow her to push the door closed.

'What were you doing on the wall, Miss Young?' Before she had time to answer, the Head Mistress continued. 'You know climbing on the wall is forbidden.' The Head Mistress took the cane from the stand and using the end, lifted the young girl's left wrist.

'Hand out,' she commanded.

Vera went to speak as tears welled up in her eyes and the first whack stung her palm. The cane pushed her hand back into position and with slow deliberation the second whack was administered.

'Don't let me catch you doing it again,' the Head Mistress warned, replacing the cane and dismissing the child.

'Yes, Miss,' Vera sniffed, the shame of getting the cane more painful than the red welt swelling across her hand. Tears rolled down her pretty face. She wiped them away with the back of her hand. This was the first and last time she was getting caned, of that she was decided. Back in class she waited for the bell rung at noon for the dinner break.

Most of the children went home, those that didn't stayed for a hot dinner served in the dining-room across the playground. Billy lived with his elder brother and father, Tim Reagan, on the other side of Kennington Road, along the Kennington Park Road. It was unlikely she would see him on her way home. Vera placed her straw Panama hat firmly on her head and walked fast on her own in the opposite direction, to 144 Kennington Lane, a Duchy of Cornwall ground-floor flat. Her mother was dishing up the dinner when she walked in: meat pudding, vegetables and tinned fruit. Her favourite. She ate it quietly with her left hand bunched into a fist, so as not to expose the tell-tale signs that still throbbed. Sitting on top of the saucepan was her father's dinner, plated with a soup dish over the top, keeping warm. She did not want to carry it up the Lane to her father's barber's shop, as this would have taken two hands. Not wishing to be told off a second time, she gladly parted with chewing gum, a popular sweet that was always disliked by teachers, to bribe her elder brother. The extra time she utilised to run cold water over her swelling. When she went back through the gates in time for the two o'clock bell, her hand was all but back to normal.

At half past four, with school finished, she was surprised to see Billy running ahead of her with his friends Johnny Middleton, Joey King and Teddy Mason. They turned out of view into Kennington Lane, but she guessed they would turn down by the White Hart, where the boys lived. She crossed the Lane before turning in case they were waiting around the corner, but they had gone. As Vera came level opposite the turning, she could see them grouped around a lamppost. Billy was hanging upside down from the crossbar, high above the pavement. She stood and watched. Billy was the only boy she ever saw doing it and she was impressed. She knew if he tore his uniform he would be in trouble – both he and his brother always came to school well turned out, which was not the case for many of the poorer kids. After hanging there for a few minutes he pulled himself upright and swung down, then she watched as they all ran off.

Vera went in through the door, sat and ate bread and strawberry jam, followed by a piece of cake. She drank the last glass of home-made lemonade before her mother chased her to take her things to her room. For the rest of the evening Vera did her homework, helped her mother with a little of the housework and played with her girlfriends in Denny Crescent. Having escaped the duty of delivering her father's dinner earlier in the day, going to the chip shop to buy supper was an errand she could not avoid. And woe betide her if it wasn't on the table for eight o'clock.

'One sixpenny fish and a penneth of chips and three tuppeny fish with three penneth, please,' Vera asked, standing on tiptoe to look over the high counter. Through the window out of the corner of her eye she thought she saw Billy Howard running across the street, but she knew she was wrong. It was the wrong side of the Kennington Road for that time of night.

Billy Howard was a year older than Vera and she knew that he wasn't interested in her. All the girls liked Billy, not that he was good-looking. His bandy legs did not add to his attraction, but he had a charisma that nobody else in the school, in fact no other boy she had ever met, had. It was difficult for her to put her finger on what it was exactly but she knew you could almost touch it. A charm, a gift of nonconformity. A talent for mischief and daring, and deep down a smile that could draw you in as easily as mock you. Whatever it was she knew or should have known, in Billy's hands, it was trouble.

Billy and Vera often saw each other in the street and never spoke. Sometimes she would see her elder brother talking to Henry, Billy's elder brother. She wasn't sure but she imagined they might have been in the same class. Billy and Henry were facially similar, but Henry was tall and slim, while Billy was shorter and thickset. They had joined the school when they moved into a flat in the Kennington Park Road with their father.

Mr and Mrs Howard originally had three children – Helen, Phyllis and Arthur. After their marriage broke down Billy's mother, Beatrice, retained the house in Walworth and took up with Tim Reagan, the owner of a fish stall in East Lane. There then followed another three children, Henry, Violet and Billy. The age gap was quite considerable between the two sets of children and certainly during the very early years of Billy's life, times were not easy. Billy suffered from both asthma and rickets, a disease caused by a lack of vitamin D in the diet, resulting in the softening of bones and often causing bow legs in children. Whether Tim moved out and disregarded the children that were not his own is unclear, but certainly by the time Billy and Henry were approaching their early teens, they were living only with their father and attending a new school. A move that clearly improved their quality of life. Vera always considered Tim's two boys to be a lot better turned out than many of the children.

The move away from the family home did nothing to distance Billy from his mother. He regularly returned to her, expecting her to perform her motherly duties right up to the time of her death. Washing, ironing and food Billy took for granted, and he scrounged the odd few pounds when pennies were short. The one thing that Billy found difficult was accepting the shame of illegitimacy, as Tim and Beatrice were never married. In 1916, when he was born, it was considered sinful. Billy later told Vera that he was shy. Although she found this difficult to believe, she put it down to his feelings regarding the marital status of his parents.

From the time he started in senior school, Billy took up boxing. His thickset shoulders made him a powerful puncher and, wishing to fight off his shyness, his dare-devil attitude made him a formidable opponent. Fights were often staged at Manor Place Baths, a swimming-pool off the Walworth Road. Although Vera was not a boxing fan, she was a swimmer, gaining the School Championship before leaving. Arriving at the baths, where she practised and swam in inter-school galas, she would often bump into Billy, but both had their own interests and circle of friends.

Billy's manor was somewhat larger than a lot of the children's: father working and mother living off the Walworth Road, home in the Kennington Road, friends in Kennington Lane and the draw of the hustle and bustle of the Elephant and Castle. The network of buses and trams cost money and were really only for travelling, on best behaviour, with parents. The preferred method of transport for most of the kids who enjoyed playing in the almost car-free streets was to jump up onto the back of a truck as it passed and skip off at a convenient point close to their destination. The drivers knew of the practice and often shouted back at them in mock anger, threatening to box their ears. Of course, if the boys tried interfering with goods stacked in the back then that was a different matter. Billy skipped up onto the tailgate of one, running along behind another and skipping on to that, never giving the speed or the height of the jump a second thought. Often other kids, the ones who knew a sense of fear, would hold back and miss their chance. 'Cowardy, cowardy, custard' was a regular chant to those who didn't chance it. Billy would simply shout that he would see them at their agreed destination.

On one overcast evening, Billy's journey was from Kennington Lane back to his mother's in the Walworth Road. He could have cut through the side streets, running along the copings or drawing a stick along the railings, probably getting an earful from the people living in the flats as he went. But he had been out playing street cricket and Jump Jimmy Knacker 1–2–3, he was weary and it looked like rain. At Kennington Cross he sat for a few minutes on the side of the horse trough. He could have hopped on the back of a horse-drawn cart just heading off to the Elephant as he arrived, but metal-ringed wheels made journeys bumpy as well as slow. Before long, turning off the Kennington Road from the direction of Westminster, a truck slowed and Billy was off the cold damp seat in a shot. He grabbed a piece of leather webbing and, using the speed of the lorry, swung himself aboard. It was the end of the day, the load had been dropped and by the look of the rubbish left behind, the lorry had been delivering fruit and veg. In the corner, behind the cab, Billy's eye caught sight of a few brown paper bags. He guessed they contained a few perks the driver had put to one side for himself. The driver's family were sure to be well provided for in greengrocery, just as his family never went short of winkles and shrimps.

Billy did not think the driver had seen him get on and in the dim light he felt confident that he could scrump himself a Cox's or two, if he was lucky, without being caught.

Parsnips and a Savoy. He knew what he could do with them, Billy thought. As his hand went into the third bag, the driver's face came out of the window, not more than a few feet from Billy's head, and shouted in a deep angry voice: 'Oi, you, get ya bleeding 'ands off. Thieving little blighta.'

Billy snatched an object from the bag, ran quickly down the length of the boards and, as the driver braked to jump out, Billy also jumped. The road was wet. It must have already rained and passed on. His shoe slipped underfoot and he nearly went down, but he managed to regain his balance and put some pace into his feet. The driver, seeing he was no match in a chase for the young urchin, did not bother getting out of the cab. Realising a chase was unlikely, Billy cooled his heels and, looking in the direction of the driver, took a good, deep bite into the large apple he had succeeded in liberating.

'Urgh!' Billy's face screwed up as the sour juice from the cooker filled his mouth. Without a second thought, using his best street cricket return, he threw the apple at the lorry, watching it shrapnel into pieces as it hit the hub. For a moment Billy thought the driver was going to climb out and attempt pursuit, but he didn't. 'The next time I see you, Billy Howard, I'll wring your neck,' the driver bellowed.

Billy tried to see the man better. The fact that he knew his name had scared him – not that he was afraid of the man as such, it was more the surprise. All Billy could think of was that the man must be a friend of his father's. Maybe he delivered greengrocery to one of the stalls down the Lane. His father would probably think it was funny and simply give him a clout round the ear if the man complained.

He was at the Elephant now and needed a lorry going back in the direction of Camberwell, along the Walworth Road. The few lorries he could see all seemed to have the backs closed up. He started to walk, the sour taste in his mouth making him want to spit. The rain had started to fall quite heavily. Billy stood back in a shop doorway, waited until he got bored and then scooted off through the large drops of water which fell noisily on the paving flags and splashed upwards. Blinded by the driving water, he darted into the next available shop doorway and wiped the sleeve of his jumper across his face and over the top of his hair. Normally, he would not have given a second glance to the truck that pulled out of the side turning 30 yards ahead of him. In the dry it would have been bad enough, but he was sure to be filthy the moment he touched it. A clap of thunder swayed his doubts. Without a second thought he was out of the shelter, pumping his legs after the now departing lorry. It braked as he launched into the air, grasping to secure his hand and pull himself aboard. Water from the wheels splashed high above the sideboards, sending spray across the pavement. Not travelling at the speed he had calculated, the corner of the back flap was higher than he had allowed. It plunged into his groin, sending a shooting pain up through his stomach and chest. For a moment he did not believe he could hold on as the lorry began to accelerate away. The surge forward was enough to pull Billy over the tailgate, where he lay in the coal-dust, his face black on the empty coal sacks. The sour taste in his mouth from the apple was now replaced with the taste of vomit. He lay there, unable to straighten out, the rain soaking deep into his clothes and wetting his skin.

He was still there when the lorry pulled into the yard. If Billy had not called out, the driver would have swung the gates closed and Billy would have remained where he lay until the driver returned the following morning. The coalman could have boxed his ears, but he had taken pity and helped the lad to his mother's a few streets away. Beatrice was less merciful. The moment Billy stumbled in through the door, blacker than a piece of coal himself, she had swiped her palm around the back of his head, nearly knocking him off his feet and sending him in the direction of the scullery. The next day the doctor was called.

The doctor told him he could have done some serious damage, but he thought that Billy would be on the mend after a few days and warned him that injuries like that could easily cause problems in later life, especially when it came time to have children.

★ ★ ★

By the age of 15, Billy was getting into scrapes and showing little sign of wanting to knuckle down. Everything had its funny side and he seemed unable or unwilling to take anything seriously. Brushes with the police did nothing to dampen his desire to buck the system. At weekends he would be seen going around with a very pretty girl, Irene Weeks, who lived with her mother over the shops and laundry in the Kennington Lane, 50 yards from Vera's home.

An incident that happened with Irene's mother, a widow of the First World War, started Billy's mind working. She was a cleaner at Scotland Yard on the early morning shift, starting at six o'clock. This was a normal practice for many women, going out early morning and early evening cleaning offices. It allowed them to be at home with the kids, when the men were out working. During one shift, being nosy as most people are and detectives being untidy as most men are, Irene's mother saw a photograph of a member of her family on the desk. Naturally, as soon as she left the building she contacted the relative, allowing him to go on the run before the boys in blue came to feel his collar.

The penny quickly dropped – the idea of having people well placed to obtain information was extremely attractive. Being one, two, three jumps ahead could shave the odds considerably. It worked, he knew, when betting on horses and he did not think that it would be any different in dealings with the Old Bill. If you were on the inside, picking the right horse was more a matter of knowing what was going on than just taking pot luck. Off-course betting was illegal, but this just encouraged the illegal activities of bookmakers' runners, who would collect bets in pubs, cafes, factories and on street corners. Tim Reagan, Billy's father, was a betting man. Billy was regularly dispatched with cash to run down the street with his father's selection. On the way he would usually take a short detour, check the paper himself and speak to a runner whose opinion he trusted.

'What do you fancy for the two-thirty?' Billy's voice would be low and conspiratorial, making the man feel important. If the answer was not the horse Tim had selected, Billy would slip the money in his pocket, to spend later. If Tim's selection looked as though it stood a chance, Billy would fly on down the road and place the bet with the runner his father favoured. This went on for years without Tim ever tumbling.

Whereas many of the kids of Billy's age smoked, Billy did not smoke, drink or gamble, apart from deciding whether or not to withhold his father's bets. The money was often spent going up West, a tuppenny bus fare, wandering the streets, taking in the bright lights and the fashionably dressed stepping from their cabs into commissionaire-greeted theatres. The prestigious gentlemen's clubs of Pall Mall, up round St James', past the Ritz Hotel, the shops of Burlington Arcade, along Piccadilly, cutting down the side of the Café Royal into Soho with its Italian-owned restaurants. These trips over the river and twice-weekly visits to the local cinema were considered money well spent. The Movietone News, a B film and the main feature provided good value. The boys who took girls along headed straight for the back row, then came the quarrels over watching the film, the boys riveted during the gangster action and the girls not wanting to be diverted when the romantic sequences filled the screen. Without television, it was not unusual for people who could afford it to go to the pictures every night, perhaps with a visit to the music hall at the weekend. The smell of hot chestnuts roasted in the street by vendors pushing barrows of glowing red coals was another call on pocket money, along with acid drops, pear drops and other boiled sweets. Small tuppenny bars of chocolate were considered a treat but, of course, gobstoppers and chewing gum were a favourite with all the kids.

Playing in the quiet streets was a free place for entertainment. Billy often saw Vera and her friend Rita playing street cricket with a group, or skating round the block, or hot and out of breath standing in Vera's doorway drinking homemade lemonade or R. White's. Sometimes he would stop and talk to kids in the group and on other times he would not bother, heading to the gym for sparring practice. On Sundays with Irene, Billy would almost without fail see the two friends coming from Sunday School at St Anselm's, a routine for most children, or later heading to or returning from Bob White's, the famous wet fish shop situated on the corner of Kennington Lane and a great rival for Tim Reagan's stall. Winkles and shrimps for the traditional Sunday tea.

In the ring, Billy was now beginning to make a name for himself. For most of the matches he was making the punches count early in the rounds. His being a southpaw seemed to put many of his opponents at a disadvantage, making it easy for him to come in under or over the top of their defences. His trainer was impressed with Billy's style of taking the fights continually forward and being prepared to take a punch without retreating. One fight that stuck in Billy's mind took place in Walworth after a great deal of build-up. The boys from the Elephant were matched against a team of lads from the East End. Billy laid a string of body punches on a taller lad who many of the local supporters believed was older than the opposing club had declared. Before the end of the first round Billy had put the other fighter on the canvas. In the second round, Billy changed his tactic and pounded home head punch after head punch. Before the bout, significant money had changed hands and now with the East End favourite cut, bleeding and swollen, the crowd were in uproar. The Eastender's corner threw the towel into the ring before the referee had time to step in front of the beaten lad to stop the fight. Billy's chest hammered like fists, his heart feeling as if it were going to crash through the ropes that were his rib cage. Sweat poured down his face, the salt irritating his eyes, and his ears throbbed with the sound of his blood pumping and the roar of the spectators.

In the street, after most of the people had left, Billy leaned against a wall, enjoying the cool air and the virtual silence. A car slowed and under the street lamp he could see the laughing faces of people he knew. He dug his hands deep into his pockets, shook his head at the shouted offer of a lift and walked off in the direction of home.

As they shoved him into an alleyway leading to the rear of some shops, his assailants hit him hard. It was almost like being bound with rope; his hands were trapped. This was a lesson he would heed for the future: hands out of pockets. The narrow distance between the two walls prevented him from going down. If he had, he knew they would have beaten him badly and there would have been nothing he could have done about it. There was blood on his face, but that was from the rough brickwork. He managed to dodge the next couple of blows then, hands free, drove a crushing punch into the throat of his nearest attacker. The sharp intake of air told him he had found a mark. The narrow alley was doing him a favour – they could really only come at him in single file, and they were no match for him on that basis.

As Billy's head began to clear, he realised he recognised two of the three men. They had come into the ring, or had been standing close to the lad he had fought earlier, before the match had begun. He guessed if they had been much good, they'd have had a bout, not just been hangers-on. Still, they were big.

The alleyway didn't seem to be going anywhere. As far as Billy could make out there was a gate at the end, blocking any chance of escape. If he stopped defending himself, turned and tried to open it or found it locked and had to climb, they would be all over him. The only way out was over them and, despite winning convincingly in the ring, his earlier efforts had taken their toll. At the same time as he felt the strength draining from him, his assailants seemed to lose theirs. The one that had taken the punch to the throat seemed to lose his enthusiasm almost immediately. Now another had pulled back, and under the streetlight Billy could see him sitting, head bowed, on the pavement. Billy made one final charge, there was a clash of heads and he brought up a left hook from deep down by his waist. The man in front of him buckled and Billy was through and out on to the pavement. It was at this moment that he should have been at his most alert, but wasn't. The blade sliced his coat, cutting a clean straight slash almost a foot in length. It had missed his face thanks to the inaccuracy of its owner, not because Billy had taken evasive action. The punch to the throat had been vicious, but the recipient had mustered enough energy to make the razor attack. Had it been on target, it would have been final. The power of the swing unbalanced his opponent and gave Billy sufficient time to react. The punch he delivered sent the man crashing to the pavement, the razor clattering into the gutter. Billy retrieved it almost before the man realised it was no longer in his grasp. Knee firmly planted on the man's chest, Billy ran the blade from one side of his forehead to the other. Then he did it again. In an instant he was gone. A mile down the road, out of breath and sure his attackers were not thundering after him, he took advantage of the shadow created between two street lamps to drop the weapon into a drain. The next day he took a bus into Brixton and bought his first cut-throat razor.

* * *

1931. Billy was out of school, and there was a second general election in two years, with Labour losing to the Conservatives' government of national unity. Billy joined the groups of men that habitually stood around the streets chatting, hanging around outside billiard halls and pubs. Billy usually found himself mixing with the groups that frequented the Elephant and Newington Butts. Not working meant that he was always looking for ways to earn money. He did odd jobs for his father and others working in the market, and he continued to pocket bets and anything else he could lay his hands on that had a value. A cuff round the ear from the local bobby, who would pocket his own share of any booty, was standard punishment. But on more than one occasion he was hauled into court and spent spells in detention.

In an attempt to put him on the straight and narrow, and against his own better judgement, Billy allowed himself to be coerced into joining the army.

Boxing in the services was a big attraction, with the honour of each battalion resting on prized tournaments. Billy was told he could do well and, had it not been for the rigid discipline, that might have been the case. Trips to the ring were only outnumbered by trips to the glasshouse. Red Caps were not slow in dishing out beatings and their dislike of the young private was not diminished when he refused to be broken by their regime and repaid the brutality in the ring by dishing out a savage retribution that would have been stopped in any other arena. Billy was cut, bruised and bleeding, but remained on his feet. The Red Cap in the ring, too proud to accept defeat, pulled himself off the canvas red with blood, over and over again. A senior Military Police officer, firmly gripping the arm of the timekeeper, prevented the final bell from being rung in the desperate hope that his man would find the reserve to finish it with a last-ditch assault. The fight brought Billy's military career to an end, certainly for the time being. The next time he was in trouble, instead of being locked up he was shown the front gate.

* * *

Billy Hill was released from prison – not for the first time – at about the same period as Billy Howard found himself back on the street. Born at Seven Dials in London's West End, Hill had no doubt in his own mind that he should rule the criminal activities around his own birthplace. Capable of viciousness and a good organiser with the air of a leader, Hill's name was near the top of the criminal ladder. But Hill was by profession a thief.

In the years approaching the Second World War and throughout much of the war itself, Hill's name was regularly on the front pages of the press, becoming synonymous with daring and outrageous robberies. Expensive jewellery and fashionable furs were a favourite target. Breaking into socialites' homes and reversing cars through shop windows in busy West End streets, shattering glass across the pavements, snatching the highly priced displays and driving off at high speeds, tyres squealing, were all part of the pattern that rapidly became Hill's trademark. Thousands of pounds were generated by this ongoing spree which the police seemed unable to prevent, when the average national wage was only a few pounds per week. Still it failed to satisfy Hill's greedy ambitions. He wanted to be known as the Boss of Britain's Underworld and later in his life he would launch his book by that name in the fashionable Soho restaurant, Gennaro's. However, Billy Hill lacked one essential skill he needed to be the boss of bosses. He lacked the ability to hold the Jewish, Italian, Maltese and British tribal interests together for any lengthy period.

The other pretender to the throne was Jack Comer, affectionately or not known as Jack Spot or Spotty. Four years older than Billy Howard, Spotty was an East End Jewish lad, born in Whitechapel of Polish parents. A fighter early on, he soon provided protection for the bookies and shopkeepers in the Jewish community. But in the long term he suffered the same pitfalls as Hill when it came to uniting the various gangs. In 1936, Jack Spot gained a major boost to his reputation. Sir Oswald Mosley and his Blackshirt followers began their anti-Semitic march through the streets of the East End where many of the Jewish immigrants lived and worked. Amongst those who fought to break up the march were Spot and a number of his strong-arm boys, who were more than a match for the Nazi bully-boys flanking Mosley. Police intervened and arrests were made on both sides, but luck was with Spot, who found himself appearing before a more than understanding Jewish magistrate, happy to see Spot walk from the court with only a small fine for his trouble.

Earlier that same year, the Battle of Lewes Races, a landmark in British gangland history, had swept terror and disorder through the racing fraternity and the bookmaking world. London's hardmen were lining up behind one or other of the gangs battling for control. Billy Howard was not at the racecourse on the day it happened, but the turmoil provided him with an opportunity to offer a commodity that would prove very marketable. Protection.

Billy already had the makings of a reputation from boxing and street fights and the belief among other gangsters and the bookmakers prepared to make use of his services that he was more than prepared to use a razor if and when the situation called for it. While some bookmakers were ready to accept the protection of the gang who finally triumphed at Lewes Races, others sought to operate a more personal service. Billy was approached, first by one bookmaker and then, as the success of his protection became evident, by more who sought to come under the same umbrella. Not having a formidable gang, Billy appeared vulnerable, but it soon became evident that any attack would be avenged. The opposing gang members involved were quietly and individually taken to one side as they left a club or the home of a girlfriend, or simply stepped outside their front door.

'Oi, you.' The man behind the voice would step quickly from the shadows where he had been waiting patiently, as the other lone man, unprepared, closed the door behind him. Before he could run or turn back, the flash of the blade would open the cheek and then, as the victim's arm went up to the wound, a second slash would stripe the back of the hand. 'I'm Billy Howard and that's from . . .' Billy would say, giving the name of the bookmaker employing him before stepping back into the shadows and disappearing into the night, leaving the man bleeding and with little doubt why he had been singled out. The beatings or a slash with the razor meted out to the lone gang members, first one and then another, soon made attacking the pitches protected by Billy an unappealing prospect.

With money in his pocket and a reputation for being prepared to dish out punishment to anyone who trod on his toes, or the toes of those under his protection, Billy Howard was now spending less time around Walworth, and more in the bright lights north of the river. By providing protection to the racecourse bookies, doors were open to provide the same bookies with protection for their other gambling interests, mainly centred on small illegal gaming rooms. These spielers were generally located in the back rooms of cafes and rooms above shops. In Soho, it was not unusual for one of the upper floors to be utilised as a storeroom, the next floor providing a parlour for a prostitute and her maid and the remaining rooms to accommodate a few card tables. Others were more plush and were located in the back rooms of the many drinking clubs and billiard halls. Drunks and bad losers were a constant source of trouble, and trouble would almost certainly result in a visit by the police. The other potential cause of trouble was jealousy. One operator doing better than another would result in an attempt by one either to wreck the more profitable spieler, or to take it over. On the premises, Billy was proving a worthy deterrent, and soon his name being associated with the owner of a particular establishment was sufficient to deter unwanted aggravation.

Spot protected the Jews, but was unable to control the Italian population of Clerkenwell and Soho. Soho was the West End, and like all villains before him Spot wanted at least a toehold amongst the bright lights. His East End operations were gambling-based and this made Soho a better bet, in Spot's mind, than Mayfair. The gambling rooms in Mayfair tended to be more glamorous set-ups, more expensive to fit out, thereby requiring a greater capital outlay before any profits came rolling in.

Big or small, Mayfair or Soho, it was usual for most establishments to be under the control of the villain that frequented them, and this often did not require the owner's consent. This was not the case when a bunch of Islington lads in a Soho billiard hall where Spot enjoyed a game decided Spotty needed to be put in his place, and that place was not Foxy's Club. At a nod from the owner, they set about the Jewish villain with billiard cues, knuckle-dusters and anything else they could lay their hands on. Unprepared for the fight, Spotty defended himself, throwing balls and chairs, but being outnumbered, it was not long before he found himself out on the street, cut, bleeding and bruised. On hearing of the problem, Billy stepped in quickly and explained to the owner the reality of the situation. Unless he was prepared to pay Billy to sort out the problem, his business was finished. It did not take much brain to realise that Spotty would not simply wipe his mouth and walk away. The next time the Islington Boys were in, someone would make a call and Spotty's henchmen would not be far behind. And so it would go on.

Having agreed a figure, Billy then visited both parties and explained that Foxy's was now under his protection. Any retribution should take place outside the West End, otherwise both parties would find themselves unwelcome in far more establishments in Soho than that particular club. Spotty dealt with the request in an off-hand manner, telling Billy that it did not matter to him where the Islington Boys got it. But there was no further trouble connected with the assault at the club while the property was under that ownership.

Billy had successfully extended his circle of influence among the owners and players of the narrow streets that were Soho. This was to become a well-trodden path over the coming years. Often members of the various gangs would be curious as to why they were pulled out of a confrontational situation by their bosses. Matters had been settled quietly and in most cases the agreements not only stuck but also proved popular with 'top management' as profits climbed in a business environment.

This did not stop the ill feeling between Jews and Italians, many of whom were interned as Italy joined the war on the side of the Nazis. Lots of the Italians were now openly anti-Semitic and, with their numbers reduced, they sought to stand their ground, lest the Jews saw them as weak and made a move to eradicate the Italian power base at the first opportunity.

A notorious fight between the two groups proved fatal for Little Hubby, the brother of police informer and pimp Big Hubby Distelman. Italian Albert Dimes, Tony Mancini, Harry Capocci and Joe Collette went into a billiard hall in Soho's Wardour Street, where a number of Jewish faces were playing and where Little Hubby was employed as a doorman. Eddie Fleicher, who had earlier been drinking in the club downstairs, started on the Italians. Cues, tables and chairs were soon flying around the room. Both Dimes and Mancini were carrying blades, but it was Mancini who pulled the stiletto and, as Little Hubby ran into the room with the intention of preventing the place from being destroyed, Mancini plunged it into his upper torso. Little Hubby died a few hours later in Charing Cross Hospital. Antonio Mancini died six months later on the gallows. Dimes, Capocci and Collette were charged with wounding Fleicher and bound over to keep the peace. At this time Dimes was also on the run from the MPs (Military Police) so he was subsequently packed off to serve in the RAF.

Billy again extended his influence, this time brokering a deal that prevented 37 Wardour Street, which housed three clubs, from falling into either the hands of the remainder of the Italian gang or the Yid gang. However, he had to handle the situation with kid gloves. Although he had been kicked out of the army a few years earlier, the authorities had seen fit to call him up. Having reported for duty, he had absconded at the first opportunity. Most of the Italians hated the Jews and the Italians had come under fire, their shops and restaurants having bricks thrown through their windows, when Italy came into the war. Being seen to favour either side could have found Billy grassed up and shipped out to fight for King and country.

Dimes and the Italians, now at loggerheads with the Jews, saw their allies as Hill's gang, which further isolated Spot's power, although it would be wrong to suggest that he could simply be dismissed. Spot was not stupid, and whereas Billy was not prepared to align himself totally with any faction, he was prepared to give credence to the Eastender, brokering deals on his behalf. It was this reputation for not being anti-Semitic that later drew the Kray twins into Billy's circle of influence. Whilst not being Jewish, members of the Kray family were of European origin and along with Irish and gypsy lineage, Jewish blood could not be excluded. During their army years, it was not unheard of for them to be referred to as the Yid Kids by some of the officers and MPs.

Another known gangland face was 'Ruby' Sparks, who had picked up the nickname as one of the major jewel thieves in the country prior to, and throughout, the war years. Finally he withdrew from this career and opened the Penguin Club in Regent Street, on the edge of Soho. Not wanting to be drawn back into business dealings with Hill, despite having enjoyed previously amicable contacts, Sparks was content to have Billy Howard in the background to ward off unfriendly advances from any direction. This set-up was to prove an attractive option for a number of club owners like Sparks in the coming years. His services were no less expensive, on a weekly basis, than most of the other protection rackets, but Billy did allow the owners to retain control of their businesses in the long term. Protection provided by other gangsters could regularly result in the owner being pushed into a minority shareholding. Maybe not on paper, but in actual ultimate profit share, they would see their remuneration squeezed to the point where it was questionable whether they should stay in business at all.

Billy had learned an important lesson early on. A milk bar south of the river had provided Billy with a steady income at first. Then, as his needs grew, Billy increased the demands. As time passed, despite protests from the owner, Billy again increased the level of demand and with it the level of threat. Not knowing which way to turn and fearful of the kind of violence Billy might rain down on him, the owner chose to die by his own hand. Although not large, the golden goose was dead. Billy had quickly discovered that there was no profit in dead people unless you were an undertaker.

Billy was now seen as one of the most powerful and fearless fighters with both fists and blade to have emerged from south London, a noted breeding ground for hardmen prepared to battle for any gang leader capable of commanding respect and offering generous rewards. This tradition stretched back over scores of years. But it was not Billy's fighting prowess alone that was the key to his increasing success. Whilst bookmakers, owners of spielers, clubs and small businesses were forming the basis of a profitable protection empire for Billy, there were two other criminal activities generating fortunes for him in excess of those being achieved by Hill's thieving. The first was the black market and the second, although initially only a sideline to further his marketeering, was the cultivation of corrupt police officers, which paid dividends right up until the time of his death. A friendly smile to the young copper on the beat, the odd packet of fags or a pair of stockings for his girlfriend, and later, tickets to a top West End show or a charity boxing match.

Little things that were appreciated and never forgotten as the copper climbed the Met ladder.

Goods of all descriptions fell off the back of lorries, a euphemism for all and any stolen goods and the basis of the black market which was an uncontrollable activity throughout the war and the years after, while rationing remained. Wide boys or spivs were the purveyors of the legally unobtainable, but Billy was operating much further up the supply chain, boxing in the heavyweight ring. He was seen as neutral by many of the gangleaders and the police were also relaxed about passing on sensitive knowledge that would be used by a third party. Dealing at arm's length was appealing to all parties. Equally the pay-off, channelled in reverse, offered the same attraction. Billy was a trusted middleman.

One of his largest coups was handling the proceeds of a robbery in Romford, Essex. The haul netted over £400,000 worth of ration books. On the street, they would have achieved 50 per cent of their face value, and 50 per cent of the street value went directly to the police. Billy stood in the middle. He was entitled to, and received, a cut from both halves. Some of the proceeds he ploughed into Soho strip clubs and spielers on both sides of the river, with various partners already operating in those areas. A substantial remainder funded his increasingly costly lifestyle.

* * *

They were both walking along Lower Regent Street, in the late afternoon. It was 1945, more than ten years since they had last seen each other and now, heading in opposite directions, they came face to face. Billy was striding up towards Piccadilly, cutting a dash in a blue serge suit, white shirt with gold cuff links, neatly knotted tie and polished black shoes. As was his style, he carried a trilby hat which was all the fashion for men, mimicking the Humphry Bogart look.

Vera wore a light summer dress, obtained without coupons from a friend in the rag trade who worked in a cutter's, and who made clothes for many of the top fashion houses. They recognised each other instantly and chatted about people at school, the war years and nothing.

'Have you got a telephone number?' Billy ventured.

'Reliance 2546,' Vera said, and scribbled it down on a piece of paper from her handbag. She was one of the few people in London at the end of the Second World War with a phone, unusual unless you were rich. It had provided her with an excellent social life during the war years, with young Canadian and Norwegian soldiers on leave in England with no family and keen to go dancing or skating, and to be able to laugh; to become human again for a while before returning to the Front and possible slaughter.

When they parted, Vera did not seriously think that Billy would call. She thought he was simply being polite in asking for her number and would have his sights set on far more glamorous girls. That evening, however, Billy did ring and asked Vera for a date.

Lots of local girls would have expected to have been taken to a place to drink or dance in south London, but Vera had found the West End as much of a draw as had Billy. At the age of 16, she had bought her first radio and had spent evenings at home listening to the popular tunes of the day played by the Savoy Orpheans, Swing, Ambrose, Harry Fox and Henry, all the sort of music played in the large hotels and small clubs around the West End. She had once been happy to race around the ice at the Brixton rink, but by her 18th birthday she was spending more time with her friend Anne, who introduced her to the West End theatres; a bastion, in many respects, of the rich and well educated as most of the casts were drawn from public school backgrounds. This certainly changed with the run of *Golden Boy* at the St James', where the cast came from Lee Strasberg's Method Theatre in New York, a breeding ground of socialist views and cult stars that in the future would include James Dean, Marlon Brando, Elia Kazan and Meryl Streep. Dating stars of the show, attending parties with stage crew and being influenced by Anne's natural socialist leaning, the values and ideologies of those she mixed with during these years broadened Vera's political horizon.

Billy hopped out of the back seat of his car, with a new haircut and smart suit and a trilby swinging in his hand. He knocked on the door, full of charm, charisma and smiles. One of the last times Vera had seen him he had been upside down, hanging on the lamppost a few yards from where he now stood. Billy's driver held open the back door of the large black saloon and closed it behind Vera. Billy sat beside her as the car swung round and turned right out of Kennington Lane, along the Kennington Road, past The Cut and over Westminster Bridge. North of the river, it cruised up Whitehall, around Trafalgar Square and up Lower Regent Street into Piccadilly Circus, drawing up outside Monaco's, a fashionable bar and restaurant next door to the News Theatre. Billy's driver did the honours with the doors. On realising Billy was entering his establishment, the head waiter began moving other guests and marshalling his staff to ensure the very best table and service was on hand. Vera was impressed. This was not an easy feat. She had been wined and dined by famous faces from the cast of *Golden Boy* and American brass, flashing handfuls of US dollars, but this was the first time she had seen waiters react with such deference. Vera ordered a gin and tonic while Billy had a bottle of Worthington Pale Ale. They sat and talked, oblivious to other guests and waiters seeking to ensure that no complaint of neglect could be made. No bill was presented for the few drinks they consumed but, as they left, Vera saw Billy push a folded large white £5 note into the head waiter's palm. Billy's driver was already standing with the car door open as they stepped out into the flashing lights and warm night air.

Over the next few months they dated, but it was not until some months later that Billy let it be known he was married. The marriage had broken up and Billy was now looking to get a divorce.

'Do you have any children?' Vera wanted to know.

'No,' Billy said and explained what had happened to him when he had been tailgating as a kid. He was convinced that he was not able to father a child. Vera's own views on starting a family were mixed, so Billy's situation, as things became more serious between them, did not seem to her to be critical.

Billy did not have Vera as a constant companion: he would pick her up and they would go out but days, sometimes weeks, could pass without him being in contact. Then he was picked up by the Military Police and arrested for being a deserter. In prison he mixed with many of the chaps he knew from the Elephant, Walworth and around the West End, who were in the same boat as himself. The connections he maintained on the outside were able to provide much sought-after black market goods, luxuries and coupons for everyday items to bribe the warders. Bottles of beer, the odd bottle of spirit that Billy used to reward other prisoners on his landing, and decent food that, in return for a share, the prisoners working in the kitchen were more than pleased to cook.

Days were boring. Exercising passed some of the time, that and discussing future opportunities with other influential chaps and making connections with men from good backgrounds who had gone AWOL and found themselves banged up and in need of friends. Otherwise, Billy lay in his cell and spent hours reading the Bible. Although a non-believer, over the years he would become almost an authority on the subject. Time passed and with each week Vera received a letter posted outside by a warder, so it would not have to go through the system. When soldiers were demobbed, Billy and the other deserters were given an armistice. From Scotland Yard, the old building off Whitehall down by the Thames, Billy telephoned Vera and asked her to come and meet him. Apart from considering this to be a bit of a cheek, she was dumbfounded to find that Billy had been given a demob suit and pay, the same as the soldiers who had actually fought for their country.

Coupons and shortages continued long after the war had ended. The black market had become a way of life and had turned virtually the whole of the British population into criminals. A full range of goods, impossible to purchase in the shops, were available at a price from someone who knew someone who had something that had fallen off the back of a lorry. Not everything was stolen. The system often operated on the basis of bartering – an extra couple of sausages or lamb chops slipped into the shopping by the butcher in return for a few coupons for clothing or chocolate. Everyone seemed to be getting what they needed. The criminal fraternity thrived, there were no bombs to dodge and no MPs to duck and dive from, as there had been during the war years. Having suffered the hardship of war, people now wanted to enjoy some of the pleasures in life. This did not mean that the Old Bill did not need avoiding. Yes, it was relatively easy to give bribes, but that was only necessary if you had been caught.

The pressure to remain at liberty and avoid getting your collar felt was real. But at every opportunity Billy chose to play the game. Why they were being chased, to this day, Vera does not know. It occurred to her at the time that the police car from which they were fleeing was only in pursuit because the car she was in was speeding away. Billy and Vera were sitting in the back, the top down in the sultry spring evening. In the front was his usual driver and one of his henchmen. One minute, the car was being driven normally and then a black police car was spotted sitting in a side turning. On instructions from Billy, the driver changed gear and raced off. Moments later the police car was hot on their tail, bell ringing and tyres squealing. The race went on for some 15 minutes, with Billy's driver weaving in and out the archways, down narrow side streets leading off The Cut, across into the back streets of Waterloo station, back round by the Elephant. In the end Vera believes the police just gave up. Billy's driver pulled into a cobbled alleyway at the back of a pub. They put the roof up and went in for a drink.

'That'll keep them on their toes,' Billy laughed.

* * *

Before the Second World War, sex outside marriage was frowned upon. Boys and girls often remained virgins until their early 20s. The war changed things. People started living for the moment, not knowing whether intensive bombing raids on the large towns and cities would grant them a personal future. Having been married for a number of years and not having fathered any children, Billy believed he was incapable of doing so. However, in December 1946, Vera, now 29, found herself pregnant. Abortion was commonplace, albeit illegal, and this was certainly considered as an option. Had Billy not been adamant that he was ready to start a family – he was very serious about wanting the child – the abortion option would have been given greater consideration. Billy had been separated from his wife for a long time and promised Vera that he would obtain a divorce at the earliest opportunity.

Billy and Vera took an apartment at the prestigious Dolphin Square, a large block in Victoria, which was convenient for Billy's interests on either side of the river. The pregnancy brought about change. As time went on Vera was less likely to accompany Billy when he went out in the evening. This meant that while he was wining and dining in smart West End restaurants, followed by visits to clubs that kept him from returning home until dawn, Vera was left sitting alone in the apartment. Often, she would take a cab back to her mother's flat in Kennington. This annoyed Billy, as she would not be at home when he returned. Not being prepared to go out without a clean shirt and freshly pressed trousers, he was further annoyed that she was not taking on all the domestic duties in his absence. When she was not there, Billy would be driven to his mother's place in Walworth so that she could iron his clothes as he stood over her to ensure the creases were ironed to his approval and the cuffs were folded back, not ironed. Jermyn Street hand-made shirts, sleeves tailored to a perfect length sufficient to allow cuff links to show, had to be handled correctly. Even when Vera was at the apartment it was not unusual for her to refuse to do his ironing. 'If you want your shirts ironed, stay in at night and keep me company while I'm doing it. I'm not standing doing your laundry while you're out having a good time. If you want a maid, employ one,' was Vera's attitude. Regular offers of ten shillings to iron a shirt failed to win the day.

* * *

1947 was a busy year for Billy. At the age of 31, he was a powerful figure behind the scenes, actively seeking to avoid publicity as sections of the police, who were not, or who were perceived not to be, on the take, began another fight for control of the streets. The battle had started early in 1945, when roadblocks were set up in and around the West End and on many of the bridges used by south London villains returning to their various patches. But those with contacts on the force simply used alternative bridges and travelled the few extra miles.

The public perception of Soho had become that of the 'Hole in the Wall', where gangsters did as they pleased and the police were unable to maintain law and order. Wherever crime took place in London, it seemed to be perpetrated by heavily armed men, using caches of weapons brought back from active service. They would then go to ground or seek to enjoy their ill-gotten gains in the West End. In the winter of 1945, the Metropolitan Police poured some 2,000 officers, many armed, into the square mile that is Soho. The raids were an exercise in saturation policing which succeeded in sending everyone into hiding for the hours during the raid. As a long-term measure it was seeking to achieve the impossible. It failed miserably.

The Ghost Squad was the next step in the fight against organised crime. Formed a year earlier, it became effective in 1947 under the operational control of Chief Superintendent Capstick. It soon became apparent that this team were going to be more expensive. They worked from locked offices in Scotland Yard, and those outside the core team were excluded, creating a feeling of resentment within the ordinary ranks of the Yard's detectives. It brought into question their honesty and gave them a reason to undermine their more highly thought-of colleagues. During this period, information was being obtained from those within the ordinary ranks who had managed to glean titbits from overheard conversations and from movements that could not be concealed, from cleaners, whom Billy had nurtured over long periods, and, much to his surprise, from Capstick himself.

John Capstick was no different from most other officers, only more expensive. Everyone has their price, was Billy's philosophy. Capstick's price was success: more than anything he wanted his Ghost Squad to succeed. Billy was not unhappy to pay the price. Again it was simple: those who came under Billy's umbrella were in the main left alone, or at least given plenty of notice of a proposed raid. In return, the gang leaders – Hill, Spot and Dimes – were required to give up bodies, whose names Billy would pass on to Capstick. Those given up would likely have upset their bosses or, on the promise of a pension, would have agreed to put their hands up. Favourites for this last option were men who were sick, who would spend most of their time banged up in the prison hospital, or on light duties. Having the ear of powerful Met officers brought kudos for Billy. It soon became rumoured that he had the Yard in his pocket and that if any problems arose, Billy was the man to sort things out.

Throughout the war years, Billy had kept some older officers, who took perks as a way of life established over a long time in the force, well supplied with the necessities and those little luxuries that made family life bearable. Billy recalled an argument at Vera's home concerning an acquaintance who was in the police at Scotland Yard and who was responsible for testing taxi drivers on their 'knowledge' and issuing the Hackney Carriage licences. Those who passed traditionally gave the examining officer a cash tip. Vera had argued this was a corrupt practice, giving the examining officer an incentive to ensure the cabby passed. The other side of the argument was that it was no different from the tradition of tipping a waiter or hairdresser for doing their job. However, it was clearly illegal and once accepting a bribe, particularly on a regular basis, the officer or any person in authority had two things to lose, firstly his job and reputation, and secondly the pleasures that the extra money had permitted the recipient to enjoy and take for granted. If knowledge is power, then prior or insider knowledge of what was about to happen put Billy in a commanding position. Those who subscribed to Billy became privy to elements of this valuable information, which could both keep them out of the nick, and ensure that their businesses were only disrupted for short periods of time. Others found themselves thrown into the back of a Black Maria and their cash flow terminated. It paid to have friends, all round.

Leading up to giving birth, Vera was evacuated to Bath, a provincial city in the west of England. Evacuation had been in effect since the beginning of the war for children and pregnant women. They were sent to what was deemed to be a safe distance from the target cities, particularly London, to places where essential services were more easily provided. Before leaving blitz-torn London, there were the arguments, usual between any husband and wife, over the naming of their child. Vera and Billy were no different. As is often the solution, it was agreed that if the child were a boy, Billy would choose the name and if a girl, Vera would have the privilege. Full of woman's intuition, Vera had settled on Veronica, and all the young children on her side of the family were well rehearsed in using the handle. Michael was born during the first week in August 1947, named after Billy's young nephew.

Towards the end of the summer, Billy Hill was arrested and while on bail skipped to South Africa, where he had every intention of setting up a new life on much the same lines as the one he had left behind. Within a short period of time, the opening of the Millionaires Club in Johannesburg took Hill into the territory of Arnold Neville, a local gangster who expected to be paid protection. Either he was unaware of Hill's reputation, or he believed that Hill was too far from home and would not have the muscle to resist the demand. Unable to settle their differences, Neville and Hill tore into each other viciously. This brought them before the courts. On bail again, Hill decided that English prisons were probably better than those in South Africa and so he headed back to the UK. He opened a nightclub in Southend and, in an attempt not to appear too provincial, he also opened a spieler in Soho's Dean Street with a Maltese who would eventually take over some of the Messina brothers' interests, although on a much smaller scale.

Jack Spot owned successful operations in the East End and had no wish at this time to push deep into the West End. He was quite content to develop interests and associations. His main cash flow was generated by a spieler in the East End, close to the City. Operating well within his own territory, Spotty could enjoy profits running at between one and two thousand pounds per week, without the burden of protection money. The same would apply later to the Krays, where their business interests remained within that boundary.

As with Hill, Southend had its appeal for Jack Spot. Although seeking to maintain the image of the Jewish businessman, Spot felt he was duty bound to stand firm against the disrespect shown to him by one of the Whites' relatives, Johnny Warren. The Whites were a powerful north London gang. Spot attacked Warren in a pub on the edge of Soho, thereby upsetting the equilibrium that many were trying to achieve. It was around this time that the gangs had sought to make Soho an 'open house'. Each gang had its own interests, but the Italians, through Albert Dimes, still had the major influence due to the dominance of Italian-owned businesses operating in the area. Gang leaders and the police looked to Billy to maintain working relationships and to sort out any situations between those not prepared to come to amicable arrangements. The results of this consensus can be seen when, in due course, the new breed that included the Krays, the Richardsons and the Knights, along with Dimes and other notables, were regularly seen drinking in Soho clubs at the same time, without animosity.

★ ★ ★

Vera returned to London towards the end of August that year, with Michael Howard in her arms. For Billy, cash was no object – the best pram, the best pushchair, the best cot money could buy, not something off the back of a lorry. Toys, toys and more toys. And then if that was not enough, even more toys. However, as far as Vera was concerned, the main problem with their relationship still existed. Vera's mobility was now even more confined than it had been before the baby had been born. While Billy obviously adored his son and revelled in the thought of being a father, his attitude was nearer to that of a generous uncle. Fatherhood did nothing to curtail his socialising. He was out most evenings, regularly failing to return until the early hours of the morning, and as often not returning from one day to the next. Had he been prepared to provide explanations, the insult might not have been considered so great.

'Vera, as soon as the divorce comes through, I promise we will get married. A big wedding and then we'll have some more kids.' This was Billy's message of future happiness.

It was not what Vera wanted to hear. 'I don't want to marry you and I don't want any more kids. I don't even want to have sex with you any more.' Much to Billy's surprise, she meant it.

Tim, Billy's father, tried to mediate. 'Give Billy time. Now he's got a child, he'll soon settle down,' he told Vera. Billy's mother, Beat, was equally assuring. Billy was Billy.

Whilst most unmarried mothers at that time only had one thing on their minds – how quickly they could get a ring on their finger – Vera was prepared to walk away and take Billy's son with her if he did not mend his ways.

'What for Christ sakes is this?' Billy demanded when she bought him a book on socialism that had been recommended to her by Stella Adler, from the cast of *Golden Boy*. The play had been written by Clifford Odet, a left-wing writer, who would eventually be blacklisted during McCarthyism, and the un-American activities hearings in the USA. The West End theatre production starred Odet's wife Luise Rainer and Luther Adler at the St James' Theatre.

'I thought you might learn something, if you stayed in a few nights and read it,' she told him.

He wasn't impressed. And so it went on.

As months passed, she spent more and more time at her mother's in Kennington. Late one evening, the doorbell rang. Neither Vera nor her mother, now also separated from her husband, were expecting visitors. Certainly not at that late hour. Pulling the curtain of the front bay window slightly to one side Vera saw it was Billy, but before she could signal that she was coming to the door he began hammering the knocker. The street was quiet and the hallway was communal, leading to the two upper flats, but that was not what was annoying her. She rapped on the pane and gestured for Billy to keep quiet, not wanting him to wake Michael whom she had only moments earlier rocked to sleep.

'Open the bloody door,' Billy mouthed, gritting his teeth.

Moments later she let him into the living-room. His arm held inside his jacket, Billy pushed his way through to the kitchen, where he held his hand under cold running water. As the sink quickly coloured red, Vera's face drained of colour.

The cut was deep across the palm of Billy's hand. Slowly the water stemmed the flow of blood and Vera was able to bandage the wound sufficiently until Billy could get to a doctor who would not ask too many questions. The razor travelling towards his face and neck could have sliced fatally into an artery. Without a second thought, Billy had grasped the shining blade, stopping it inches from its target, but allowing it to cut deep into the flesh of the hand providing protection. Turning, his own razor had whipped instantly in retaliation. One slash, another and then a third. His hand holding his opponent's razor, Billy had relaxed and plunged his fist into the face now streaming with blood. The assailant fell back, crashing over tables and up-turning chairs as he stumbled, screaming, across the room. Within minutes, the whole fracas had ended, and those still capable of walking had melted into the night. Until that time, Vera had convinced herself Billy's activities were only based around the black market; her view now changed.

Before the end of the decade, Billy was to make his promise of a divorce true. On 14 October 1949, the papers came through and on 30 November 1949 the decree nisi was granted. Billy's marriage to Ellen Howard was now over. He felt sure that this would finally change Vera's mind and he set plans for their marriage in motion. However, Vera had taken her decision and would not be persuaded otherwise. In addition to Billy's playboy lifestyle, which she would not tolerate, the fact that Billy's business activities went well beyond the black market supply of goods gave rise to the strong possibility, in Vera's mind, of Billy being sentenced to long terms of imprisonment in future years. The potential absences and the environment created by his criminal activities were not, in her belief, suitable for bringing up a child. The relationship was firmly over.

The fact that Billy and Vera were no longer together soon became common knowledge and a number of Billy's girlfriends with whom he had had affairs over the previous few years began to surface. A blonde woman, who Vera guessed must have lived in the Newington Butts area, stopped one day, walked up the short path and rang Vera's doorbell. Vera had seen her on numerous occasions passing the Kennington flat, but now they were face to face.

'Are you Vera?' she asked.

Vera confirmed that she was, while examining what appeared to be a black eye.

'I hope you don't mind me calling, but I just wanted to know if you had finished with Billy. He did this,' she said, pointing to the bruised eye. 'And I wasn't going to see him any more, because he said you two went together. But if that's not the case, I thought I would give him another chance. If you're still interested, I'll stay away.'

Vera smiled at the thought that the woman would even consider going back after getting her eye blackened. 'If you want him, he's all yours.'

When Billy came around a few days later to pay Vera the money they had agreed for the support of Michael – an amount that varied according to the cash Billy had in his pocket at the time, although it was rare that he called without bringing a toy of some sort – he apologised for the blonde woman calling and told Vera that he had smacked her in the face and broken her nose for her effort. He assured Vera that she would not bother her again and that she should let him know if any other unwelcome visitors made a nuisance of themselves.

* * *

Hill was soon due for release after what proved to be another short spell inside. Prior to the case going to court, Hill had approached Billy to see if anything could be done to lessen the gravity of the sentence. Billy told him the same as he would later tell the Krays – the more publicity you attract, the more difficult it is to make any arrangements. Billy had spread some money around but had promised nothing. In any event, the sentence had not been too draconian, though it was impossible to be sure if the cash had landed on fertile soil.

Meanwhile Spot considered his own situation strong, financially, and was reluctant to have Hill coming back on to the street knowing he would be in Hill's sights. Spot arranged a meeting with Billy Howard in the bar of a West End hotel. He did not want to come down hard on Hill, but thought that it might be the only way of preventing Hill from trying to muscle in on his spielers. Billy was certain that Hill could put together sufficient muscle to cause trouble for more than just Spotty. However, he was equally sure that Hill's financial position had taken a dive with the downturn in his large-scale robberies and the losses he had sustained in the Johannesburg affair. Billy suggested that Spot make a personal approach to Hill on Hill's release, to tempt him into some sort of mutually agreeable alliance that would ensure Hill received some sort of income early on without the bother of putting a team together and risking going back inside. Spot took the advice and also offered Hill a storeroom of furniture that would enable Hill to re-establish himself.

Within a few months of coming out of prison, Hill was on the rampage. It seemed to Billy that the last stretch inside had had an effect on him. Normally, if Hill was upset with someone it would result in a casual beating or a single slash from his razor. However, as part of a reprisal, a minor villain who posed no threat was slashed over and over again. Had any one of the cuts been an inch or so deeper or longer, or repositioned, a cut artery could have quickly pumped the life out of the victim and Hill could have found himself off the streets forever. Spot was concerned that his flourishing empire of cash cows could be destroyed by this kind of uncontrolled behaviour. He discussed the matter with Billy, who again counselled bringing Hill closer into Spot's organisation. Spot was sceptical but there seemed to be little alternative. Billy explained to Spot that bringing Hill in close would allow Spot to keep an eye on what Hill was up to and, where necessary, undermine any action of which Spot did not approve. If nothing else, Billy assured Spot that it would buy him time. Pushing Hill away now would almost certainly create a confrontation, which was exactly what Spot was trying to avoid.

Spot brought up a second problem: an American interest in fixing Anglo-American boxing tournaments in the UK. This was an area in which Billy was unsure of his own position. He had already been in talks with some American players, a fact that he was not prepared to disclose to Spot. Spot had declared his position to keep the Americans out, but Billy was not so sure the right course of action was quite so clear-cut. He told Spot that he thought they [Spot and Billy] should talk again over the next few days, which gave Billy some time to see if the appropriate meetings could be arranged. The two men shook hands, Billy telling Spot not to let Hill get under his skin. Had the meeting been between Billy and Hill, he would have counselled the same.

Spot and Hill had both favoured Southend at various times in their careers, particularly when things in London were looking a little hot. Spot knew that Hill still had a hankering to own a club, and he felt that with the offer of a joint venture, in line with Billy's counselling, Hill's attention would be diverted from the West End, where he was continually getting into trouble. Spot was not seeking to exclude Hill from the West End, simply to reduce his free time in the capital. The choice of people to run the club surprised Billy and he was further surprised that Hill had accepted Spot's suggestion. The two men whose names were put forward had been part of a gang closely associated with Spot, the Upton Park gang. Hill later told Billy that at first he had argued that one man should be from Spot's firm and the other traditionally associated with Hill. But Spot's business mentality won through, seeing that it would be bad for the business if the two men running the club were at each other's throats. Spot's choice was agreed, although Hill did have previous connections with the gypsies with whom one of the men, Jackie Reynolds, was associated. The second man was Teddy Machin, who had bookmaking interests and had been involved in the Heath Row robbery of 1948, when the airport was a strip of concrete, a few Nissen huts and two words. As it turned out, no love was lost between the two men, and in time they would be in a knife fight with each other so vicious it was fortunate neither was killed.

Spot's second request had to be weighed carefully. Billy was sure that Albert Dimes had connections with the Italian-Americans: it was a matter of cultural background, language and families back in the old country. If Spot was not connected with the Jewish Mafia in America already, Billy felt sure that Spot would have an affinity with Meyer Lansky's people for similar reasons. If discussions were allowed to take place, the Jewish factor would provide a natural solidarity and Billy did not want to be left on the outside, believing whatever action he proposed to Spot, his own personal agenda must always be his first concern. After due consideration, Billy arranged for Spot to travel to Paris for a meeting with the Americans to discuss the British boxing scene. Billy had made numerous contacts with Americans from various backgrounds during the Second World War, when US troops were stationed in the UK. Gambling, sex and black market goods were all commodities they found of interest, both from the point of view of supply and that of demand. When the war was over and the US troops returned home, many of the contacts remained. But it was not through one of these contacts that Billy now needed to work. On this occasion, a more sophisticated approach was required.

* * *

The Bag O' Nails public house in London's Victoria stands a short walk from the back of Buckingham Palace and Wellington Barracks. This was a favourite haunt for young homosexual Guards officers, many of whom were high-class rent boys. At this time, homosexuality was a criminal act in the UK and members of the homosexual community operated in the same underground way as the criminal fraternity. On many occasions, their paths crossed. Lord Boothby, who was later exposed as a friend and sexual partner of Ronnie Kray, and other members of the government, the civil service, the Royal Family and foreign embassies were also known to use the establishment. On one occasion Boothby, along with a group of young men and a member of the Canadian Embassy, attended a homosexual party in Brighton. Whilst the police tended to avoid confrontation with Royals and government ministers, it was not unusual for them to blackmail the lower ranks of that community.

The Canadian had been brought to Billy's attention by a senior member of the Brighton Police Force who was looking to trade favours. As far as Billy was concerned, the Canadian had little to offer, although the opportunity for London criminals on the run to obtain Canadian passports, visas or emigration clearance had obvious attractions. Having invited him to a couple of parties, where Billy knew other homosexual guests would be circulating, the relationship became more amicable, as the Canadian did not view Billy as a potential blackmailer. It transpired that back home the Canadian had enjoyed a number of encounters with a member of the Seagram family, one of Canada's most powerful distilling dynasties. During the years of Prohibition, Seagrams had been heavily involved in the supply of liquor, much of which was smuggled over the border into the USA. Later, as Prohibition came to an end, mob money accumulated from the illegal trade was ploughed into legitimate brewery and distillery companies, one of which was Seagrams. Billy requested that the Canadian Embassy official make a telephone call.

Spot was impressed. Billy had decided to cross-match the introduction, arranging for Spot to face up to a notorious Italian mobster in Paris. Ralph Capone, the elder brother of Al Capone, a man in his 60s who had been heavily involved with his brother in bootlegging during Prohibition and had spent time in prison for fraudulently handling over $8,000,000, was the contact.

Billy did not have delusions, as was the case with the Krays and some of their henchmen that were to follow. He did not see himself at the head of the British arm of an American Mafia family. He was always pleased to provide a service, as he did for English gangs, but never to come under the direction of foreign mobsters. He was never prepared to be anything but his own man. 'Better to be down and out, than have someone on your back,' he once told a friend.

CHAPTER THREE

A Tonic for the Nation

The Whites, a north London gang whose dominance had grown during the war years and reached a pinnacle in the mid-1940s were, as the decade drew to a close, almost completely out of the picture as far as Soho was concerned. Albert Dimes, who was born in Scotland of Italian parents, two years prior to Bill's birth, was handling the Italians. By 1931 he had been to borstal and had spent a couple of short spells in prison for minor offences. On arriving in London, he had naturally joined up with the strong Italian gang under Darby Sabini. But after Sabini was pushed to one side, Dimes had been perfectly happy to side with the Billy Hill and Jack Spot alliance to rid London of Harry White and his boys. Dimes always remained his own man, a fact that Bill never tried to change. The Messinas seemed to have the girls under control, plus Hill and Spotty were achieving a working relationship. At times, it even seemed that they were friends.

Billy Howard had graduated. In his maturity, and particularly to those who were close to him personally, he was known simply as Bill. He now directly controlled a string of spielers and drinking clubs in Soho, Mayfair, Walworth, Kennington, Streatham and Brixton. To show that he approved of the Hill–Spot relationship, and along with three other investors, he bankrolled a spieler in Ham Yard, at the end of Archers Court in Soho. The hope was to provide profits on the same level as Spot's operation in the City and the joint Hill–Spot operation in Southend. The decor was more Mayfair than Soho, and from his experience there Bill retained in the back of his mind the thought that Brixton could also support a similar stylish club.

The club in Ham Yard paid protection to nobody. After all, it was the property of a consortium of London's most feared villains. But even so, large amounts of cash each week were going out of the door with bag men from West End Central and Scotland Yard, freebies and handouts to council officials, to this squad and that – everyone wanted their cut. At one point Bill considered pulling out of gaming and drinking clubs altogether, simply concentrating on protection and charging a fee for easing situations between parties – gangland confrontations or problems with the legal system.

★ ★ ★

As the 1950s dawned, the public looked to leave behind the austerity of the war years, a sentiment heralded by the Festival of Britain, which involved the whole of the country from major cities to towns and villages. London was to be the venue for a 27-acre exposition on Lambeth's South Bank, an area along the river stretching from Waterloo Bridge to County Hall. This rebirth of a nation after the dark years of war was to be modelled on The Great Exhibition held 100 years earlier. Themes included innovation; the arts and music; gardens; medicine; seaside resorts; cafés; the Festival Hall building; and industry. A total of 36 different focuses provided attractions for millions of locals, day-trippers and tourists, and acted as a magnet for criminals. A five-month business opportunity for pickpockets, thieves, con men, spivs, gamblers, pimps and prostitutes, dubbed 'A Tonic for the Nation', it was certainly an elixir to the underworld of the capital.

Greedy gangsters muscled in on traditional spiv pitches. Top names could see the potential for soaring profits, with criminal penalties far less onerous than those for armed robberies and smash-and-grab raids. One of the most lucrative sites was readily identified at Trafalgar Square. A short walk past the Houses of Parliament, Downing Street and the Changing of the Guards. A must for any visitor to the capital.

Billy Hill was determined to take control of the photographic 'concession', a con operated with no film in the camera, where the spiv pretends to take a photograph of a tourist, pockets their money and provides a receipt. Having taken their name and address, he promises that the photograph will be sent immediately it has been processed. If the tourist refuses, the photographer becomes threatening, insisting he has already taken the shot and that if they did not want it done they should have stopped him before he took the picture. Not wanting to become involved in a brawl in a foreign city, most people would finally, if reluctantly, pay up. Over the period of the Festival, tens of thousands of pounds were expected to be bagged.

Finally, it was agreed that the right to operate unhindered would go to the winner of a bare-knuckle fist fight. The last man standing took all. In a narrow cobbled street between Trafalgar and Leicester Squares, one of the longest, most brutal fights London had ever seen took place.

'Kill the bastard.' The shout turned into a raucous chant from the ranks of the excited, expectant crowd.

'Kill the bastard. Kill the bastard,' other voices joined in.

'Go on Billy, give 'im a left hander on the chin,' a cockney voice shouted encouragement above the roar.

Bill did not know if the crowd were shouting for him or against him. Probably some of each, he thought. Then he was fighting again. He led with his right, jabbing into his opponent's ribs. The man, whom he did not recognise, took little notice. He had only just stepped up to take the challenge. He was the sixth, and Bill had hardly broken sweat. Suddenly, without warning, the short, barrel-chested man lunged forward, swinging wildly. Bill side-stepped the attack and drove his fist squarely into the face that was closing quickly on him. The already flat nose cracked under the power of the blow. Bill felt blood ooze across his bare knuckles and heard another roar from the crowd. The blooded man fell back, only to be pushed forward again by the spectators forming the front line of the ring. Some just wanted to see more claret, others knew the line was long and the more punches Bill wasted, the sooner tiredness would set in and the chances of Bill losing would increase. Plenty of money was changing hands and those hoping Bill would lose his edge were betting against him.

Those who knew Bill well, the ones that no longer called him Billy, recognised that he was a long way off being beaten by fatigue. But there were good fighters in the crowd. The proven hardmen, and the hopefuls, who operated on the streets and in the clubs of Soho, had been joined by men, young and old, from the other manors who fancied their chances. Like those punters looking to see Bill get knocked out, the serious challengers were hanging back, happy to let the less likely contenders soak up the poundings.

Another blow and it was all over. The barrel-chested man was on the cobbles, his blood flowing into the grouting, mixing with the small red rivulets from previous losers. Fast-moving hands exchanged cash, payments were made and new bets taken quickly before another fighter stepped forward determined to finish Billy Howard.

Bill had been here before. His hands were already mounds of reset broken bones, the knuckle joints on each fist irregular and bulging like carbuncles from more fights than most people could recall. Each man stepped forward and, regardless of the fact that Bill was usually punching above his weight, each one was either hammered into unconsciousness or, when cut and bleeding, threw in the towel. Some spectators say they counted 20 fighters who succumbed to the unforgiving rain of blows that Bill maintained round after round. Many thousands of pounds changed hands.

It was a tournament that Bill could not ultimately win. Every time a man went down, another stepped forward. It is not absolutely clear but it would seem that the fight was won by Tony Mella. Certainly, this fight against Mella was one of the two most memorable street matches that Bill took part in, along with another earlier one against Arthur 'Spindles' Clawson.

Billy Hill put the final winner forward and it was Hill, not Tony Mella, who took control of the Trafalgar Square concession. Bill was annoyed. It was not that he objected to losing. The fight was fair and square and he believed that had he been fresh and of a similar age – Mella was quite a bit younger – he would have flattened the contender. What irritated him was the fact that Hill had obtained the concession without stepping into the ring in person. When the opportunity arose, Bill took Hill to one side and marked his card. Hill appreciated the implication and, understanding that Bill had been behind much of the negotiation to form the alliance between himself and Spot, came to an agreement that saw Bill benefiting from the pot generated by the racket throughout the period of the Festival.

* * *

Mad Frankie Fraser was years younger than Hill and Spot, and his little team were starting to have an ongoing ruck with the Carters, a south London family. This worried Hill and Spot, as it looked as though it might bring unwanted trouble and be disruptive to their businesses that were developing profitably. The police were also not looking to have a war develop that would bring their operational procedures into the public spotlight again. Hill was pleased that he had not allowed Bill's displeasure to fester over the Trafalgar Square business. When Hill approached Bill about the problem, Bill had already been contacted by an Inspector from Camberwell nick. Bill agreed to speak to someone in the Carter family and left Hill to talk to Fraser, with the understanding that if things did not sort themselves out, Bill would bang a few heads together. Bill's reputation was now that of a mediator as well as a man who could provide strong-arm answers.

Unlike Bill, Hill was drawn to foreign parts and towards the end of the year, unable to persuade Bill on a French adventure, Hill headed off with Spot to holiday in the south of France and to investigate opportunities for expanding their club empire on the Riviera. It was not long after this trip that Bill had dinner with Hill and Spot at Isow's restaurant in Soho. Spot and Hill put a proposal to Bill over the future of London's underworld. Spot's wife Rita was pregnant and he wanted to retire from activities that could result in a prison sentence. His future role as a family man was to be given top priority. Hill, a habitual criminal, knew the next time he was found guilty he would go down for the best part of ten years. They had taken the decision to concentrate on activities in legitimate business. Bill was not only confused by the purpose of the dinner, he was also amused. It was not clear to him his role in their conversion.

'What we want you to do is have a word with the Old Bill and see if it's possible to sort something out,' Hill explained.

'Sort what out? They're not after either of you for anything, are they?' Bill asked.

'Who knows? What we thought was that if you could talk to someone at the top, not Inspectors, someone at the Yard, who could put a finish to everything . . .'

'For a sum,' Spot butted in.

'So we could be sure that in the future nothing would come back to haunt us,' Hill continued.

'I mean, if a drawer full of files could be lost, that would be worth quite a bit,' Spot suggested.

'The problem is that you're both a bit well known. You keep putting yourselves about. Photos in the paper. If you'd have kept your heads down it would be a hell of a lot easier, if the public had never heard of you,' Bill explained, offering the same advice he would be giving to the Krays years later. He agreed to see what could be done.

'Then there is also all our interests that we can't put on our tax return,' Spot said. 'We thought you might be interested in buying us out,' he added.

Bill looked at him to see if he could detect any hint of a smile. He could not. Spot and Hill were shrewd and Bill could not fathom out what it was they were really looking to achieve. Bill was already getting a cut from the Soho clubs in which Hill and Spot were involved. He was getting a further rake off from the money he was passing to the police on a regular basis, and if they really intended to walk away from their illegal business interests, surely they must believe that there was a good chance Bill would be in a position to command enough power to simply walk in and take over whatever was up for grabs in Soho and the West End. As for Spot's East End investments, Spot was fully aware that Bill had never had any aspirations to extend his influence into that area of the City. Dinner ended in a friendly enough way, with Bill promising to speak with a 'good' copper at the Yard and to consider the suggestion that they come to some accommodation concerning their respective business interests.

As it turned out, before any of the matters could be pursued, Spot and Hill appeared to have a change of heart, putting their good intentions to one side. This may have been due in the main to Hill splitting up with his wife Aggie, followed by his making another trip overseas, this time to North Africa. On Hill's return, both he and Spot were involved in attacks on various members of the criminal fraternity and it was only by virtue of the fact that those involved refused to press charges that Hill remained free. However, his lust for overseas adventures proved to be financially ruinous. Again Hill sought to involve both Spot and Bill, but on this occasion both refused the offer. Spot, seeing that Bill was not drawn into Hill's escapades, invited Bill into a joint venture to expand their collection of clubs in Soho, just as Billy Hill faced the biggest financial disaster of his career.

Albert Dimes had been drinking in the New Cabinet Club in Soho, which Hill's wife Aggie retained after the split. French Tony, well known in the West End as a wide boy, offered Dimes a deal with an Arab. Not having had dealings with the Arabs previously, Dimes invited Hill, who he knew had experience in

Tangier, to accompany him to the meeting. Through a translator, it became clear that the Arab was looking for a team of mercenaries who would undertake to kidnap the Sultan of Morocco from a house in Madagascar where he now lived in exile. A fee of one hundred thousand pounds was agreed, 50 per cent to be paid in two parts prior to the kidnapping and the remainder on completion.

The Fourth Lady, registered in Costa Rica, was purchased, refitted and renamed *The Flamingo*. It left British shores from Torquay for Tangier, an open city under international administration until 1956 after which it became part of the Republic of Morocco and was granted the status of a freeport. Hill had recruited an experienced master mariner to captain the vessel, but the crew, whilst being trustworthy, had little maritime expertise. They consisted of Georgie Cole, Eddie Chapman, George Walker – brother of boxer Billy Walker and later to become head of the casino, hotel and leisure company, Brent Walker, which collapsed during the recession of the early '90s – Teddy Machin and Patsy Murphy.

Dimes and Hill joined the vessel in Tangier after flying out from Heathrow. But even before they arrived, things were not as they should have been. The guns needed for the assault in the Indian Ocean had failed to materialise, leaving George Walker the only member of the crew armed. A lack of instructions from their 'employer' left them sitting idle, so to pass the time and subsidise their stay, they embarked on a series of smuggling trips transporting cigarettes into Portugal. Finally sailing orders arrived, but not from the Arab. The orders were from the Chief of Police in Tangier who, having contacted London, decided the vessel and its crew were no longer welcome. The captain sailed for Genoa, while Dimes flew ahead to liaise with the local Italian families. No instructions from their employer reached them. That, and the adverse publicity plus a fight on board that ended with a fire, brought the mission to an end. Dimes, Hill and Walker flew home, mission aborted.

Hill needed large amounts of cash, and blagging was what he knew best. A bullion robbery in the City of London was looking for a financier, which appealed to him. If things went wrong, he could place himself well back from the action. Having decided to put money into the project, he took over the position of architect, taking responsibility for planning the raid. Whether Hill did not actually have sufficient cash, or was reluctant to place all the cash he had at risk, is unclear. The robbers demanded assurances that he could not or would not provide. It was standard practice that the money man was required not only to provide sufficient funds to underwrite the cost of the actual robbery, but also to guarantee funds to retain barristers, bribe police officers and get at juries if things went badly. If things went very badly, the backer would also be expected to ensure that the families of anyone who was sent down were supported financially during the period of incarceration. Hill approached Bill, a move which he believed would add credibility to his status as financier. If he could tell the leader of the gang going in that Bill was involved — Bill's reputation was second to none for his ability to influence evidence and coerce juries — it would calm the nerves of those worried about a potential custodial sentence. As it turned out, the robbery, which took place outside the offices of KLM, the national Dutch airline, just off Theobalds Road in September 1954, went without a hitch. Gold bullion valued at £45,000 was stolen from a van and neither the robbers nor the gold were ever traced.

Ironically, the inflow of cash was now becoming a problem for Bill. Whilst outgoings in the form of bribes and day-to-day running costs remained high, money that could not be declared or banked was mounting. Unlike many of the American gangsters who looked to snatch the American Dream, their British counterparts were at their happiest when they remained within their own environment. They rejected the large house and the film star lifestyle. Some were simply happy to park a luxury car outside their council flat and put pressure on the housing officer to give their son or daughter the one next door so that they could knock through and double the size of their 'family home'.

Once again, Hill left British shores, this time sailing for Australia, leaving Bill to expand into legitimate clubs.

* * *

Already parading himself as the King of Soho, Spot misguidedly took the opportunity, in Hill's absence, to strengthen his elevated position. In many respects he fell prey to believing his own publicity, and the action he instigated returned him to his earlier belief that the time had arrived to retire into legitimate business. The tussle was never between Bill and Hill, or Bill and Spot. It had always been a Spot and Hill thing. This was probably due to the fact that both Hill and Spot headed large, powerful gangs, whereas Bill had been much more of a loner, bringing in muscle and expertise when and where it was needed. With Hill heading for warmer climates, Spot wanted to secure his position, knowing full well that Bill would back him by virtue of the fact that if he were to take control, Bill would be backing the winner. The problem was Albert Dimes. Spot needed to move against Dimes before Dimes moved against him. However, before Spot could make his move, Hill was back, having had his entry into Australia blocked because of his criminal record. Spot was undeterred, but it did mean that he was always keeping an eye over his shoulder to see what Hill was up to.

The fight that took place was the well-publicised 'Fight That Never Was'. Spot attacked Dimes in a running assault along Old Compton Street in the heart of Soho, the road that had been Dimes' bookmaking pitch for years. Spot's bookmaking interests had previously been restricted to Dean Street, but now his activities had encroached on Dimes' business. Betting was a busy pastime on the narrow streets and out of necessity more than one operator was required. Each held to their own patch and as long as this remained the case, profits could flourish for everyone.

The Soho streets were crowded as usual. Cars swerved to avoid the brawling men and the police were quickly on the scene. But not before the owner of the local greengrocer's, on the corner of Greek Street, a Jewish woman by the name of Hyman, laid into both men with a heavy pan for upsetting her pavement display. Dimes and Spot both sustained stomach wounds and ended up in hospital, and court. The wounds healed and the victims refused to press charges or to give evidence. This was not unusual in Soho and the West End, where over 500 clubs were operating, some legally, but many illegally. All of those not directly owned by a major gang leader were paying protection to one of the major gang leaders, and many in turn were paying additional insurance to Bill for police protection.

Bill had two other main interests. The first was maintaining control in south London, centred on the Brixton area, and the second was on the gambling scene. The Brixton situation was easy and straightforward. Having grown up in the area, Bill knew everyone. With the ever-increasing respect he earned in Soho and the West End, nobody was interested in bringing Bill's potential power base down against them.

There were three main strings to Bill's gambling interests. The first was at the races, where Bill took little direct action. Dimes, however, was heavily involved and Bill was pleased to provide insurance to Dimes for a price. Protection rackets on the racecourses in the early days were vicious. With fast-moving, running battles, many bookies were bludgeoned and slashed at even a hint of non-payment or misdirected allegiance. This form of extortion was not confined to the major race meetings or large courses; a point-to-point held on farmland with amateur riders was equally fair game. Leasing pitches to bookies on a subcontracting basis was against the rules, but this did not prevent many racecourse executives from operating the system, using London gangsters to make the cash collections.

First Harry White, then one of Spot's men, had held the contract at the East Essex point-to-point. But with Spot's attention to racing diminished, Dimes had taken over the work on behalf of the Secretary, Captain Soames, who was also a director of the brewing company, Watneys. The bookmakers, who had sought protection and had turned to Bill years earlier, remained in his stable, so to speak. Dimes had quickly decided that it would be him, not Soames or the East Essex point-to-point, who would be the benefactor of the money, and there was little they could do about the new arrangement. On one occasion, while Dimes was in Manchester, where he was developing a gaming interest, one of his henchmen in London, an old-time hardman by the name of Dodger Mullins, was beaten to death with an iron bar. In a show of retribution, setting a standard that gang interests should not be encroached upon, Bill located the attacker and cut the culprit to ribbons.

Another request for Bill's expertise to be exercised in favour of Dimes occurred following the William Hill Gold Cup, run at Redcar in 1963. Faultless Speech was heavily doped and, very much out of character, the Jockey Club called the police. Doping had been a regular practice over a three-year period and there were plenty of ways the police could trace these offences back to Dimes. Darkie Steward was the stable lad charged, and Dimes was of the opinion that Darkie might be a bit milky and say anything to get off. Although Bill had enjoyed the fruits of the business, he had never been directly involved. However, it was now essential to keep Darkie quiet. A co-conspirator, Eddie Smith, was being held at Lewes gaol and had agreed to turn Queen's Evidence, so word had reached Bill through a prison warder. Bill decided to kill two birds with one stone, an unfortunate turn of phrase that was to cost Smith his life and ensure that in the future Bill would take care to express the degree of punishment without ambiguity. The intention had been that Smith should be given a good hiding, a message that would be clear to Darkie. In the event, Smith 'fell' from the balcony at Lewes gaol and died. Darkie got the message and Dimes, whose name was mentioned at the trial, was not charged.

Bill's second string of gambling interests comprised the permanent spielers and those set up for special occasions. The spielers were generally run by front men who managed the place, collected the cash and paid it over to Bill in return for wages. The spielers set up for major racing events in hotel rooms, in the back rooms of pubs and, where the course was a long train journey out of London, in a carriage on the train. Set up correctly, many punters would arrive at the course completely skint, having been fleeced within hours of leaving London. The overnight train to Ayr was one of the best runs, a long boring journey with plenty of time to pull the suckers in. The guard was the first person to be squared – race weeks could prove highly lucrative for him. Regardless of who was on duty, they were all prepared to play ball, many even pointing out the big tippers and those they had seen carrying large wads.

Bill handled a deck of cards with speed and a sleight of hand far swifter than his gnarled knuckles would have you believe. One of his favourite party pieces was to shuffle a new pack, cut it and then ask for your favourite number of players at poker. Three, five, six, whatever, he would then deal your hand and the remaining number specified. Your hand would be almost as good as it could get, a hand worth playing to the full. His hand would always prove one better. A good trick, but with its obvious drawbacks when playing with well-seasoned gamblers, particularly those who were accompanied by minders. If a sore loser wanted to take back his money and dole out some punishment, it was usually left until the train pulled into the station, thereby allowing the attackers to escape into the crowds without fear of being trapped in the confined carriages. If they felt they had been tumbled, Bill and his team would regularly slip off the train, on to the track, as the engine slowed at a strategic point, shortly before pulling alongside the platform. Cheltenham was another favourite, full of Paddies there for the horses, but determined to gamble on anything at every opportunity. A suite at the Queens Hotel, at the top of the Promenade, always attracted high rollers, as did the boat train returning to Holyhead for the Irish ferry.

The third area of gaming interest was the corporately owned, formal casinos. By the mid-1970s, Bill was barred from all the major casinos in the UK. A company having problems with a player would have his or her photograph circulated to all the company-owned units up and down the country. Barred from one, barred from all.

Bill operated scams in these premises on three levels, bouncing stolen cheques and handing in stolen goods to the cashiers and managers who were unable to report the situation because of the illegal nature of the items, and who would not refuse to accept them at the time of presentation for fear of receiving a good beating or a slash with a razor as they left the building. Similarly, he worked in collusion with the croupiers, predominately calling bets which, if they won, would be paid, and if not, would not be collected. Alternatively, the croupier might conceal high-value chips amongst stacks of chips of a lower value, which would often require the acceptance of the inspector. All involved enjoying a cut of the 'winnings' at a later date at best, or at worst, escaping a slashing or blackmail over some act of which they would prefer their employer, wife or the police not to be aware.

Bill also used a more complex scam that involved a wide variety of highly skilled manoeuvres, often carried out by a small team who would divert the attention of the casino staff at the moment the ball on the roulette wheel dropped, or dice, which had been tampered with, were introduced or withdrawn from a crap table. As the little white roulette ball lost speed, dropped and bounced between the numbered slots, a judgement would have to be made with speed and accuracy. Of course it was somewhat easier if a member of the staff had earlier been persuaded to slightly broaden the gap between some of the numbers, making it easier for the ball to drop into a particular slot. Pairs of protractors were used at the beginning of each shift to ensure all the gaps on the wheel were equal, so any tampering had to be done between that time and the time of the table opening. 'Pushing' was also popular, normally operated from the end of the table. One member of the team would have a stack of chips ready just outside the column box. An accomplice would shout a code word if the ball dropped into the appropriate number and the pusher would quickly slide the stack of chips into the corresponding column box, paying two to one. On other occasions, as the croupier called 'no more bets' and the ball dropped, a stack of low-value chips, with a high-value chip at the base is placed on the winning box. The player pretended not to be concentrating, and appeared not to be concerned if the croupier noticed, as he surely would. 'No bet,' went the cry. The player apologised and lifted up his stack of low-value chips, leaving behind the high value chip. If this chip was queried, the player said it was not his, but an accomplice could claim the chip, which he said was placed earlier, long before 'no more bets' was called. Standing well out of reach of the number, it looked clear that the accomplice could not have put the bet down at the last minute. At odds of 35 to 1, the croupier, inspector or pit boss would usually know they had been had, but they would pay out. Efforts would be made to isolate the team, close the table and generally make it difficult for the team to play. For stunts like these Billy Howard soon became *persona non grata*.

* * *

The Kray twins had not dissimilar backgrounds to Bill, although when they were born in 1933, Bill was already 17. They grew up in the East End and like Bill they enjoyed boxing and were gutsy punchers. By the time they reached the age of 17, they had already been part of a gang that enjoyed fighting, both with fists and blades. It was this that led to their first formal visit to the Old Bailey, to answer charges involving assault and wounding. At the age of 19, like all other young men at the time, they were called up to do their National Service. Unlike Bill, they boxed less when they were drafted into the Royal Fusiliers, where their lack of interest in girls slightly set them apart. Before long they were AWOL and on the run. They had naturally wanted to avoid their home in Vallance Road, Bethnal Green, the first place the MPs would look. So, instead, they had gravitated towards the West End, and Soho in particular, hanging around the billiard halls and drinking clubs.

When they fell under the eye of Bill, he recognised their potential. Bearing in mind their home ground, and Spot's increasing lack of control, having failed to secure a victory over Dimes, it seemed that the Krays would undoubtedly be contenders for Spot's East End manor. But there were two things Bill felt might prevent their move up. All of London had its tearaways, many more vicious than the gang leaders they followed. What these tearaways lacked was the capability of turning violence into cash. Running a gang costs money – gang members had to be able to earn a living and it was the boss's responsibility to stump up the cash. The more that was paid out, the more loyalty that could be commanded.

The other problem they faced was a lack of direction. Criminality, like any other business that is going to be successful, needs to channel its strengths. The Messinas were pimps. They concentrated their efforts into running girls – high-class prostitutes at one end of the market through to streetwalkers at the other end. Billy Kimber saw his goal in the racecourse protection rackets. Dimes looked after the Italians, Hill at his best was a thief and Spot had the backing of the Jewish East End community. Gang leaders needed a power base. The Krays were still tearaways, kicking around, and it was not long before their immediate future was decided. The MPs swooped and the Twins were held in lchester Military Prison for many months before finally being kicked out of the army with a dishonourable discharge.

The Twins were bright enough to know that if they wanted to reach the top of their chosen profession, they needed an in while they found their feet and established their position. Spot was the obvious person to fulfil this role but, whilst he was prepared to have them carrying out errands on his behalf, he was not prepared to treat them as his anointed successors, as Dimes would with Zomparelli, or as Bill would when he was pleased to place his hand on Ronnie Knight. The Twins turned to Bill, as they could logically sell the idea that they would not be a threat to Bill's south London manor. And to have them as allies, running the East End, would give stability after Spot either stepped down or was pushed aside – a fact that was becoming increasingly clear to everyone, probably most of all to Spot himself. The approach to Bill was made in Soho, at the Caterer's Club in Frith Street. The Twins had chosen this place that, although originally a club for the waiters and chefs who worked split shifts in Soho, had been taken over by a variety of celebrity afternoon drinkers from many of the West End theatres. It was also a place frequented by Dimes, so the Twins did not expect to accidentally bump into Spot, who would have become highly suspicious.

The following day Bill, sitting in the back of his V8 Pilot, told his driver to head for the East End and to take a tour around the streets. It was not an area Bill often frequented, although he had, from time to time when he was younger, been on raiding parties with members of the Elephant gang, mounting assaults on lads the Elephant Boys thought had been taking liberties, and more recently, attending the occasional opening party of a pub or club under new management. After an hour or so, Bill told the driver to find 178 Vallance Road. As they drew up at the pavement, the Twins, dressed in cheap but smart dark suits, white shirts and plain ties, stepped from the front door. They had learned something from being in the Army, Bill smiled to himself. Walking, shoulders back, arms swinging. Not ridiculous, but noticeable.

Bill had selected half a dozen places, small and therefore probably beneath Spot's interest level, although possibly businesses that young members of Spot's gang may have been putting the squeeze on. The Twins told Bill anything they knew about the businesses, which was practically nothing. They finally settled on a second-hand car lot, no petrol or garage work, just little more than a hut, a sign and half a dozen small cars on what appeared to be a flattened bombsite. Bill was not sure how best to handle it. Ideally he thought it was best for the Twins to go and speak to the owner on their own, but he was worried that they would come on too strong and end up smashing the owner instead of letting him off in return for a payment. If Bill fronted it himself, there was a danger that Spot would get word and think Bill was trying to take over his patch, which would cause all sorts of trouble and benefit nobody. The Twins' chomping at the bit made up Bill's mind. He suggested that they start inspecting the cars, one using a razor to pick at the paintwork, the other poking at the tyres with a flick knife, while he spoke to the owner within earshot.

Seeing the V8 pull up at the curb, the owner of the site left the hut and began to approach the prospective customers, but seeing the size and shape of the men he quickly felt uncomfortable. They did not appear to be his normal style of clientele. Bill was noted for being eloquent, swearing and shouting at people he found to be counter-productive.

'Excuse me, do you own this site?' Bill asked the man.

He had told the Twins that it was always best to make sure you're dealing with the owner before you start causing trouble. If you threaten a worker, he can just go home and not come back, the owner has had some warning and the next time you visit there are some heavies he's brought in from a rival gang. And you still don't know what the owner looks like.

The man nodded uncertainly.

'Do much business?' Bill asked, looking around.

'A bit,' the man replied, starting to relax a little.

'Been lots of trouble round here lately.' This was more of a statement than a question.

'Has there?' The man was on his guard again. 'Looking for a car? Any particular one you got your eye on?' he continued.

'Any one of them catch your eye?' Bill asked the Twins.

The owner then caught sight of what was in the Twins' hands. 'Oi,' he said, barging forward, 'you can stop that.'

Bill tripped him as he went to go past. The man, who looked as if he were an ex-RAF officer, but was probably nothing of the sort and more than likely had spent as much time in Colchester as the Twins, stumbled against another of the cars. Bill pulled him up by the scruff of the neck and punched him in the stomach. Not too hard, just enough to take the wind out of his sails. Then he pushed him in the direction of the hut. The Twins followed. Bill saw a crucifix hanging on the wall, which surprised him a little. There was an ex-army type desk, a wooden chair and a small gas ring with a kettle on it. What it was connected to, Bill wasn't sure.

'What do you want me to do with him?' Bill asked the Twins, but before they could answer, he pushed the man down into the chair. From the table he picked up a pencil and from his pocket he took out a razor that had been taped open. Using long strokes, which ended only inches from the man's face, Bill sharpened the lead.

'My bosses here,' Bill pointed to the Twins. 'they are in the insurance business and they tell me that a car site this size should pay £40 a week.'

'I've already got insurance,' the man mumbled.

'Well, now you've got some more,' Ronnie said, speaking for the first time.

'I can't afford that. Some weeks I don't make that,' the man argued.

Then Reggie piped up. 'Then you'd better work a bit fucking harder, 'adn't ya?'

'Honestly, look, that's all the money I've got.' He tried to pull a wallet from his pocket, but it fell on the floor.

Ronnie moved to pick it up, but Bill gently put his foot on it.

'So how much can you afford?' Bill asked.

'I might be able to manage twenty,' he replied, watching Bill running the blade across the palm of his own hand, without drawing blood.

Bill bent down and picked up the wallet. Inside was £70. Bill counted out £25 and handed it to Ronnie, returning the wallet to its owner.

'Let's call it a pony. They'll be round each week like the Prudential. I only get paid once for doing house calls, so I don't want to be having to come back. If you've got any problems, let the Twins know when they come round.'

In the car Ronnie offered Bill the money back.

'What you collect in the East End is yours, or yours and Spot's. Anything else, we talk about. If you have any problems with the Old Bill, call me. But if it's something that needs sorting out, don't leave it until it's about to go to court. Call me straightaway or get your brief to give me a bell. Whatever it costs, I'll cover it, you square me up later. OK, you've got your first place, how do you fancy a cup of tea?'

They parked up. Bill spoke to his driver and sent him in first to a little corner cafe.

'Why did you stop us picking up the wallet?' Reggie asked. 'I'd 'ave had the lot if that had been me,' he added.

'That's why I didn't let you pick it up. Take everything and the man can't run his business. You're not looking at being robbers. You take it all and you've robbed him. You take a little from a lot of people and you've got a pension for the rest of your life. Or the rest of his life, anyway,' Bill explained.

A few minutes later Bill went into the caf with the Twins. They ordered three teas and sat at the only empty table.

'Why did you want to come in here?' Ronnie asked, not really believing Bill was so desperate for a cup of tea that he wanted to drink out of a chipped mug at a greasy table.

It happened before either of the Twins knew what was going on. Bill's driver came from a door at the side of the counter, snatched up the bald little man in a dirty apron, and smashed him into a stack of unwashed plates. 'That sodding pisser is a disgrace. I wouldn't use yours to have a piss in a dirty hole like that,' he screamed in the man's face, pulling him forward again.

The cafe owner hung in the arms of Bill's driver like a dirty wet dishcloth. Bill gave the Twins a shove. 'Go and throw that troublemaker out,' he told them. 'If the owner offers you anything for helping him out, refuse. Tell him he can buy you a breakfast tomorrow.'

'I don't want to eat breakfast in this filthy hole,' Reggie protested.

Bill smiled, 'Just do what you're told.'

The Twins hustled Bill's driver out of the door without too much fuss, though he put on a bit of a show. The owner did not offer them any money; he just offered them some food, a drink. They said they would look in for breakfast the next day. As they went back to their seats, some of the people at the other tables gave a muted clap.

'Tomorrow refuse breakfast and tell him you'll have a couple of quid and you'll look in each day to make sure everything's OK. Then up it to a fiver when he gets used to the idea,' Bill told them as soon as they were outside.

By two o'clock Bill was back in Mayfair, drinking a large gin and tonic and arranging for a couple of wooden tops from Brighton to spend the afternoon doing the rounds of the Soho strip clubs, followed by drinks with a couple of hostesses in Mayfair.

Before the day was over, Spot was on the phone wanting to know what was going on.

'Jack, I should have talked to you about it first, but the Twins were chomping at the bit. Better they've got something to keep themselves busy than planning all sorts of things that are going to cause lots of trouble. Let them get on with a bit. Just keep your eye on them and everyone will be happy,' Bill suggested. He knew it was the thin end of the wedge and he bet Spot knew it too. Although Spot was moving on, Bill knew Spot would not want to appear to have been pushed out.

'Bill, I'm telling you, if they start getting too big for their boots, I won't stand for it.' Spot was laying down the law, but unless he acted against the Twins now, Bill thought, it would not be long before he would not have the power to come away winning.

Bill did not return to the East End until he was 40, when well-known Soho character Tommy Smithson was dead. Bill attended the funeral as a pallbearer, sorry to see the man go, gunned down in a hotel room by an unknown team. He had carried out the odd job for Bill over the years, but most of his dealings were with the Maltese and the prostitutes they ran. He had been noted for always carrying a gun and Bill had told him more than once that he should restrain the violence he dished out, although there was no doubt that he was equally capable of taking it. He was the sort of man that you had to kill. If you didn't, however badly he was injured, when he was back on his feet he'd find you. It was a philosophy Bill understood and admired. He just thought Smithson should have done it with more brains. Prior to Smithson's brutal killing, he had been set upon by Spot and Hill, a revenge attack for an assault with a razor Smithson carried out on a hardman by the name of Sullivan. The two gang leaders stood by while a gang of Sullivan's friends and a few family members slashed Smithson, inflicting injuries that would almost certainly have caused his death from loss of blood had he not been found in time.

Spot was also to bear the scars of a vicious attack. Hill and Spot were no longer the allies they had been during the earlier part of the decade. Dimes had sided with Hill, and Spot's attack on Dimes in Old Compton Street was seen just as much as an attack on Hill. Only a matter of weeks before Smithson's death, Mad Frankie Fraser, Bobby Warren, Battles Rossi and Ginger Dennis were all given long prison sentences for an ambush on Spot and his wife Rita outside their flat in Hyde Park Mansions, Bayswater, in which they were both beaten and Spot sustained a gaping wound to his face. Hill was not yet finished.

Known to regularly be on his own, Bill was easy to corner and fell prey to an attack. Coming out of the dark quickly, after his driver had dropped him off, four men waded into Bill with pieces of timber and an iron bar. As he fell to the ground, unarmed and unprepared, out came the knives and razors, cutting deep into his back, shoulders and side. Bill couldn't remember the exact words Hill spoke from the open window of his car as it cruised along the gutter, but they amounted to the insistence that Hill was now the Boss of London's Underworld. If that were the case his tenure lasted weeks, not months and not years. Bill's wounds were deep, long, curving cuts. First penetrating clothing, then skin and then flesh, in some places down to the bone. They took weeks to heal, not months and not years.

To Bill retaliation was not a gangland affair. Hill, Spot or Dimes and their predecessors would have called together their loyal hardmen and mounted an attack. This was not Bill's way. It never had been. Once Hill knew that Bill was on the warpath, Hill would surround himself with men he could trust, or he would go to ground. Bill realised that Hill had to be the first on his list. Before Bill could make his move, a Chief Inspector had been dispatched to ask him not to go up against Hill's mob. There were serious concerns in the police and the judiciary that before long the whole of London's gangland would explode into a gang war, with each gang looking to take control of the West End for themselves. Within days of Fraser being sent down, Dicky Frett and Dave Rosa were also given seven-year sentences for cutting Johnny Carter, a member of the notable south London family and closely connected to the Elephant Boys. Billy Blythe, who also had south London connections, was sent down with Battles Rossi and Bill Dennis for the assault on Spot, and Spot had been in court, but walked free, for a razor attack on Dimes' driver Tommy Falco, outside Bertie Green's Astor Club in Mayfair.

Bill declined the invitation, but sent word back through the Chief Inspector that the way things were did not benefit anyone, and that given a little time and a blind eye he would sort things out. The police and the underworld waited to see what was going to happen, waited to see who would make the move that would spark things off and settle the discontent once and for all. The police had been keeping a close eye on Hill, but this was now relaxed. Bill made his move. No razor, no gun, no knife, just fists. He wanted to prove to Hill that one to one, he could take everything Hill dished out and then come back for more. Bill stepped from the rear of his car, strode across the pavement and without speaking, drove his fist into the side of Hill's head. To his surprise, Hill did not go down straight away although he was disorientated. A blow to the gut and another to the head sent his legs buckling. Bill grabbed him by the throat, held Hill against the wall and pounded with one body punch after another.

'Next month they're going to abolish hanging, but if they don't, next time I'll swing for you,' Bill shouted into the red gasping face. Bill removed his hand from around Hill's throat and allowed him to drop to the floor, stamping on his ankles as he lay at his feet. Even if the ankles were not broken, Bill knew that Hill would not be able to walk to the edge of the pavement without assistance. It took Bill a month to locate the others that had attacked him. Again, he took them individually, but in these attacks he repaid cut for cut.

Hill stepped back, content to shun the limelight. Any thought of heading a power struggle had gone from his mind and the idea of retirement to warmer overseas shores was again becoming appealing.

Spot also needed to be spoken to, as it became clear that along with having no stomach for attempting to restamp his mark at the head of a gang, he also did not have the funds to pay his rent, let alone mount a costly challenge. Dimes was the one person Bill wanted to remain in place. It was necessary to have an Italian in control of the Italian community in Soho and Clerkenwell. Tough, but with an easy-going manner, Dimes was the man for the job. The Messinas had been splashed across the front pages of the tabloid Sunday papers again, and it was made clear to Bill in discussions with the Chief Inspector that any reorganisation in the West End should not include a long-term future for the Messina family. Rounding up the hardmen of the Elephant and Castle, in much the same way as Billy Kimber had done years earlier, Bill began working his way through Soho and the West End, not at the head of a raging mob, but quietly talking to the owners of drinkers, spielers, strip clubs – everyone that was not Italian, all the time letting it be known that the muscle of the Elephant Boys was ready and waiting. Bill had someone in mind for the future, but for the time being he was happy for Dimes to have his backing, and he had successfully persuaded any possible contender that a war was in nobody's interest. Soho became what it was best at being, not a war zone for every gangland hopeful or jack the lad tearaway, but a playground for the whole of London's underworld. In Soho everyone showed respect.

No sooner had Bill put a plaster on Soho, Brighton became a festering sore.

* * *

'I don't run the bloody country,' Bill told the man sitting at the table with him. 'I can't protect everyone. Sometimes, some people just have to go down.'

'Something's got to be done,' the man told Bill, with one eye on the floorshow and the other on Bill.

Bill had seen the show a hundred times before and at that moment was about as interested in it as he was in what was being suggested. 'What?'

'We thought we'd leave that up to you.'

'Why don't you just let them go if that's what you want?' Bill said with his usual grin.

'We can't do that.'

A scantily clad girl in sequins and feathers draped a broad feather fan in the direction of Bill's guest and then saw Bill's look of disapproval. She moved away.

'Well, you're the Old Bill. If you can't, who can?' Bill told him.

'Mr Howard, there are a lot of very nervous people, not only at West End Central and the Yard, but also in Chambers. If a Chief Constable goes down, nobody will feel safe. You have to protect him. There's a lot of people watching this case.' Bill's guest had taken his eyes off the girls and was talking seriously. He was not talking to Bill on his own behalf, he had been sent with a message. He swallowed the remainder of the liquid in his glass.

'Ted, there's three of yours and two of mine. What's the deal?' Bill asked, at the same time signalling to one of the waitresses to bring them fresh drinks. He didn't like having to ask, she should have been there already. He would speak to the maitre d' later. She could find another job.

'Are you sure there is nothing you can do for Ridge at your end?' Bill asked. He would have preferred if papers could have been lost and evidence corrupted, rather than having to talk to witnesses.

'Not as far as Ridge is concerned. That part of the investigation they've got battened down as tight as a duck's arse,' Ted Bland explained.

'If we see the strength of the witnesses at the committal, scare a few so they're not as keen when it goes up to the Bailey,' Bill suggested.

'We'll leave that to you.'

'And the other two?' Bill asked.

'I'll try and get them to go softly with the evidence on one. Which one do you want?' Bland asked.

'Have to be Lyons.'

'Might cost.'

'So might Ridge,' Bill added.

'Let's just see how things go, we can work out what's what then.'

Bill agreed.

Bland had been on the payroll for a long time and Bill could see that his climb up the Met ladder still had some way to go. Before they left Bill put a couple of tickets for a West End show in his pocket. 'Take the missus, everyone says it's a great show. I'll let the doorman know and you can take her backstage afterwards, she'll enjoy that.'

Later, in the Spanish Garden Club in Mayfair, Bill started to make some phone calls. From time to time he was paranoid about phone tapping, which had become an issue since the Hill telephone-tapping scandal. On this day Bill was being extra careful. He arranged to see the people he wanted to talk to back across the other side of the river.

In the upper room of a Brixton pub, Bill started to put together plans that he hoped would satisfy the agreement he had made with Bland. Two people, a man and a woman, were dispatched to Brighton. The woman was to cover the court, the man picking up the talk around the pubs and clubs.

'Pick some likely faces and a few of the boys can get down there and put the frighteners on them. And any of the chaps down there stepping out of line, you can let them know we'll torch their places if they open their mouths too wide,' Bill told the small group of men sitting round the table.

★ ★ ★

'Just set fire to the place. If Page goes ahead as pros witness, torch it.' Bill was in no mood to play games. Bland had confirmed that, for a price, he had been able to get to one of the prosecution team. All things being equal, Tony Lyons should be able to get a not guilty, but Bland wanted assurances over the Chief Constable. It had taken more pressure than Bill had anticipated, but by the time the Old Bailey jury had reached their verdict in what now had become nationally known as 'The Brighton Affair', the right result had been achieved. Bill would have liked Sammy Bellson to have got off as well, but it was unrealistic to expect the Old Bill to carry the can alone.

Bill was being particularly careful and things were working out quite nicely. Spot had declared himself bankrupt and, along with Rita and the kids, he had been thrown out of their Bayswater flat. The word was he was on a boat heading for a new life in Canada. Hill was taking a back seat with much talk that he was looking to open a club or shop somewhere in the suburbs. The interest Bill had in Churchill's Club, Bond Street, had turned sour, with Bruce Brace splitting from the co-owner Meadows. Bill had sided with Bruce, whom he considered a friend. The loss of this interest was not only substantial financially, it also greatly reduced the influence he was able to exert over many of the well-placed clientele. However, the setback was short-lived. Tongue in cheek, Bill and Bruce had opened a club of similar style, and a short distance from Churchill's. They named it Winston's.

Spot received the same treatment at the hands of the Canadian immigration department as Hill had with the Australians. Whether Spot enjoyed his sea voyage nobody knew, and fewer people cared. His status in gangland did not improve on his return, although he was able to sort out his bankruptcy and open a club using his wife's name. The Highball opened a short walk from the flat Spot had been evicted from 12 months earlier. Whether Lancaster Gate was considered the West End or not made little difference. Spot and his new club were not welcome. Within weeks of it opening, much of it was wrecked. Undeterred, Spot reopened.

'What do you think should be happening with Spotty?' the voice on the other end of the phone said, more in conversation than as a request for advice.

Bill's thoughts were much the same as they had been for Page's club in Brighton eight months earlier. 'Jewish lightning,' Bill replied.

Knowing Spot was on his uppers, Bill's attitude was that Spot could make an insurance claim and have enough cash to finally disappear from the scene. Within days, the Highball Club was burnt down and Spot, with his family, had retreated to Ireland.

Hill grabbed some publicity with Lord and Lady Docker, when Lady Docker had her jewellery stolen and he arranged for it to be returned. He also had a bit of a fight in a pub with Joey Wade, but apart from that and his involvement in a shop in the suburbs, he was talking of returning to Tangier or Spain to spend a quiet life in the sun.

The 'Swinging '60s' were about to erupt on the scene, bringing with them new faces, not only in the criminal world, but throughout the Metropolitan Police and the entertainment industry.

CHAPTER FOUR

Unacceptable Behaviour

Bill enjoyed women and liked being seen with beautiful women. But he lived in a violent world and in many respects treated them the same as the men he mixed with. By men and women alike, he was considered charismatic, eloquent, well dressed, and conveyed considerable humour and authority. However, when he gave an instruction he expected it to be carried out and when it wasn't, the men with whom he circulated were not surprised to find the instruction repeated with a right-hander. The women were more surprised. Vera seems to have been the only person who was not subjected to this violence, and remained completely in control of her own destiny.

The 1960s were a time to party and this had now become very much Bill's business, providing an exclusive club scene for the rich and famous, and enjoying the benefits of it personally. The Soho strip clubs and vice had given Bill a constant string of interested, attractive young women more than happy to be the centre of attraction for one night, or however many nights they remained in favour. They all enjoyed the large tables of influential guests Bill hosted in top West End restaurants, rarely settling the bill but assured of lavish service by maitre d's and waiters who knew they would receive a tip, often higher than the wage bill for the whole restaurant for a whole month.

Churchill's, Winston's and Bill's Brixton club, The Beehive, provided an inexhaustible supply of starlets, celebrities and wives of the rich and powerful. It had not taken long for Churchill's to slip into second place behind Winston's, which had become the number one venue in the West End. Good writers, choreographers and performers had achieved a cabaret that outdid all of the other clubs. The chorus girls and hostesses were noted for being the sexiest in town and Bill acted as the lavish host, ensuring the club pulled in the crowds that were prepared to spend.

Danny La Rue, who really started at Churchill's as a young lad and who in his early years had come under Bill's care, developed into a major attraction and was brought over to Winston's by Bruce Brace and Bill. His act proved to be pivotal in the making of Winston's. Barbara Windsor, with her bubbly personality and a keen interest in socialising with anyone who took her fancy, and who was later to marry Ronnie Knight, also gained much success at the club, along with comedian Ronnie Corbett, who met his wife, Anne Hart, while they were working at the club. It really was a breeding ground for many television personalities who became household names during subsequent decades. But it was not only those seeking to make a name for themselves in film, TV and the theatre who were associated with the club. It also attracted many established stars. Patrick McGoohan, of *Danger Man* and *The Prisoner* fame, was a regular. Judy Garland, Noel Coward, Bing Crosby and Peter Finch, who enjoyed a rather unsavoury reputation with the hostesses, also frequented the club. Finch was a big drinker and a good spender.

'Peter, it's good to see you as always,' Bill welcomed the lone male, already somewhat the worse for drink. As Bill spoke, the man stumbled and had it not been for Bill throwing an arm around him, the man would have toppled a table and sent another guest crashing to the floor. Bill guided Peter Finch to a table close enough to the stage and the cabaret to make him feel that he was sitting near the front, but sufficiently far enough away to prevent Peter from interrupting the performance.

'Peter, are you after a girl tonight?' Bill asked, knowing that rarely on his regular visits to the club did he leave alone. Peter asked if a particular girl was at the club that night. Bill confirmed that she was, but that he was not sure if she was already spoken for. Bill lied, but he knew the fuss the girls were starting to make.

'Send her over and tell the waitress to bring a bottle of champagne,' Peter said, ignoring the suggestion that the girl he had stipulated might not be available.

'Peter, I know you like to have a bit of fun with the girls and sometimes it gets out of hand, but a lot of them are starting not to want to go home with you.'

'Bill, don't you worry about any of that, you just send her over. They always get a good time and no one can accuse me of not being generous.'

'Peter, one of the girls you took home last month couldn't work for two weeks, she was so badly bruised and had a split lip. Even if they're putting up with it all, most of them have to work. They need the money. They can't afford to have weeks off,' Bill explained.

'I'll make sure things don't get out of control. How's that?' Peter said, making a promise that Bill believed he was unlikely to be able to keep.

On the way back to the bar, Bill sent a waitress in the direction of Peter's table and then picked up the house phone. He dialled two digits and waited for one of girls in the Cage, the term applied to the room where the hostesses waited to be called to a table, to answer. When eventually someone did, Bill told the voice on the other end to answer quicker in future and to send someone up.

'Who for?' the girl asked.

'Peter Finch.' Bill knew that this would provoke an argument. He had heard them talking amongst themselves about it a few nights ago. He could persuade them to put up with a bit of beating, but none of them liked being off work. 'If there's any trouble tonight, I'll see something goes on his bill the next time he comes in. Now let's have one of you at his table straightaway.' Bill replaced the receiver before there was time for any backchat.

Bill had not taken more than a few steps from the bar when there were more problems. The doorman wanted him. 'Mr Howard, do I let him in or not?' the doorman asked.

The man that the doormen were uncertain about was the wealthy son of a large brewing family and was well known around the West End, causing an uproar the last time he was in doing his party piece.

'Bill,' the man said with a tone of appeal in his voice, as Bill approached him.

Bill nodded to the doorman to indicate that the man could come in. He was a good punter and Bill would have been sad to lose him, but it was going to cost.

'You're welcome but it's a hundred quid if you want to come in,' Bill told him.

'A hundred nicker? There isn't a club in London that charges that kind of money,' he exclaimed, somewhat indignant.

While the man had been a little drunk and easy-going, the idea of paying up that kind of money to get in had rather sobered him up. He slapped Bill on the shoulder and made to walk past. Bill checked the man's advance. 'Sorry, but it's a hundred to get any further.'

The man took out his wallet, counted out the notes and handed them over.

'That's the cost of entrance from now on. And don't piss over any of the customers,' Bill told him.

The last time the man had been in he had stood at the edge of the stage and urinated over the chorus girls. That was one thing, but turning his aim on the club's more important guests sitting close to the stage almost caused a riot, if not a lynching.

'You look like you need a cup of coffee, Mr Howard,' a small Asian man said quietly as he approached Bill. 'I will make you a very strong one.'

'Thank you,' Bill replied.

The small man standing next to him operated the coffee franchise in the club. A very lucrative business, particularly the way he operated it. Offering guests a variety of speciality coffees, he ensured that the service was immaculate and that his attitude was always deferential. Guests paid him there and then, the cost was never added to the bill. And the coffee man never had any change. Regardless of the large value of the note the guest handed over, the coffee man would take it, thank the guest profusely for his or her generosity and proceed to the next table. Guests were too embarrassed to say that was not their intention.

The club operated a similar scam with the cigarette girl, but Bill had to admit that the coffee man had the edge. Hostesses were required, when asked what they would like to drink, to order champagne, which was brought to the table in an ice bucket and served with a linen napkin wrapped around the label. With most punters the make was cheap, but the price tag was not. The hostess was also required to ensure that the guest bought her cigarettes. Calling the cigarette girl to the table, the guest would ask what brand the hostess would like and the cigarette girl would put a carton of 200 of the brand requested on the table.

'Just a packet, darling,' would be the usual comment from the guest.

'We only sell cartons, sir.'

The tight customers would then look to offer the hostess one of their own cigarettes.

'I can only smoke that brand,' she was instructed to say.

The guest would then have little option than to purchase the carton at a highly inflated price.

Before leaving with the client, the hostess was also required to ensure that he bought her a large teddy bear, on sale in the foyer. The cost of this would be £25 and she would be required to return it the next day, when she would be given half the purchase price back. What clients thought the girls did with the hundreds of teddies they were bought is a mystery. One girl said she visited a children's hospital each week and they always expected her to take a teddy along for one of the really sick kids.

The coffee man showed Bill to a table at the back of the room, where he had put the cup of coffee, a quiet spot where he thought Bill could sit and enjoy the expertly prepared brew. 'Mr Howard, you must come to my house and have Sunday lunch with me this week,' the coffee man suggested.

This was the umpteenth time the coffee man had given Bill the invitation and Bill had refused it on every occasion. The thought of spending Sunday lunch with an Indian, being served Indian food, was not something Bill relished.

'Please, Mr Howard, I would be greatly honoured if you would do me the courtesy of visiting my home. It would be a nice change for you and I assure you, you will receive the best of my hospitality.'

Bill felt that it was becoming impossible to say no again and still remain on good terms with the man. 'That would be very nice. Thank you,' Bill said and, having agreed, immediately regretted it. Sunday morning, after a late, busy Saturday night, was not the best time for him to be venturing outside his normal routine. But it was now impossible to retract.

'If you are at The Cumberland Hotel at noon, I can drive you to my house from there,' the coffee man said with a note of pleasure in his voice. 'Please try not to be late, we do not want lunch to be spoilt.'

Bill assured him that he would be there in plenty of time. The next Saturday night, the coffee man made a point of reminding Bill that he was lunching with him the following day and reconfirmed the details.

Wearing a blazer, grey flannels, white shirt and cravat, Bill felt a little overdressed for his lunch invitation, but the coffee man had arranged to meet him at The Cumberland, so wearing anything less formal would have looked out of place. The mini-cab dropped Bill off at 11.45, five minutes before the bar was officially open, except to residents who in theory were allowed to drink on the premises 24 hours a day. Bill informed the barman he was a resident, ordered a large gin and tonic and told the barman to take one for himself. He did not know the barman and the barman knew that Bill was not a resident, but still the drink was served. Before Bill had time to add the tonic, a uniformed man, wearing a blue suit and peaked cap, approached him.

'Mr Howard?' he enquired.

Bill looked at him and waited for the man to continue before admitting to his identity. 'I've been asked to collect you for your luncheon appointment,' he added by way of explanation. 'The car is waiting at the side door. I hope that will be convenient, it will save me driving you round the block.'

Bill nodded, drank his drink in two gulps and left a ten-bob note on the counter before following the chauffeur to the waiting car, which turned out to be a black limousine. The chauffeur opened the door and with Bill safely lounging in the back, the car pulled gently away from the kerb, joining the light traffic flowing down Park Lane.

The journey seemed to go on and on, firstly through the leafy suburbs and then into the green fields of Surrey. It crossed Bill's mind, at one point, that he might have been led into a trap and should have been tooled up. He leaned forward and tapped on the screen. The driver informed him that it would only be a few more miles. Then within minutes the car swung into the driveway of a large country house, standing proudly in its own grounds. The coffee man walked down the front steps to greet his guest as the car drew to a standstill and the chauffeur got out.

Lunch was served in the dining-room, with each man sitting yards apart at opposite ends of the highly polished table. Servants waited on the two men in silence, retreating after the dishes had been served and not reappearing until the host lightly rang a small bell he kept for the purpose, a short distance from his right hand. For once in Bill's life he was stuck for words. At three o'clock, after a fine lunch, Bill sank back into the rear seat of the limousine, a Romeo y Julieta clouding the air with smoke and fine aroma.

'Where would you care to be dropped, sir?'

Many places were quiet on a Sunday, a lot were closed. He decided to go home.

'Battersea,' he told the driver through the haze.

Before they came within a mile of his flat, he had changed his mind.

'Can you make that the Savoy?'

'Certainly, sir.'

The staff at the Savoy knew him. Checking into a room without luggage for someone just walking in off the street would have posed a problem, but not for Bill.

Lying on the bed in just his pants, waiting for the girl with whom he had been friends long before his second marriage, a smile came to his face as he remembered another time, involving a huge bunch of flowers in the same hotel foyer.

'Jan and I have decided to get married.' Bill, Jan and Harry H. Corbett were sitting in the bar of the hotel when he made the announcement. Harry, a great friend long before he became nationally famous as the son in *Steptoe and Son*, which ran on television originally from 1962 to 1965, was truly pleased for them both. In a moment of exuberance, he strode from the bar into the hotel foyer and, scooping up a huge display of flowers, returned to present them to the happy couple. That was Harry! Bill looked out for him, kept trouble away and ensured that Harry wasn't bothered. Until now his successes had been in *The Last Mile* and in *The Emperor Jones*, both television productions of the much praised Armchair Theatre series, and in the 1959 film *The Shakedown*, and, like many of his contemporaries, with Joan Littlewood at the Stratford Theatre, in London's East End. Harry, nine years Bill's junior, had a cheeky smile, in much the same way as Bill was a smiler. He smiled now, lying on the bed, and knew that Harry would disapprove.

'Come in,' Bill called.

The girl entering the room was of a similar age to his wife, Jan, though with dark hair, slightly fuller breasts and sallower skin, but very much the same look. He had known her for a similar length of time and his long-term relationship with her was no secret.

★ ★ ★

Bill had met his second wife, Jan Macauley, when she was still 16 or 17. Bill was driving a Bentley and would regularly pick her up for lunch from the West End office where she worked as a receptionist. Blonde, tall and bright, she would have turned the head of any man, let alone one almost 25 years her senior. Jan's father, Archie Macauley, was the well-known Arsenal footballer and later the manager of Norwich City Football Club and was responsible for putting the club on the map. Bill had driven up to Norwich and proposed to Jan, only to be refused. She had already consented to marry a bookmaker named Victor. Bill returned to London crestfallen. But in less than two years Victor was dead, struck down with terminal cancer. He had provided well for his young widow and baby girl, leaving them cash and three flats in Battersea, so Jan did not have too many financial worries, though she was alone with a small child. Bill decided that having lost her once, he had no intention of making the same mistake again. On this occasion, his proposal was less romantic.

'Right, we're getting married,' Bill told her. And they did.

At first they were all for holding the reception at the Savoy Hotel and then other glamorous venues were discussed. Finally, Bill decided on the ideal location. Despite the high standard of fixtures and fittings, The Beehive had required new carpets for a while and, as it is traditional for the bride's family to pay for the wedding, Bill held the reception at The Beehive and charged the cost of recarpeting to Jan's father. Jan was soon expecting her second child, but even before she was pregnant, Bill's old habits returned. Just as he had left Vera at home, preferring to go out on his own, he expected Jan to take on the housewife role. When Bill required shirts ironed and Jan did not have time or the inclination, Bill would, as in prior years, take a cab from the flat in Battersea to Walworth, for his mother to iron a shirt or press his suit. From there he would go directly to Winston's. But, much to his annoyance, it would not be unusual for Jan to be there waiting, or to arrive shortly after. Jan claims to have been very naive at this time and would simply be positioned by Bill at a quiet table with someone and left to watch the floorshow, later to be joined by members of the cast, but rarely by Bill.

'I wish I could lick my arse like that,' the woman sitting next to Jan said, looking at the cat Bill always had roaming around the club, which was now sitting preening itself. Jan was taken aback. Dorothy Squires always seemed to have the ability to shock. That evening, the woman Bill had invited to the Savoy after his Indian lunch, and who regularly shared his bed, sat at the adjoining table. Later the tables would fill with iced champagne and bottles of spirits for the mounting number of guests. By the end of any evening, the list of table guests could easily have sounded like the roll call of top gangsters or Oscar hopefuls. Such names as Danny La Rue, Barbara Windsor, Victor Spinetti, Ronnie Corbett, Anne Hart, Noel Coward, Victor Mature, Nureyev, George Raft, Meyer Lansky, the Cellini brothers, Judah Binstock, the Knight brothers, the Kray brothers, Albert Dimes and Bert Marsh.

* * *

Bill sat in the basement of The Establishment club, in the heart of Soho, talking to Dorothy Squires and listening to a jazz quartet. Dorothy was drinking, so was Bill, but Bill could handle it better. She was grossly unhappy. Her marriage to the young actor Roger Moore had just broken up in California. She was 14 years his senior and as his career had started to take off, he had started to mix with a younger crowd.

The club was packed, it attracted British, American and international celebrities from both the screen and the music industry. Within a short time of opening, it had a membership of over seven thousand. Peter Cook and Dudley Moore, the owners of The Establishment, had not only seen their own careers take off with satire on television and in the theatre, but had now achieved success with the club, Dudley, of course, providing an added attraction with his own mastery of the jazz piano.

When Bill arrived with Dorothy, Pete and Dud, as they were affectionately known by their friends and audiences alike, were not in the club, although it was them Bill had particularly called in to see. In other circumstances, this lateness would have caused him some irritation, but The Establishment was a pleasant place to be and Bill was enjoying it. It had an air of its own that was hard to define. It certainly wasn't a Winston's and it wasn't even a Ronnie Scott's. It was probably the relaxed feeling of the place, without the hostesses and hard sell of Winston's, and Dudley's jazz in the basement was a pleasure, where at Ronnie Scott's it was a duty. Serious stuff.

'Mr Howard, Mr Cook is in the office now. He asked if I would show you through,' a member of staff said quietly into Bill's ear and then stepped back waiting for Bill to follow.

'I won't be long,' Bill excused himself from Dorothy, who waved him away without a second thought of being left at the table on her own.

They shook hands. They had met before but Bill did not know Peter Cook, nor for that matter was he acquainted with Dudley Moore. Pete came straight to the point. 'I've had Ronnie and Reggie Kray round looking for insurance payments, I think they called it. I'm not paying.'

'Peter, everybody pays,' Bill told him.

'I've got insurance and I don't want any more. And I am definitely not going to pay money to a couple of thugs in dark suits with an IQ of a park bench.'

'That could prove expensive in the long run, even dangerous. And I'm not sure why you are telling me this, what is it you expect me to do?' Bill really wasn't sure what the man was expecting of him.

'I could have gone to Albert Dimes, that's what Ronnie Scott advised, but you are a club owner yourself, I'm told you have always looked after Dan and Harry well, and a lot of people in the theatre speak highly of you, including George Raft and Billy Daniels, and you are sitting outside with Dorothy Squires. All of these people are well respected on both sides of the Atlantic.'

Bill assumed that the reference to Dan and Harry referred to Danny La Rue and Harry H. Corbett. Why Cook was hinting at the American connection, he wasn't sure.

'I still don't quite see what it is you expect of me,' Bill said.

'I'm not paying the Twins, and if I have any trouble I'll walk round to the police station and have them arrested. Dud and I are very busy, it's time we can't afford to waste. You get them off our backs and it will save everyone a lot of trouble.'

Bill looked at him with raised eyebrows.

'I think you can do that,' Pete added when Bill continued only to look at him.

'It'll cost. And if you're paying me, maybe you might as well be paying the Twins.'

'A one-off payment for a satisfactory service?' Pete suggested.

'If the Twins go away, then there'll be someone else trying it on,' Bill explained.

'I will not pay protection. We'll sell before I pay money to scum like that.'

'I hope you are not including me in that, Peter?'

Peter was silent. For a moment Bill thought the scene was set for Dud to walk in through the door and start a skit.

'Peter. What is it you want?' Bill realised he needed to clear the air as it seemed their conversation was going nowhere.

'We want to be left alone to run our business without some idiot coming round thinking they can steal it from us,' Pete said.

'Strictly business. How many members have you got?' Bill asked, already having a good idea of the answer.

'Six thousand.'

'Don't cheat me, Peter, not if you expect me to be on your side. I'd say it was nearer seven.'

'Six and a half.'

'Two pound a member, per year, paid quarterly.'

'One pound.'

'And you pick up the tab whenever I come in,' Bill countered.

'As long as I don't see you too often.'

Bill stretched out his arm and the two men shook hands.

The following day, Bill had two telephone conversations regarding The Establishment. The first was from a senior police officer at West End Central Police Station, telling Bill to expect a call from Peter Cook, the comedian. 'He said that he did not want to make an official complaint, but that he had been approached. I suggested that if he wanted it kept off the record, he could do worse than talk to you.'

Bill told the officer he had already sorted the problem out and that they should get together for a drink sometime in the near future.

The second call was to Reggie Kray. Bill arranged to meet the Twins at The Dorchester.

Laughing Boy was his usual smiling self as the Twins crossed the elegant foyer and approached the sofa where Bill was sitting. He rose to greet them. 'Now which one is it I kiss and which one do I shake hands with?' Bill was one of the few people who could get away with such a comment, without fear of retribution. Later, it would transpire he could just as easily have kissed them both. Being homosexual was not a trait that Ronnie particularly hid, but it was not an allegation that many people were prepared to make to his face.

Since starting the Krays on their career of extortion and protection, it had been part of the unwritten agreement that Bill would benefit from the takings. Takings that never amounted to the sums of money Bill considered potentially available. At one point he had considered the possibility they were creaming some of the profits, but discreet enquiries with publicans and billiard hall owners satisfied Bill's curiosity that many were only paying a nominal fee, often as low as £25.

'This thing with The Establishment,' Bill started. Stopped. And then signalled to a hovering waiter to bring whatever his guests wanted. 'Cook has been to the filth. I've smoothed things over but it's one you're going to have to let go and wipe your mouth,' Bill continued.

'I'll cut the cunt's legs off and the place can have two midgets running it,' Ronnie had sat forward in his armchair as he spoke.

Bill signalled with a downward movement of his hand to keep the noise level down. 'If there's trouble, it'll end up all over the papers. These people are well liked and I can tell you, all the celebrities you entertain will disappear. Nobody will want to know you. I'll talk to them, see what I can do, and in the meantime whatever you were expecting from the place, you can deduct from my wedge on the other places.'

Ronnie wasn't happy, but Reg put much value on the prestige of their position and it could not be argued that they both enjoyed mixing with the stars.

'If he gets mouthy about giving us a knock back . . .' Reggie said, not finishing the sentence, though the implication was clear.

Bill accepted the comment as a reluctant agreement. Ronnie was still not happy.

At Winston's, it was now time for Bill to make his own strategic climb down. At the time he knew it was the sensible thing to do but later, looking back, he realised how dreadfully he missed the club and how it was a fight that he should not only have fought, but could have won.

Another club owner had pinpointed Winston's as the West End venue he needed to acquire if he were to achieve success in the world of London nightclubs. He was backed by a team of young tearaways, headed by Jimmy Evans.

Here was a brash villain, a new breed, who was prepared to put aside the climb up the ladder of broken knuckles gained from punching his way to the top, and the scars of knife and razor attacks. Evans carried a gun and was not afraid to use it. He had arrived at Winston's with a small team, laughing and joking, apparently looking for a good night on the town. But, in reality, that was the furthest thing from his mind. On this evening, he was looking to make his move. He did not expect to be leaving Winston's until he had shot Billy Howard. Taking the club from Bruce Brace was feasible only if Bill was out of the scene. He said he intended to knee-cap the man, but those with whom he had discussed the plan knew of the attempt made by Billy Hill and that if they weren't prepared to accept retribution, it needed to be one bullet clean, not two.

Why Evans did not simply shoot Bill is not clear. A bullet in the head as Bill stepped from the rear of his car was all that was needed. But that was not the line Evans chose. Possibly in an effort to justify the shooting, he sought to provoke Bill into a fight. The provocation he chose was exercised in the solitude of the men's toilets. Evans had waited until his target headed for the gents and followed him in.

'That's a good-looking little brass you've got hanging about up there.' Evans can't recall the exact words he used when referring to Jan, but they were designed to wind Bill up, to make him have a go. 'Bit young and lively for you. She'd be better off letting me give her one,' he added.

Bill turned from the urinal as Evans, with a derringer concealed in the palm of his hand, made to comb back his hair. Bill stepped alongside him and swung a tightly clenched fist across his chest into the palm of his own open hand. The clout echoed round the walls. Bill smiled and walked on by. Later, Jimmy Evans and his lads were congregating on the stairs outside the ladies toilets when Jan emerged. They blocked her way and laughed. One tried to put his hand up her skirt as she pushed past. Despite being really scared, she chose not to run to Bill, in the knowledge that he would go berserk. Again Evans failed to achieve his aim.

Bill may have avoided a confrontation that day, but he was not cavalier enough to ignore what was going on. Troops were being assembled. If a gang war broke out, people would die or at least be seriously injured, customers and the star cast would run for cover and Winston's would be finished, whoever won. It would not be long before Jan would give birth to Bill's child. She had already lost one husband and father of a young child, he didn't want a repeat of that, or a similar result of her man being banged up for years. And then there was the other matter to consider, the emerging opportunity on the gambling front. Any prospect of developing links with the Meyer Lansky empire would be wiped out at the merest hint of a gang war.

Bill arranged a number of meetings to discuss the implications of the future of gaming in the UK, the implications of a gang war based around Winston's and, most interestingly, any major potential American desire to gain interests in British casinos. Lansky and one of the Cellini brothers met Bill at an office a short distance from Marble Arch. At the end of the conversation, Bill was satisfied that the action at The Colony Club in Berkeley Square, under the management of Alfie Silkin and Fred Ayoub, was directly controlled by Lansky, not the Italian-American-based Mafia families who had invested in the casino operations. Connections that the Krays were attempting to develop and those families represented in the UK by Pasqualino Papa, Bert Marsh, did not have controlling interests. Bill believed he had backed the right horse and was set to handle one aspect of the Jews' gambling operations on this side of the Atlantic. Judah Binstock, Bill accepted, would be the money man. This was in line with Bill's philosophy of providing a service in preference to becoming part of a team.

Bill had opened The Beehive Club at 10 Beehive Place, Brixton, with much ado, spending a great deal on fitting out the property with a black and white decor, finished to the same standard as any top West End club. Magistrates reviewing the licence application insisted on a visit to the property in the belief that the photographs being shown to the court were in fact not of a club in Brixton, but of a Mayfair establishment. They were wrong and the licence was granted to Albert Fitch, a front man for Bill, to operate a Members Club on the premises. This was a standard method for club owners to evade the laws concerning the sale of intoxicating liquor. Although the proprietor would own or lease the property, a committee in whose interest the club was operated would run the club. Market traders who worked early in the morning and finished just as the pubs closed for the afternoon, for instance, could set up a club, say The Porters, so that the members – market porters – could enjoy a drink after work. This of course was generally a front and went ahead with the proprietor persuading the required number of market porters to put their name to the application, thereby facilitating a trading period beyond the traditional licensing hours.

With other interests in place, Bill was ready to walk away from Winston's. But he was not inclined to walk away empty-handed. Looking to obtain a big wedge from Evans' boss, Bill rightly believed, would provoke the very situation he was seeking to avoid. Whatever arrangement Bruce Brace made with Joe Wilkins, Bill decided Bruce would have to take responsibility for making a cash settlement.

* * *

Evans was not the only person gunning for Bill. The Beehive was closed and the doors were locked, with Bill, a few staff and one or two customers remaining on the inside. At first, Bill had believed the attempt to break down the door was a police raid. Whilst this would have been almost unthinkable without prior notice, it would not have been the first time such a thing had happened, either in Soho or Brixton. On one occasion, money had been handed to the desk sergeant in Kennington, a substantially higher payment than was usual, on the basis that Bill was hosting a major high-stake game in a spieler within the Kennington area, and right at the height of the play, uniformed and plain clothes filth were trampling all over the show. In danger of getting his collar felt, Bill had quickly grabbed the wrist of the most influential player, and cuff to cuff marched him out of the door and down the street. Most raids involved officers from various nicks and it was not unusual for many of the officers not to know others in the team. With the right front, it was not too difficult to slip away.

The other problem, had it been a raid, would have been the embarrassment of the police storming in only to confront senior members of their own station relaxed and enjoying a drink. The Beehive was a favourite haunt with officers at all levels from south London and from the West End, seeking a place to pass away an evening where their faces were less well known, or where they could openly arrange rewards for the favours they had performed. A list of names was regularly left behind the bar so that officers who had carried out requests successfully, or required a down payment in advance, could be handed the agreed amount as part of their change when they came to the counter to purchase a drink. The most powerful of the officers who participated in the corrupt practices would be invited by Chief Superintendent Ted Bland to join a large table which he hosted almost on a weekly basis, and at which Bill lavishly provided the food and drink without charge.

Over the years, the relationship between Bill and Bland had progressed from purely business to that of family friends. Bill and Jan had become frequent visitors to Bland's home, and when it was time for Bill and Jan's baby boy to be christened, Bland insisted young Billy be given Bland's name as his middle name. Jan went along with the naming in the church, but nominated a family name when it came to filling in the baby's birth certificate. Pictures taken outside the church after the service, which was attended by a number of officers from the Met and their wives, show people tucked out of sight behind large pillars, or with their arms raised, to hide their faces from the camera.

But on this occasion, it was not the filth. When the banging stopped, the kicking and shouting began. Then a pistol was pushed through the letterbox, the barrel waving from side to side.

'Howard, I'm going to blow your fucking bollocks off, you bastard.' The voice outside was angry. It did not take Bill too long to recognise who it was and to guess why. The Mad Axe Man, Frank Mitchell, had obviously got wind that Bill had been seeing Mitchell's girlfriend and it appeared from his reaction that he was not too happy about the arrangement.

When Frank Mitchell was sprung from Dartmoor, where he was serving a long sentence, it had been the Krays' intention to use him in their firm to put the frighteners on the Richardsons. However, Mitchell was too well known and too easily recognisable to be allowed a free run. Despite being provided with a girl from Winston's to keep him company, he became impossible to control and was finally murdered on the instructions of the Krays. Albert Donoghue, a member of the Krays' firm, was told to put his hands up for the killing, which had been carried out by one of the Krays' lieutenants, Freddie Foreman. Under questioning, Donoghue looked to save his own skin and put Foreman in the frame. Unlike most people, Bill was able to reason with The Mad Axe Man.

Arranging to meet him on his own gave Mitchell the respect he deserved. Bill apologised for taking liberties and the matter was sorted out without spilling blood.

During the 1960s there was, however, plenty of bloodshed. Much of it involved the Krays and the Richardsons, but as it did not infringe on Bill's south London or Soho interests, he generally stood to one side. Where mediation was requested over certain issues, he was prepared to assist, but he did not see the point in taking sides. At one particular juncture it looked as though both firms would fall; an outcome Bill considered would only be to the advantage of the Knights. But the killings were not confined purely to gangland battles. Deaths of innocent members of the public, or so it seemed, were starting to fill the headlines, as the police sought what appeared to be a serial killer.

★ ★ ★

Dorothy Squires had achieved success worldwide with her voice and the songs she made into hits. Her name sat easily alongside all the greats of the '50s and '60s. At the time of the break-up of her marriage in 1961 to the man who was to star in *The Saint* and as James Bond, Roger Moore, which finally ended in divorce in 1968, she was distraught. Her moods swung into depths of sadness and her drinking reached epic proportions. Much of that time she spent with Bill. He was with her in her London apartment when, during one of those bouts, she wrote the chilling song 'Say it with Flowers', a hit which she recorded with her pianist and fellow hit-maker Russ Conway, whose chart successes in the early 1960s included 'Side Saddle' and 'Roulette'.

On one occasion Dorothy had been up most of the night when she telephoned Bill and asked him to come over. When Bill arrived, she had all but changed her mind, although talking to Bill seemed to be her only option. Russ Conway had confided in her a story that she would have preferred not to have heard, in the same way Russ had the story told to him. For both of them, it was now just too much. Russ had been at the apartment earlier and she wanted him to come back before she was prepared to talk to Bill. She did not feel that the burden of the knowledge he had entrusted her with should be her responsibility to settle. When Russ arrived at the apartment, his mood had changed and he had decided to tell his story to the police. The only dilemma he faced was how to go about it without putting himself in the centre of an investigation. It appeared that using Dorothy's friendship with Bill, he had, in telling Dorothy, already devised a way of achieving what he had decided to do. He had wanted her to persuade Bill, of whose reputation he was well aware, to approach the police and, in return for the information, have his name kept out of the affair. Bill was certain that Russ would, with or without his help, speak out, but it was not something he felt personally comfortable becoming involved with. Like Russ and Dorothy, it was a secret to which he would have preferred not to have been party.

Russ went over the details, the pain of the knowledge clear in his speech and his anxious, unsettled movements. Why the singer Michael Holliday, who had topped the British charts with his soft casual style in such songs as 'The Story of My Life', a Burt Bacharach number in the late 1950s, and 'Little Lost Boy' in 1960, had confessed to Russ, Russ wasn't sure – probably their similar age, both born in the late 1920s, both having been in the Navy, and their similar career paths and lifestyles. Guilt eats some people away. With Holliday it had taken four years, Russ two, and Dorothy only hours. Dorothy and Russ had not been involved, but just having the knowledge filled them with guilt.

Michael Holliday had confessed to Russ, two years earlier, of having a homosexual affair with the ex-light-heavyweight champion of the world, television personality and Soho club owner Freddie Mills. On occasions their sexual exploits, mainly instigated by Mills, had involved picking up girls and performing mild sado-masochistic acts on them for titillation before Holliday and Mills had sex with each other. If the girls from the clubs around the West End could not be persuaded to partake in the games, Mills was in the habit of picking up prostitutes. In his confession to Russ, Holliday maintained that Mills had killed one of the girls by mistake when things got a little out of hand. Mills had apparently arranged for the body to be disposed of and prevented Holliday from going to the police. Bill guessed this did not take too much argument as, in 1959, Holliday would have been at the pinnacle of his career.

The practice cooled and Holliday had indicated that the relationship had also become less active. They had returned to incorporating girls in their sexual games, but on Holliday's insistence had reduced the activities to mock aggression. This satisfied Mills less and less and, during one night in the early 1960s, Holliday said a second girl was killed, again the body being dumped by Mills. Shortly after confiding in Russ, and while Russ was still deciding whether or not to tell the police, Michael Holliday took his own life with an overdose of drugs. Russ saw no reason now to go to the police, in the belief that with Holliday dead, Mills would cease his activities. For Russ, Bill realised, Holliday's suicide had been an easy way out. Within days of the suicide, the second body was discovered.

If it had ended there, it would have been over. But it didn't.

Throughout 1964, the killings accelerated, each one exhibiting a greater degree of rage. Seven more prostitutes' bodies were discarded, either in the River Thames or around the Shepherds Bush area of the capital, their teeth smashed in, with evidence of those involved having been made to perform oral sex before being throttled. Either the killer had found a less reluctant lover or had waged a war on the women for driving Holliday to his death. Alternatively, there was a thought that a third party had been involved from the beginning. Russ was, according to his story, now terrified that he would be implicated, at least for withholding evidence. Since Holliday, the source of his information, had died months earlier, it was clear that he had been in possession of the evidence long before this run of killings had taken place. With no sign of the killing spree stopping, Russ said he could no longer keep the secret to himself and had on a number of occasions been near to suicide. What he wanted was to be able to pass the information on to a trusted police officer, privately, and then having unburdened himself, be able to walk away. Refusing to go anywhere near a police station, Russ agreed to meet a Met contact in a large Brighton hotel. He was adamant that the officer not have prior knowledge of the reason for the meeting. Bill could see that Russ had spent considerable time planning how he wanted things to happen. It did cross Bill's mind that Russ may not have been simply the friend and recipient of the confession, that the account Russ gave may well have omitted a third participant – himself. Later this was something Bill discounted. Russ's health declined, he began drinking and, in 1967, suffered a nervous breakdown that prevented him working for a lengthy period.

As a Soho club owner, Freddie Mills had enjoyed Bill's protection. So Bill decided to give Freddie some forewarning of what was likely to happen in the near future, not out of sympathy for the man, only because he believed everyone was entitled to some dignity. This would give Freddie the opportunity to line up a brief; after all, the story Russ had outlined might well have been flawed and Holliday could have been seeking to protect someone else with the accusation. But deep down Bill felt that Freddie was not an innocent party, and after he had marked his card, Bill was even less concerned that the accusation might be without foundation.

'Fred, you seem to have got yourself into a bit of serious trouble,' Bill had told him, using the Italian expression, serious trouble, which is often used to refer to death. 'You are about to get your collar felt, so I'd arrange to have a brief on call,' Bill had added.

Freddie hardly answered, muttered something that Bill could not understand and left.

When the news broke that Freddie Mills had been shot, later confirmed as suicide, in his car outside his Soho club in the early hours of a July morning in 1965, Bill was on holiday with Jan in the Scilly Isles. Bill had done what had been asked of him by a very dear friend, and had also handled the matter in a way with which he felt comfortable. Mills had made his own decision. But this was not to be the last request for assistance Billy Howard was to receive, where murder was involved.

* * *

The Krays were free and were riding high on their perceived invincibility. They believed the courts could no longer endanger their liberty. Setting aside Bill's advice to keep a low profile, they flaunted their win not only in criminal circles, but also in the face of the police. Referring to themselves as 'untouchable', they openly allowed the media to announce their status to the general public and to the powerful within the establishment, a brazen image many were not prepared to tolerate. However, there was another incident that further fuelled the demand by the faceless men in high places to have the Twins removed from the public arena, and not just for a few months or a couple of years.

The Krays contacted Bill by telephone and asked to see him immediately. Reggie was clearly in a panic and Ronnie had taken the telephone from him telling Bill they could not talk over the phone. They met at Dolphin Square less than an hour later. Ronnie was calm, relaxed and confident, Reggie was anything but. Any thought that a casual onlooker would believe they had simply met for a drink was rapidly being eroded by Reggie's obvious paranoia, so much so that Bill refused a drink and suggested they talked outside. Ronnie thought Bill was being unnecessarily cautious, but his twin was halfway to the door before Ronnie could voice his dissent. Reggie wanted to walk. Bill had assumed they would sit in the car and chat about whatever it was that was causing concern. This suggestion seemed to drain the colour out of Reggie's face. They walked.

Ronnie had been in the habit of picking up young men in pubs and at parties and, to satisfy his homosexual desires, had on occasions taken his 'friend' to the nearest block of luxury flats or upmarket houses. Having located a property where the owners were not at home, he would break in and make use of the bedroom and other facilities. Slipping a catch often meant they could enter without causing damage. Ronnie regularly wondered if it was the husband, or wife, who was blamed for bringing their bit on the side back, and how many screaming matches and divorces would result.

Early one evening, the Twins were heading for Bertie Green's Astor Club in Mayfair, but at the last minute Ronnie had changed his mind. Being in the car on their own, he had told his brother that he wanted to go for a drive round the West End first.

Whether Ronnie had picked the young lad up from the 'meat rack' outside the Regent Palace Hotel in Piccadilly Circus, or had visited the gardens in the centre of Leicester Square, another popular place, particularly for wealthy older men, to pick up rent boys, Bill was not clear. But having left Reggie in the car for only a few moments, Ronnie had returned with a pretty blond kid in tow. Reggie expected Ronnie to make the lad give him a blow job in the back seat, while he drove the car around the block a couple of times, before kicking the kid out. But Ronnie sat in the front and they headed off down Pall Mall, round past the Ritz Hotel and straight through into Knightsbridge, making a left into the Sloane Square area. They toured the large Georgian houses until Ronnie located a property that he felt he could access from the rear. Five minutes later Ronnie was standing at the top of a short flight of stone steps in an open doorway, calling Reg to lock the car and bring the lad into the house.

What happened next Reg was reluctant to elaborate on. If looks could have killed, Bill believed Reg would have at that point happily seen his brother struck dead, as Ron, with excitement in his voice, began to go into detail.

'Give Bill the cash and let's piss off. The longer we hang about . . .' Reg's voice trailed off. Ron was going to have his say and nothing was going to stop him. It transpired that the lad and Ron had stripped off, and while Ron insisted Reg found a bottle of something, Ron got the lad to perform oral sex. When Reg returned with a decanter of brandy, they all gulped a lot down. The lad was lying naked on the bed, Ron's hands fondling him, then Ron told his brother it was his turn. As Reg dropped his trousers, Ron rolled the lad on to his stomach. As the lad took Reg into his mouth, Ron, without using any cream, mounted the lad and viciously entered him.

'You should have heard him squeal. Just like a little pig,' Ron laughed.

If this was the first time they had shared a sexual partner, neither of the Twins commented. Reg ejaculating and the boy trying to scream in response to Ron's continual pounding caused the boy to vomit and at the same time roll from under Ron. In the bizarre pursuit that followed, bottles toppled, tables and chairs were upturned and the bathroom door was felled.

'Grab him,' Ron panted.

Reg, almost stepping in more vomit and tripping over his trousers, fell on to the lad, then dragged him back into the bedroom and threw him on to the bed, holding him down, head over the end, until Ron was finished. Whether the boy had choked on his own continued attempts to vomit or the weight of Reg pressing his windpipe across the foot-board was not clear, but the small half-clothed body now lay in the boot of the Krays' car. Reg was pressing the vomit theory, but Ron didn't seem to mind either way.

Bill wished they had chosen to handle the matter within their own firm. At the beginning of the story Bill had thought the lad had nicked something and the Twins wanted Bill to have a word with the local filth to see if it could be returned and the rent boy told not to take liberties in the future. By the end, an end that seemed to excite Ron as much as it seemed to scare Reg and horrified Bill, Reg handed Bill a bundle of notes. 'Can you go round to the house and tell the owner something when he gets back? There will be smudges all over the shop. The last thing we need is a pull with that in the boot.'

Bill got a minicab over to the address they had given him and after knocking on the door to check that the owner was not already back, stood in the square until well into the early hours of the morning. At one point a squad car went round and a few minutes later went round again. At first he thought he had been spotted and then he wondered whether he had been set up. But with the Twins' prints all over the place, he could not see how he could find himself in the frame.

Four days later Reggie phoned to see if Bill had been able to square things with the owner of the house. They arranged to meet again at Dolphin Square.

Bill had not realised Ronnie would be joining them but he was there and this made Reg noticeably uneasy. Ron was still flying.

'The man was a gentleman. He was far from pleased and was not sure that he should not call the police anyway. But he took the cash and said my employer would hear no more about the matter,' Bill said.

'What the fuck did you tell him?' Reg asked.

'I told him I had been asked to apologise on behalf of my employer and his friend. They had broken in as a joke, thinking the house belonged to friends who were giving a party and then realised it was the wrong house.'

'He went for that?' Reg asked.

'I told him the person throwing the party was a friend of Princess Margaret and that she was expected to show up, and that the whole thing would be very embarrassing if the mistake was made public.'

'It wouldn't be the first time they've topped a few kids,' Ron said, with a broad grin.

'What, are you saying Princess Margaret picks up little boys and then kills them?' Reg said, slapping his brother on the shoulder with the back of his hand, a tone of anger in his voice.

'Not Margaret, but the Old Fox has dipped his wick and looked the other way when it was all over,' Ron said with more than a little smugness in his voice.

If Reg knew who the Old Fox was, Bill was not sure, but Reg was immediately jumpy again. He swallowed his drink, straightened his tie and walked, almost marched, out of the building. Minutes later, Bill and Ron followed.

'What happened to the kid?' Bill asked.

'Squealed like a pig in shit. Fed 'im to the pigs in shit. Well, the pigs in Norfolk,' Ron said with almost a roar and talking fast.

If Bill did not know better, he would have said that Ron had just taken a load of speed. 'Is that where the Old Fox lives?' Bill asked.

But before Ron could answer, they were outside and Reg was at his brother. He had seen them argue before, but had never seen them turn on each other with such wildness in their eyes. They were not fighting, not punching, just gripping each other's arms, with Reg trying to shake his brother. Bill pulled them apart. 'Get in the car,' he told them. 'Or is there something else in there I don't want to know about?' Bill added.

Quieter now, the Twins sat, one in the front, the other in the back, with Bill.

'Right, what's this all about?' Bill asked Reg.

'Ask him. He's the one with the queer friends.' This was out of character coming from Reg. It was said that George Cornell had been topped for calling Ron a poof. It was something everyone knew and accepted. When meeting them on their own, Bill had regularly greeted them with 'Right, which one do I kiss and which one do I shake hands with?' But Reg speaking like this, particularly after what had happened in the flat a few days earlier, Bill considered strange. What happened next Bill considered stranger and seemed to take Reg by as much surprise. Ron burst into tears.

'You don't think Lord Fatso is the only one at these parties,' Ron said between sobs. Bill knew he was referring to Lord Boothby, who had been named as one of Ron's lovers in press headlines a couple of years earlier.

'Ron, who you mix with is up to you. But he's a fat old man, not a little boy,' Reg said quietly.

'Yes, and not many of them want fat old men,' Ron replied, now more composed.

Ron confessed that at homosexual parties in Buckinghamshire and Brighton, young boys were regularly passed around and that on one occasion things had got out of hand and a lad had died. Ron said that he had been pushed into arranging for the disposal of the boy's body and that it had been cut up on a fishing boat, and the bits thrown overboard into the Irish Sea. After that, he had not been to many more of the parties. The three sat in the car in silence for what seemed like a long time.

'What's this got to do with Princess Margaret?' Bill asked, more to break the silence than anything else.

'Nothing,' Ron said. 'I didn't kill the kid. I didn't even have him,' Ron added, knowing he had alienated the two men in the car with him.

'There's not been anything in the papers about a missing boy over the last few days and I don't remember a string of missing kids being investigated. Why is nobody looking for them?' Bill asked.

'I don't know about that one a few days ago, but a lot of the boys around Piccadilly are runaways, you know that. The boy at the party wasn't English. Some of the boys are rent, they're picked up off the meat rack and dropped back in London the next day. But sometimes someone brings an Arab boy with them. The boy that died was one of them,' Ron explained, now quite matter of fact.

'And where do these Arabs come from?' Reg asked his brother.

'Most are invited to spend some time in England by friends visiting Tangier,' Ron replied.

'How do they get in the country?' Reg persisted.

Ron just shrugged.

'I suppose Princess Margaret brought them in as a favour to this foxy bloke,' Reg said, his impatience starting to show.

'I don't know how they got to England and I don't know how they got back. All right.'

Bill could see that it was not going to take much before they were at each other's throats again. 'What's the story with Mr Fox then?' Bill asked with a bit of a grin.

'He's one of them and he's got a tattooed fox going up his arse. OK. Now

I'm going for a drink.' And with that Ron got out of the car, slammed the door and jumped in a cab as he reached the end of the road.

'I'd do anything for Ron,' Reg said, not really knowing what to say after his brother had stormed off. 'But I don't want to go down as a nonce.'

'I think you need to keep an eye on him.' That was all Bill said on the subject.

Although Bill's drinking had reached levels that would have seen most people drown – three bottles of Gordon's a day, equal to his consumption while hosting the *Alfie* film crew at The Beehive Club – the information that the Twins had shared with him would not go away. Between bouts of drinking and vomiting, over the days following the admission he was not even getting drunk. He thought of Michael, his son, who must now be only a year or two short of 20, of young Billy, still little more than a baby. How would he react if they found themselves prey to a pair like the Twins or Ronnie's bunch of peers? There was such a thing as right and wrong. Maybe his did not match the rest of society, but there was, he believed, some common ground. Ronnie worried him. He had seen how excited that Kray twin had become when he was first talking about what had happened. Bill also hated the idea of people in power using their position to break the law. Bad cops were good cops, and bent judges and council officials were one thing, but if what Ron had told him was only half true, it had made Bill's stomach turn. Ron and his friends were not at the end of the road, of that Bill was certain.

'What you do with it is up to you,' Bill told Ted Bland.

It had not been an easy decision to take, or maybe it had been an easy decision and that was why Bill had mulled it over in his mind for the few days it took before telephoning the Chief Superintendent. The Twins had already walked boldly from the court after the Hideaway fiasco. Bill knew that it was easy to be wise after the fact, but had he known then what he knew now, he would not have been a string to the Twins' bow in ensuring the case against them failed when the jury were encouraged to make a wise decision.

Bland sat through the story Bill outlined without asking questions or showing much sign of any emotion. He cracked a smile at the idea of the fox tattoo, but that was as far as it went.

'After the Boothby and the Profumo scandals, they're not going to want to have a thing like this coming out, if this foxy fucker is a peer of the realm,' was Bland's only comment.

Bill had passed on the information and what happened to it after that was up to them.

★ ★ ★

Soho is located within a square mile to the north of Piccadilly, where the streets are narrow and littered with rubbish. It has the reputation of sleazy clubs, offering gambling, sex, restaurants and entertainment. The legitimate businesses tend to be film and music based, still, not really Old School, all crammed into small converted buildings, with different owners operating their businesses from different floors of the same substandard property. But there is another clubland, situated in the square mile south of Piccadilly, bounded by Piccadilly in the north, the Mall to the south, Trafalgar Square at one end and St James Street and the Ritz Hotel at the other. This is the land of leather armchairs, palatial buildings, impressive facades, wide boulevards and tree-filled squares. The members of the gentlemen's clubs located in this area are often found drifting into the dark corners of the clubland to the north, but it is rare to find those whose natural home is in Soho lounging in the elegant society of the clubs of Pall Mall.

It was here, to one of the establishment clubs, that Bill had been summoned less than a week after his talk with Ted Bland. A top-hatted, frock-coated commissionaire pointed Bill in the direction of the porter's lodge, where a porter requested Bill follow his lead through rooms and corridors that appeared a cross between a country house and a museum. Large oils in heavy frames, depicting uniformed military men or others involved in country pursuits, looked down from their lofty positions.

'Mr Howard.' It was not a question, and the use of the word 'Mister' did not sound a term of respect coming from the lips of the man who spoke them.

Bill nodded and stretched out his hand, a gesture his host ignored. Without speaking, the man indicated in which seat his guest should sit. An ageing waiter arrived immediately, placed drinks on the table before the two men and retreated slowly. They were seated at the far end of a long room away from the other members. The door clicking closed was the only disturbance in the austere silence – copies of *The Telegraph* or *The Financial Times* were begrudgingly lowered if the reader was stirred. Unlike Bill's Soho clubs, this was a male bastion.

'Large gin and tonic. I believe that is your usual drink,' the man said, pouring a little water into his own small whisky.

Bill realised this was intended to send a message. The man sitting opposite him was younger than he had thought when he had heard his voice on the telephone, and, on closer scrutiny, possibly younger still. Bill knew Savile Row suits, Jermyn Street shirts and hand-made brogues when he saw them. What the club didn't say, the clothes did. This was old money and probably a few hundred years of power. But despite the air of superiority, it was still all based on killing and stealing, legitimised by another name. Bill noticed that, although he gave his name to the porter, his host had not only failed to shake hands, but had also specifically not introduced himself.

'Information you made available reached my desk, and I thought it merited comment.'

Bill went to speak, but the figure in the opposite chair waved him silent.

'The two men to whom you refer have already slipped through the net once. I might add, due much to your own activities. You, yourself, have also escaped extremely lightly in your confrontations with the legal workings of the State. They will not be so lucky in the very near future. Men like that should not be free and I can presume when this comes out, they will not receive your patronage. Any information concerning this matter that was to reach the ears of the press would see you joining your friends. Please finish your drink in your own time.' The man stood and walked from the room without saying another word.

The Kray Twins were arrested in May 1968. In March 1969, they were sentenced to life imprisonment, not for the death of a young rent boy, or in Ronnie's case disposing of the body of another young boy, but for the murders of George Cornell and Jack McVitie. Charles Kray, the elder brother of the Twins, and one of their henchmen, Freddie Foreman, both got ten years for helping destroy the evidence after the killings. The establishment had thrown the full force of the system into removing Ronnie from society, thus preventing another national scandal.

Reggie settled into prison life with a certain amount of calm acceptance. Ronnie remained a troubled soul until the authorities allowed the two to be housed in the same unit. Bill was always of the opinion that Reg had suspected Bill's course of action and Reg had made a point, on more than one occasion, of saying that Bill was a villain for whom he had a great deal of respect. Along with their elder brother, Charlie, the Krays all died without gaining their freedom. Reggie was released in August 2000 with terminal cancer, taking his last breath a few weeks later in the bedroom of a Norfolk pub. He had been released into the silent world of death, not freedom.

Interests in south London required less of Bill's skill at maintaining the status quo than the jealously sought-after cash cows of Soho. The Richardsons appeared happy, with one brother being particularly business-orientated and the other pleased to torture his way through the day. This is not to say that both did not enjoy a bit of violence, but where the Krays had been celebrity seekers, the Richardsons demanded profits, which was considerably more straightforward.

Bill had brought on a number of Met officers, many since they had been young and wet behind the ears on the beat. Others had simply been pleased to jump on the gravy train when they had reached positions of authority. As well as Chief Superintendent Ted Bland, Bill had in his stable a DI Bernie Robson, Chief Superintendent Bill Moody and Commander Ken Drury, along with an assortment of others who had not progressed beyond sergeant or constable and those who were friends of friends in divisions outside the area in which Bill usually operated. Drury had been on the books for years before he had become a Commander and it was as a middle-ranking officer that Bill assigned him to handle any problems the Richardsons might experience. Rather than putting the squeeze on Eddie and Charlie Richardson and for them to question the need for Bill's protection, it had been more effective for Drury to act as bagman, cutting Bill into the payments that were earmarked for the various stations. The same had applied to Moody, who was raking in thousands from Soho pornographers operating with virtual immunity, accepting the arranged raids and offering up of pre-agreed bodies to satisfy the paperwork.

The Beehive Club had acted as a clearing house over many years, but bent coppers and various levels of villains were not the only clientele. The film *Alfie*, directed by Lewis Gilbert and released in 1966, with Michael Caine depicting the life of a young south London wide boy, brought the film crews and cast, which included Jane Asher, Shelley Winters, Alfie Bass and Millicent Martin, along with many others, into the area, and Bill the ever genial host ensured The Beehive was their watering-hole. Free bottles of spirits and complimentary food rarely ran out. It was during the riotous party atmosphere, enjoyed by this ever-ready-to-party celebrity cast, that Bill's drinking involved serious amounts of alcohol. Three drinks an hour between the hours of noon and three, nine drinks, and, pouring unmeasured from the bottle, few people pour less than a triple. Doing that again early evening and again late into the night, before you know where you are, you're a three-bottles-of-gin-a-day man. But the more it flowed, the more it flowed. Everyone drank, but according to Jan it was at her expense.

Even after the birth of their son, Bill remained excessively protective over Jan. At Winston's, she had been sat to one side, at The Beehive she was confined to behind the bar, ensuring the counter acted as a barrier between her and the customers. This did not prevent Gilbert, the director of *Alfie*, showing an interest and offering Jan a walk-on part in the film, requiring a woman with a pram to walk across the set. Jan did not need to ask what Bill's reaction to the suggestion would be.

The takings and the expenditure were apparently seen by Bill as amounts of money that bore no relation to each other. He saw the cash in the till as his profit. At very regular intervals Jan restocked the bar from her own money, a situation that occurred again when they opened a bar at The Ellerslie Hotel in Crystal Palace. Another strange accounting practice Bill perfected was selling a share of the business to a third party. Bill seemed to be of the mind that when he had spent the money the new partner had paid to purchase a share in the business, the new partner's interest in the club had expired. After a great deal of protest, the financially injured party, not wishing to be physically injured, wiped his mouth and walked away.

* * *

Throughout the 1960s gaming boomed, both in London and in the provinces. The Italian-American Mafia had sought to gain a foothold in the UK, particularly in London. Bert Marsh, their British contact, had naturally put forward Albert Dimes as the man with whom to do business. The Krays, however, had other ideas and made contact with several other Mafia families, only to be dropped like hot potatoes once their name became so widely publicised. They were shown respect, but there was never any question that business in the UK would be developed through the Kray firm.

The man trusted by the Italian families to exploit gaming was not Italian at all. Meyer Lansky, with his partner Bugsy Siegel, had created Las Vegas. Bugsy was eventually hit, in the belief that he was skimming profits from the Vegas operations, but this had not prevented Lansky from remaining the main man. Lansky was Jewish. Although born in Russia, he grew up in New York's Hell's Kitchen on the Lower East Side, mixing with many of the Italian mobsters, including Luciano.

Gaming in the US had been illegal from coast to coast, so Cuba provided an offshore facility of major hotel and casino operations, like the glamorous Hotel Nacional in Havana, for many Americans on vacation. The party atmosphere had been brought to an end in 1959 with the overthrow of President Batista by Castro and Che Guevara. Losing the use of this lucrative island paradise, Lansky had moved his operation to the Bahamas a few hundred miles across the Caribbean Sea, overseen from his home in Florida, a heavily populated Jewish area. Along the way, he developed the idea of casino cruise ships with actor and friend George Raft and, in light of the 1961 Gaming Act, London was also looking attractive, exploited through the plush Colony Club in Berkeley Square. Raft and top casino mechanic Dino Cellini and his brother represented Lansky's interests.

Dino's Mafia connections became clear to the UK authorities after the British Gaming Board were involved in a Mafia investigation in the Bahamas, those islands having been British colonies. As a result of this Dino Cellini was refused entry into the islands and was deported from England to Holland. As a Lansky man, he became a sales representative for Bally fruit machines and also advised Dino Trafficante on the scam establishment of hard currency casino operations in Third World countries. Raft was not deported – his step into the spotlight would come later.

Lansky was a criminal genius and a specialist in complexity. He had visited the UK as a member of a junket prior to Cellini's forced departure. Following a meeting with Lansky at the time of the junket, Bill was prepared to provide the necessary connection to the police, the judiciary and council officials. However, he could not provide the next step Lansky was seeking – access to members of the British government. Bill explained that it was possible to bribe, blackmail and corrupt enforcers of the law to look the other way or, in some cases, simply not to perform, but it was beyond his capability to get the law makers to change the laws of the land. It was not possible to have what was illegal made legal. Lansky knew that one well-placed politician could obtain results that a hundred well-armed gangsters could not achieve in their wildest dreams. Over time, and during a visit to the UK some years after this first trip, Lansky sought to place this goal in the hands of the solicitor and financier Judah Binstock, who would prove to be a man of wizardry equal to Lansky himself and of a similar background. Binstock's childhood was in the Jewish ghettos of London's East End and, also like his American counterpart, he was prepared to do whatever it took to get out, get rich and become powerful. Unlike Lansky, Binstock also sought the pleasures and trappings of the international playboy.

Bill had met Binstock on more than one occasion and in varying circumstances. Binstock had numerous dealings with the East End millionaire scrap metal dealer George Dawson, who had moved his operations from the dirt and grime of his East End yard to executive offices overlooking Hyde Park. In the same block, Chris Glinski, the man who had been in the public eye as a witness in both the Spot and the Richardson trials, was also located. Regularly appearing in court, sometimes on the side of the prosecution and at other times on the side of the defence, his credibility was supported by his receipt of the Croix de Guerre, the wartime French military decoration. It would seem he was one of many professional witnesses in Bill's stable, like the aptly nicknamed Willy the Witness and the vicar, Basil Andrews. Payments ensured a statement under oath before a jury that would be unaware the witness could have obtained a season ticket for the number of appearances he had made over the years.

Binstock had taken an interest in casinos, particularly London's Victoria Sporting Club on the Edgware Road, which was owned by the New Brighton Tower Company of which Binstock was an active director. It was not as palatial as Lansky's Colony Club but was reputed to be the highest earner of all the capital's gaming houses. During an audit of the Vic's accounts, Department of Trade inspectors found they showed the tables were running at a loss, even though they were being leased for £100,000 per month. It is believed that Binstock was skimming £35,000 per week from the takings, a greater figure than Lansky, who was achieving £4,000 per day from the Colony. Later in the USA, Lansky was charged with tax evasion on his earnings from the Colony, but the case was dropped.

Bill was certainly in direct discussions with American criminal families as to the security of funds being pumped into the UK. The Philadelphia family, headed by Angelo Bruno, was looking to place $25 million in the UK leisure industry. Lansky had lost a similar sum, $20 million in cash, when Castro closed down the Cuban operation and held on to all the assets. It was not a situation the families wished to repeat.

The 1969 Gaming Act not only required unacceptable backers of British casinos to be silent, they were also required to be unseen! Eric Morley, of Mecca and Miss World fame, discussed the purchase of the Vic with Binstock but no deal was forthcoming. Morley was questioned as to the interest Mecca held in a Salford casino with Binstock, but said he was unable to confirm if Binstock was a principal or a nominee.

Now not in a position to front casinos or launder cash in a big way on the British mainland, Binstock moved his operation offshore, taking the Palace Hotel and Casino on the Isle of Man. It is believed that he managed to amass ownership of 20 per cent of all the property on the island, involving various nominee companies, including: Orisa; Manz Overseas Investments; Isle of Man Overseas Estates; EIC Eurosecurities (owned by EIC Expansion Industrielle et Commerciale SA); Central European Company for Insurance, Re-insurance and Investment SA, registered, in Liechtenstein; East Mediterranean Shipping Limited; and H King Limited, a beer-bottling plant controlled by Binstock's interests in betting shops in the north of England. Binstock travelled continuously between the UK, America and Italy, and it was during one of these trips that he was stopped by a British customs officer.

During Binstock's interview, he took a sheet of paper from his briefcase and, in the belief that he was not being observed, tore the sheet, containing highly incriminating information, into small pieces and discarded them in the bin. This action was probably the best available to him in his confined position. However, it led to the death of Sir Eric Miller, a personal friend of Prime Minister Harold Wilson. After being allowed to continue on his journey, the pieces of paper were reconstructed by customs and subsequently formed the basis of the C11 dossier on Binstock.

Miller's company, The Peachy Group, had slipped into severe financial trouble and was coming under the eye of the Department of Trade. In an effort to balance the books, a meeting between Miller, Binstock and Lansky had been arranged. A loan from Miami was agreed, which when repaid would have a source, providing a laundry for black money. Between agreeing the loan and making the necessary arrangements, Miller's stress levels mounted to a point where Binstock believed doing business with the man would be an extremely high risk, and he finally aborted the deal. Sir Eric Miller shot himself in September 1977. At the inquest the court was told that Miller lived in constant fear of Binstock. There is no reason to disbelieve this statement. Power over Miller and his influential friends would certainly have been appealing to Binstock and, through him, to Lansky.

Binstock liked to stay one jump ahead of the game and he prided himself on having one of the best information services in the world, involving the Italian and American Mafia, the French Union Corse, who were specialists in processing morphine for the heroin markets, the Triads, from whom the Italians bought raw opium, and Scotland Yard, courtesy of Billy Howard. To ensure the credibility of the information, Binstock sought to establish various sources to actively gather news. Binstock's bodyguard, Michael Franklin, was an ex-C11 detective. While there is no suggestion that Franklin made use of his previous contacts, it would be naive to believe it was not on Binstock's mind to exploit all avenues.

Not all providers went unchallenged by the authorities. Under the 1911 Official Secrets Act, Detective Chief Superintendent John Kilby Groves was found guilty of passing on information to Miller, who in turn passed it to Binstock, enabling him to remain his one jump ahead of the opposition. Kilby Groves was also found guilty of bribery charges. The Detective Chief Superintendent was only one of many members of the British police force who had enjoyed similar lavish entertainment as Bill's closest contact, Detective Chief Superintendent Ted Bland. It was a trough that, over the years, Bill had had the foresight to keep full. Binstock was known to be equally generous.

CHAPTER FIVE

Mind Bets

Chief Superintendent Edward Bland formally tendered his resignation. It was sooner than most people had anticipated and was a subject that he had not discussed previously with his colleagues in the force or friends outside.

Ted Bland's patch, just south of the river, stretched from Vauxhall across to include Streatham, the same area that formed Billy Howard's manor in south London. As far as Bill was concerned, the news was potentially devastating. Their friendship had been long, stretching back to when Bland had been a pliable, more junior officer at West End Central and before. It was unlikely the new Chief Superintendent would be promoted from one of the local divisions. It was equally unlikely, Bill knew, that it would be someone already on the payroll.

On advice, he had walked away from Winston's, an act that caused him a great deal of heartache and self-recrimination; an act he now considered his greatest mistake. To have held on to the club could only have been achieved by a bloody battle that would have been both excessively violent and public. Without a doubt, people would have been killed, and at that point all his contacts assembled over decades, MPs, judges and senior police officers would have run for cover. All the pressures, friendships and dirt would not keep them within his influence. Publicity and fear would have scared off the vast majority of customers, decimating the business. Loss of influence and cover for other wide-ranging criminal activities, both directly and indirectly, would have vanished and a strong possibility of a long stretch for GBH, or even murder, would have been difficult to avoid. The public outcry would have called for the heads of people that had to be protected. This was a fight that could not be fought.

It now looked as if one of the most influential people in Bill's hand had chosen to pull the rug himself. This, Bill knew, could only be an indication of the heat Bland believed was about to be unleashed. Billy Howard's business interests were now seriously under threat. If the friendly faces in the Met saw a rift between Bland and Bill over the resignation, more filth would consider their positions. The threat of exposing past illegalities was of little substance when players now were no longer in the game. The only option was to grin and pray for the best. On 10 November 1966, printed invitation cards were posted, inviting over 100 people to Chief Superintendent Ted Bland's retirement party to be held on Tuesday, 29 November 1966, at Billy Howard's Beehive Club. Bill and Jan and a few other close friends continued to enjoy private dinner parties in Ted and Ruby Bland's home.

Within months Bill received information that left him with no doubt that he had become an active target. Times were changing. There were people in the Met that wanted him out. Bland had stepped down but there was only one way they could rid themselves of Billy Howard. He had to go down, and go down for a long time. It would take all Bill's power to stop them getting a result. The only place Bill considered himself vulnerable was at The Craywood Club. It was the only place where he was personally involved and John Bland (no relation to Ted), a Detective Sergeant who despised Bill, took a personal interest. Bill assumed that the new faces could easily put pressure on both John Bland and the staff at The Craywood Club, and put a case together.

As the days passed the pressure began to mount. Black clouds began to gather over Bill's horizon. He was beginning to feel the same depression he had experienced after walking away from Winston's. He drank too much and knew it. Before he drank as a social function, now he was drinking for the sake of it, angrily. When there wasn't a glass at his lips, there was a cigarette. Chain smoking and serious booze. In this state, if he didn't keep a tight grip on himself, he knew his frustration could get the better of him and he didn't like the person he could become. As he knew he should not have walked away from Winston's, he knew he should now walk away from his interest in The Craywood, but he was not prepared to lose another fight and certainly not to the filth John Bland.

Weeks passed and the heat seemed to cool. Bill was beginning to think that he had made the right move. Then, early in November, the call came, not to his flat in Battersea, where the caller rightly believed the telephone had been tapped, but at the public house that was Bill's local. The caller had tried three times earlier but had chosen not to leave a message. Having been given the nod, Bill considered his position over too many large gin and tonics.

He should have been stumbling but he wasn't. The clouds had returned and were now blackening out his entire reason. The power with which he crashed through his front door all but shook the entire building. Not knowing why, he took a hammer from under the sink unit and, rushing from room to room, methodically smashed every piece of glass he could find. Bottles, mirrors, glasses, TV. Only a single mirror remained, which he left unscathed, using the same reasoning he had in selecting all the other items to be destroyed. None. Holding their young son in her arms and standing before her husband, Jan brought the carnage to an end. Jan knew she was safe with young Billy held close to her. Dropping the hammer, Bill stood his ground. His hand darted for his breast pocket. Suddenly, terror flooded Jan's mind as she waited for Bill to flash the razor across her. Bill smiled, removed the comb, ran it through his hair and replaced it before walking past her in silence, his feet crunching coloured glass fragments into the carpet as he stepped out on to the street.

The night air was cold but a sweat had broken out across his brow and all over his body, despite not wearing an overcoat. He could feel his white shirt clinging to his armpits, his suit trousers to his legs and his socks wet in his shoes. The pubs were closed but there were plenty of places he could get a drink if it had been a drink that he had wanted. At that moment, alcohol was not the poison he craved. He wanted something stronger. His feet took him on to Albert Bridge and slowly, but with direction, he began to cross. A few taxis and the occasional private car cruised by, heading either north or south, but he paid little or no attention. His eyes were drawn through the metal balustrade and down into the dark swirling water of the Thames. The more he looked away, the louder it called. First a whisper, but by the time he had reached little more than halfway it was screaming to him. Left, along the Embankment, the screams died away only to be replaced by a more welcoming soft melodic voice, backed by the lap of the water on brickwork below. A chill went through his body – the sweat had begun to evaporate. Ahead he could see no one. He stopped, looked over the parapet and then glanced back in the direction he had just walked. He seemed to be the only person on the Embankment at that moment. The voice was sweeter than any he had heard recently. It was a voice that understood him. The words of the song were words he knew only too well. Humming to himself, he began to count quietly, the beat of the song, the pieces of debris travelling in the current. From his pocket he removed a packet of cigarettes and by sheltering his head in his jacket managed to keep the flame on the lighter from blowing out long enough to half-light the tobacco. He sucked the smoke hard into the depth of his lungs and, leaning on the cold damp stone, enjoyed his last cigarette.

★ ★ ★

The Craywood Club had in many respects been an opportunity, not to replace Winston's, as it did not possess the glamour and celebrity glitz of the West End's top club, but it did provide a channel for his energy and regular cash for his boys. It was a game. His Soho connections, the services he provided to London's top gangland figures were a good source of revenue, as was cash invested in armed robberies and other criminal ventures. But they were not a game. Billy Howard needed to be a player. He needed to play the game. And whilst Streatham was not Mayfair, it was in the area of the world he also loved. It was south London. It was a home game in front of a home crowd.

When The Craywood had first opened in 1965, Bill had paid it little attention. He was otherwise occupied. In early October 1966, Bill identified the club's potential and as a result, in the early hours of 26 October 1966, Henry Wagland and two other chaps closely associated with Bill visited the club. It did not take long for a disturbance involving the three to bring the gambling activities in the club to a standstill. The management quickly stepped in and requested that they leave. The request was greeted with a torrent of abuse and the door staff were asked by Mr Glassman, the duty manager, to escort the troublemakers from the premises. Knowing the reputation of the men involved, they refused. Glassman then telephoned the police, but neither the knowledge of the call being made nor the arrival of the police some time later persuaded Wagland and his friends to leave.

At the door, Glassman explained the situation to the officers led by Inspector Colls. The inspector and the other officers then followed Glassman across the club to two men standing by the coffee bar. Glassman placed his hand on the nearest and formally asked them to leave, as is required by law. They refused and were then escorted from the premises by PC Kevin Procter. During this exercise Wagland remained standing at the end of one of the gaming tables. Glassman approached Wagland and moved his hand to repeat the procedure, but before he could do so Wagland, a powerful man physically, who gave his occupation later in court as a building labourer, grabbed an ashtray from the green baize table. Lifting it above his head, he made to crash it down on Glassman. The blow was intercepted by PC Williamson.

'Which nick you from?' Wagland asked, as he was being hustled towards the exit.

'Brixton,' Inspector Colls replied.

'Hm,' Wagland sneered.

The incident had proved to the management of The Craywood Club that the staff employed on the door were either not capable or not prepared to handle any trouble that broke out in the club. Shortly after this fracas, Bill spoke to Mr Bruce, the manager of the club, and suggested that they employed Sammy Clarke on the door, and that he could guarantee there would be no trouble if Sammy were employed. This was agreed and, shortly after, another of Bill's associates, Tony Sams, joined the door staff. Trouble was not totally eliminated but it was dealt with decisively. The cost to the club was a wage to Fat Sam and Tony Sams of £40 each a week. Bill enjoyed entrée, coming and going as he pleased without the indignity of paying a membership fee or getting a ticket at the door. As weeks went by and he became a regular, local tearaways avoided the place. During the same period, his power within the club was enhanced.

'What the fuck you doing?' one of the numerous Cypriots that used the club shouted at a young man standing close to him.

Boghurst, another regular at the club, quickly tried to move away and withdraw his hand from the pocket of the punter standing to one side of him. The Cypriot grabbed Boghurst's arm and held it.

'Piss off,' Boghurst replied, angrily trying to pull himself free, but the Cypriot's hand held firm. Without a second thought, Boghurst's free hand swept up a glass from the table and plunged it into the face of the man restraining him. The cuts opened and blood ran quickly. The man released his assailant, putting both hands to his face, blood oozing between his fingers.

The following day, the doormen received word that a gang of Cypriots was coming to the club to cause trouble and smash the place up. Fat Sam telephoned Bill and asked for some assistance. That evening Bill turned up with a few boys from Brixton, who sat in the Horse and Groom pub next door to the club, waiting for it to go off. Nothing happened. The next day, Bill went to talk to Costas, the head of the Cypriot firm, and was able to sort things out. Although not directly any of Bill's concern, a financial consideration was involved. Apart from other costs, the Brixton chaps had to be looked after. Bruce had to put his hand in his pocket.

Bill's earnings from the club at this time were varied, but Bill did bring Jan to the club and used it to entertain friends. The 2/6d entrance fee was never requested from Bill or his guests and payment was never offered. Refreshments were taken on the same basis. Betting was handled in a slightly different manner.

At the poker table the pot could be sizeable and betting was against other players, not the house. This was strictly cash. The club games, American roulette, French roulette and blackjack, were different again. 'Mind' bets and 'call' bets provided substantial payouts. Mind bets were the most rewarding because there was no possibility of losing, only confirming the wager after the ball had dropped.

The process started with call bets.

'No more bets,' the croupier announced, scanning the table and turning his attention to the ivory ball about to fall into a numbered slot.

'Ten pounds on 27,' Bill called.

'No bet,' the croupier barked. Call bets were against the house rules.

Bill looked towards the inspector at the head of the table but before any appeal could be launched, the ball had fallen beyond 27, missing 13 and dropping into 36. Bill turned away and walked over to another table.

'Four and neighbours. Ten pounds.' Bill's voice was sharp and clear as he watched the ball bouncing first in one slot and the another, before coming to rest.

Calling the number first meant it had been spoken before the ball had actually settled. Adding the bet 'neighbours' compensated if the ball took another bounce. The bet refers to the numbers either side of the specified number on the wheel, not on the table. Four and 'neighbours' would not be 3, 4 and 5 but 21, 4 and 19.

The croupier looked at the inspector. 'Pay Mr Howard.'

In calculating the amount to be paid, the croupier multiplied 10 by 35 and then began to divide it by three.

'That was a ten pound bet,' Bill said.

'Ten pounds over three numbers,' the croupier corrected.

'No. Ten pounds on each number,' Bill said, holding his ground.

The croupier shakily glanced over to the inspector, who nodded reluctantly. Three and a half stacks of chips, valuing £350, were pushed across the baize in Bill's direction. Bill took a few chips from one of the stacks and tossed the tip back across the table.

Early the next evening when it was still quiet, having waited for the same staff combination to open a table, Bill, the only player at the table, placed a few chips here and there, happy to win or lose a few pounds.

'Fifteen black,' the croupier called without enthusiasm, then lazily leaned forward and, using two hands, swept the few scattered chips in, chipped them up and pushed them in to form a stack next to the wheel.

Bill, using his index finger, tapped the table twice and pointed to the wheel.

'It was fifteen, sir,' the croupier said.

'Yes. I had ten quid on it,' Bill replied.

'The number was clear, sir,' the croupier declared nervously.

'Yes. But I've been on there all night. It was a standing bet.'

'If the chips are not on the table, sir . . .'

'What's the problem?' the inspector asked.

'This gentleman thinks he should get paid out on the last number, but he didn't place the bet.'

'How much was it for?' the inspector asked.

'It's ten pound every spin. That stack there is yours. They're the ones I lost. It's easier than putting it on every time,' Bill said pointing to a small stack of chips standing slightly to one side of his main stack.

'Yeah. That's fine. Pay it,' the inspector authorised.

The croupier almost shook his head in disbelief.

As the winning stacks were pushed over, Bill picked up the small stack of losing chips and tossed them over. 'You can put them in the tip box.'

Later, when a poker school had assembled, Bill would decide on its strength and if he felt it was wide open, he would sit in. If not, he would hang around and have a few drinks. Much later, as was the case the previous night, if the inspector was not on the count, he would slip him a pony and also tell him to straighten the young lad that had been dealing. As the night progressed, the roulette and blackjack tables began to fill, but no faces came in that Bill particularly wanted to get into a card school with. The size of the pot, he felt, would not be worth the effort. He was just about to call it a night when Bruce approached him.

'Bill, I've spoken to the directors and they aren't prepared to let you have a franchise on one of the tables. Sorry about that, and I've also had a complaint about you calling bets. It's a house rule that all bets have to be placed before the ball drops.' Bruce was talking to Bill in an almost casual way. It was clear that he hoped by taking this tone, Bill would respond in the same way. He was wrong.

'This place is nothing without me and the directors should understand that. If I get taken for granted here, I'll finish the place. And, Bruce, if I want to call bets, I'll call bets and not you or anybody else will stop me.' Bill's attitude scared Bruce, but he persisted. He knew that if he could not control the situation now, control would move completely to Howard.

'I'm sorry, Bill, but if I let you get away with it, everyone will want to do it.' He was trying to appeal to Bill's common sense.

'That's your problem.'

'Look, Bill, if you continue to call bets, I won't have any alternative than to close the table.' The option of barring Bill was not something he even considered. The thought of even threatening it terrified him and he knew that it would be completely unenforceable.

Bill turned his back on Bruce and walked over to the nearest table. He pushed himself in between the players and tapped his index finger on the only box not containing a stack of chips.

'Ten pounds.'

The dealer placed a card, face up, in front of each of the six boxes and one in front of his own. Bruce walked into the pit and, before the dealer could draw second cards to each of the players from the shoe, announced that the table was closed. The players picked up their chips from the table but were not happy. The dealer locked the trays and drop box and headed for the staff room. Bill headed for the next table. First Bill called bets on all the blackjack tables, which were immediately closed by Bruce, as he followed in Bill's path. With the card tables closed, Bill moved to the French and American roulette tables, calling bets on each as he went. It had taken less than half an hour to bring all gaming tables at The Craywood to a standstill. Impasse. Bruce was angry. He had been boxed into a corner. He had made himself look stupid in front of a club full of punters. His credibility was in serious question. As much as he did not want to face the situation that had developed, he could not see any way back.

'Either you leave, or I'm calling the police.' Bruce was fuming.

Bill stood defiant.

Bruce was now the centre of attention, everyone waiting to see what his next move would be. He stood, unsure of himself for a long moment, then he walked past Bill to the manager's office.

The door had hardly closed behind him when it was flung open, shaking the room and all but parting the hinges from the frame. Bruce lunged in the direction of the wall-mounted phone, grabbing at the receiver. Before he had any opportunity to dial, Bill pushed him away. Bruce's iron grip on the receiver had the effect of virtually pulling the wires from the main box. With a loud crash, Bill had torn the box from its mount and hurled it across the office, wrenching the receiver from the terrified manager's hand. As Bill advanced on him, Bruce took sanctuary behind his desk. Leaning on both fists, Bill shoved his face across the wooden divide. 'If I have any trouble with this club and you talk out of turn, I'm going to have this place burnt down and your car will get blown up with you and your family in it.'

Bruce backed himself against the wall. Bill picked up a tray of coffee and threw it at Bruce's head. 'If you want to end up dead, you're going the right way about it.' With that threat hanging in the air, Bill walked out of the office and out of the club.

The next day Bill visited Brixton, drank in two or three pubs, shook hands with their landlords, passed the time of day warmly with a couple of bookmakers and called into the council offices to deliver an envelope containing a small amount of money for one of the officials who was prepared to ensure a problem a local businessman was experiencing would go away. By late afternoon, he had mini-cabbed over the river into the West End. The Astor Club was quiet. Bertie was out. There were a few faces but he did not feel like staying. Walking out on to Piccadilly at the Ritz, Bill turned left and off in the direction of the Circus and Soho. It was a magnet.

At the Italian-owned places, he nodded to the proprietors and staff if they were outside as he passed. He left direct contact with these to Dimes. The English-owned properties, very much in the minority, Bill entered, greeted the owners and enquired if all was well. In some, members of Ronnie Knight's firm would be making regular visits. In others, protection money would be collected by lieutenants of Hill, and in one or two the Twins' firm had a foothold, mainly due to the fact that the operators were East End boys. Peter Cook and Dudley Moore's Establishment Club, on the other hand, paid respects directly to Bill. By this time no set amount, no set collection day, just an *ad hoc* payment whenever Bill dropped by. It was an arrangement that Peter felt comfortable with, which had in the first instance prevented the Kray Twins from muscling in and, in the long term, kept the tearaways from trying it on. Bill liked Peter's humour and particularly Dud's piano playing. He felt they were a pleasure to be around, so he remained happy not to drain the place.

Back at The Craywood, trouble had broken out at one of the tables. Fat Sam gave the punter a good straightener and broke his jaw. Fat Sam reported the incident to Bill and told him that Detective Sergeant Bland had given him a bollocking. Bill told Fat Sam not to worry but in the back of his mind he felt uneasy. He could not convince himself that DS Bland's motive for habitually being around The Craywood was directly concerned with legitimate police work. Bill wondered how many people were getting a bite of the cherry. A wedge of the cash he was collecting was already finding its way to Brixton nick, so he hoped no one was getting greedy.

It was not too many days later when Fat Sam was again passing on information. This time it was a warning. The news was not new, Bill had already been made aware via a nod from the Old Bill. All this did was provide confirmation and strengthen the case that John Bland was out to nail Bill. If Fat Sam was aware of what was going on, DS Bland's confidence appeared to be strong. Fat Sam had suggested they should watch out, as the police had met with the directors of The Craywood. The information had come through Bob Bruce, which indicated Bruce was not considered to be involved in the blag. With Ted Bland now a lame duck as far as Bill was concerned, a full police investigation taking place and the possibility of certain members of the police looking to move in, Bill's options in south London were rapidly closing down. Money and violence were now the only tools that remained available in Billy Howard's arsenal.

This was a retrograde step. For more years than Bill cared to recall, his reputation for violent acts, long gone, was sufficient to keep people on both sides of the law, in line.

* * *

A hand from below the table slowly worked its way up Jan's slender leg and under her dress. She quickly swung her legs away in the opposite direction and at the same time slapped the intruding hand.

Tables at Danny La Rue's club were arranged in terraces to enable all guests to get an uninterrupted view of the cabaret. Harry H. Corbett was laughing up from the table below. With the lights dimmed, Bill and Jan had not seen their close friend when they had been shown to their seats. Two bottles of champagne later, and Bill was clearly in a mood. The alcohol and the situation surrounding The Craywood were preying on his mind.

'Phone Bruce and tell him if there is any trouble over that place, he's going to get a bomb thrown through his window.'

'I can't do that, Bill,' Jan replied.

'I said go and phone him and tell him he's going to get bombed.' Bill sounded as though he was going to explode at any minute.

'I don't have his number,' Jan said, trying to find an excuse not to go.

'Phone directory enquires. Ask Dan for a telephone book.' Jan could see that it was no good arguing with him. She picked up her bag and headed off in the direction of the call box.

'You look a bit off colour. Is everything all right?' Harry asked, moving up into the seat Jan had vacated.

'Yes. I'm just a bit out of sorts. Lot going on at the moment,' Bill said, lifting his head from his hand and glossing over things.

'Jan said you've been drinking a lot ever since you came out of Winston's.'

'I've been drinking a lot for years.'

'Yes, but not on your own in the flat.'

'Jan talks too much.'

'Bill, if it's money you know we'll all get together to get you another place.' Harry was obviously concerned and Bill knew that his offer was genuine.

'Harry, thanks, but it's not money. You're a good friend.' With that Jan returned and Harry slipped back into his chair at the lower table.

'Did you tell him?'

'I couldn't get through,' she lied. 'I'll try again later.'

Early the following week, Bill had his card marked again, this time from a constable at Brixton nick. He still had contacts, the problem was they did not carry sufficient clout to change what was happening, only to pass on information gained during briefings or by keeping an eye on witnesses that were brought in for questioning.

The management and staff at The Craywood now had to be taught a lesson. Arson is a powerful weapon. It attacks all the senses. The smell of petrol, the heat of the flames, the roar of the fire and the charred black lingering look of equipment that is expensive to replace. Even the smallest fire sends unmistakable smoke signals.

The blaze quickly took hold, assisted by lighter fuel sprayed on to the curtains. The property sustained only superficial burns but it was clear that the time for playing games was over and anyone making themselves too busy with the law would have to suffer the consequences.

* * *

'Everything all right, sir?' The voice was deep and came out of the shadows.

Bill had been in another world. The sound startled him, he turned and peered into the darkness. Now emerging from beside one of the trees he could see the helmeted silhouette of a bobby.

'Yes. Just enjoying a quiet smoke before going home to the wife.' Bill did not know if he knew the constable or if the constable would have recognised him, but in half-shadows, both were just figures.

'Well, just make sure you do. Don't want no trouble, do we?'

Bill could hear the PC's footfall as he was again swallowed by the night. He squeezed his hand around the empty fag packet and lobbed it into the river. Taking a final drag on the cigarette, he flicked the butt up into the air and watched it fall like a mini-firework flickering down until it was gone, washed away by the Thames below.

Somehow he did not trust himself to walk back. The feeling had passed, but walking back over the bridge would have sent a shiver down his spine. Seeing a cab, he stepped quickly out into the road and flagged it down.

'Albert Bridge Road,' he said, knowing his money was in the overcoat he had been wearing earlier, but had left over the back of the sofa without thinking as he left the house.

'OK, you can drop me here.' Bill tapped on the glass partition and climbed out on to the pavement 50 yards from his own address as the cab pulled to a halt. Before the cabby could ask for the fare, Bill stuck his head through the open window.

'Right. Next stop The Craywood Club in Streatham High Road. Tell the manager you've just dropped me off here and tell him Billy Howard said he was to give you a tenner for the fare.' With that Bill walked off and disappeared into a doorway. If the nod he had been given turned out to be true, he knew that would probably be the last money coming out of The Craywood. He smiled to himself, watched the taxi drive off and then walked briskly home.

The lights were on, but Jan and the children were gone. He threw his jacket over the back of the sofa and was tempted to search out a bottle of anything he had not smashed. Instead, systematically and with care, he began collecting up the pieces of broken glass, working his way from one room to the next.

Sleep came easier than he had expected. He woke early with a raging thirst but he knew nothing other than the water in the tap had survived his rampage. He checked the step but no bottles had been left. Not even any milk. He found a clean white shirt in amongst the ironing and with his usual thoroughness ironed it and pressed the trousers to a dark suit. Woman's work, never done.

The pub was not open, it was still too early, but the side door was unlocked and the barman was bottling up. 'Morning, Bill. Don't usually see you up and about this time of the day. Or are you on your way home?'

Bill hoped that he looked too well groomed to have been out on the tiles all night, but he let it go. The barman poured him a large Gordon's and tonic. Bill picked up a copy of the *Daily Mirror* that still lay on the mat and settled into a banquette seat, leaving the barman to finish his chores.

* * *

Later, from The Beehive Club, Billy Howard was brought to Streatham Police Station and questioned. Detective Chief Inspector Reginald Davis of 'L' Division subsequently prepared the following statement.

> On the 1st November 1967 with Det. Sgt. Bland I saw the defendant Howard at Streatham Police Station. I cautioned him and said to him, 'You know who I am, I want to ask you questions about money which has been obtained by you, Sammy Clarke and Tony Sams, from the Craywood Club by putting them in fear, but before I do I want to tell you that the wife of the officers in this enquiry has received a threatening telephone call, telling her to tell her husband to lay off. It

has also been said by Sams that if he makes himself too busy Sgt. Bland will be crippled.'

Howard said, 'No never me, you know I'm no angel, but I would never threaten the law. I swear on my babys life.'

I said, 'Clarke and Sams are a couple of your boys, is that right.'

He said, 'Well they used to work for me, but they now go their own way.'

I said, 'Before they became doormen at the Craywood Club, three men went into the club and caused trouble, do you know who they were.'

Howard said, 'I think it was Chandler and Wagland. That Waglands a good lad, but when he's had a drink he goes mad.'

I said, 'They are both friends of yours.'

Howard said, 'Yes, I suppose you could say that.'

I said, 'just after that your boys became doormen.'

Howard said, 'Yes, I'd heard they had trouble so I sent Sammy out there to see if he could help. They took him on and then later took on Tony.'

I said, 'What do you mean, you heard they had trouble. You sent Wagland and the others to cause trouble, so your boys could get in.'

Howard said, 'No, I didn't send them up there.'

I said, 'Is it right that Sammy introduced you to the Manager.'

Howard said, 'Yes, I told Bruce that if Sammy worked here there would be no trouble.'

I said, 'weren't Sammy and Tony working for you.'

Howard said, 'Well, I wouldn't say they worked for me, but they haven't been ½ an inch away from me for the last couple of years.'

I said, 'How much did you pay them.'

Howard said, ' I never paid them anything, but they were always on the tap for money and when I had it I gave it to them.'

I said, 'Did the Craywood Club pay you money, as well as paying these two?'

Howard said, 'No, the club has given me nothing.'

I said, 'Has Bruce the Manager ever given you money.'

Howard said, 'No.'

I said, 'Have you ever borrowed money from Bruce.'

Howard said, 'Yes a little bit.'

I said, 'How much altogether.'

He said, 'Certainly not more than £15.'

I said, 'Are you sure.'

He said, 'Course I am. A couple of fivers that's all.'

I said, 'Did you pay him back.'

He said, 'Yes.'

I said, 'It is alleged over a long period that you consistently borrowed money from Bruce in the region of over £200 and that you had no intention of paying it back. It had been made clear to Mr Bruce either by you or your two boys, that if you were upset somebody was likely to get their arse cut or a bomb put in their car.'

Howard said, 'You must be joking.'

I said, 'I've never been more serious.'

Howard said, 'Who says this, Bruce. He wouldn't say it to my face.'

I said, 'You owed Bruce money yet you still went to him for more. If these were genuine loans why did you not pay him something back on the previous loans.'

Howard said, 'He never seemed worried about the loans. If he had asked me I would have paid him back.'

I said, 'That's correct, he never asked for the money because he was frightened of the consequences.'

Howard made no reply.

I said, 'Have you ever called bets in the club.'

Howard said, 'No.'

I said to him, 'Be careful what you say, I know that you have called bets frequently on a number of tables.'

Howard said, 'Well, I have called some bets, but only on the dice. I once called a bet for £1,000 in Esmeraldos Barn.'

I said, 'When you called bets at the Craywood and you lost, did you pay.'

Howard said, 'Yes.'

I said, 'Who did you pay.'

He said, 'Bruce.'

I said, 'What, at the time.'

He said, 'No, sometimes I used to let it go for a few days, but I always paid within three or four days.'

I said, 'But it is a rule of the club that call bets are not allowed.'

Howard said, 'Everyone in gambling calls bets.'

I said, 'What without paying at the time. There is no credit betting at Craywood.'

Howard said, 'Bruce didn't mind. I always paid him sometime.'

I said, 'Do you remember the night when you went round all the tables calling bets and Bruce followed you refusing your bets and closing down the tables.'

Howard said, 'No.'

I said, 'Now don't be silly, there were a lot of people in the club that night.'

Howard said, 'Yes, that's right, but it was only a giggle.'

I said, 'Do you call it a giggle when Bruce nearly collapsed in fear at having to take this action.'

Howard said, 'No, it wasn't like that. Bruce is a friend of mine.'

I said, 'You stood in the centre of the casino and shouted that your name alone had kept trouble from the club and then threatened Bruce and his wife and family together with the fact that you would blow up the club if you could not call bets.'

Howard said, 'Well I was a bit upset at my concession being turned down.'

I said, 'Yes, about that concession, you asked to be allowed to run a table at the Craywood Club and the very night that your concession was turned down there was a fire in the club.'

Howard said, 'Yes, a lot of people have put that down to me and the other 2, but you can take it from me, I don't play like that.'

I said, 'When Bruce told you that there was no concession you made a fuss and said that your name had kept trouble from the club. What did you mean.'

Howard said, 'Well, the club has been using my name without permission as belonging to the club so as to keep off all the tearaways.'

I said, 'Did you ever stop trouble in the club?'

He said, 'Yes, many times, if there was any trouble I would go over and sort it out before it came to a punch up. For instance Rice's boy caused trouble in there one night and I sorted that out. There was no trouble.'

I said to him, 'Did the club pay you for this service.'

He said, 'No.'

I said, 'Then why did you do it.'

Howard said, 'Well I don't want no trouble do I.'

I said, 'The night after the night when all the tables were closed down and you were prevented from calling bets you went into the club with Tony Sams and the manager told you you were barred. The doormen refused to put you out because they were frightened and so the manager went into his office saying he would phone the police. You followed him and pulled the telephone wires from the wall.'

Howard said, 'That's a lie.'

I said, 'Are you sure.'

He said, 'Yes, that is a lie.'

I said, 'Are you a member of the Craywood Club.'

He said, 'Well, I filled in a form.'

I said, 'Did you ever pay your membership fee.'

He said, 'No.'

I said, 'Did you ever pay your entrance fee.'

He said, 'No.'

I said, 'Why not.'

He said, 'Hundreds used to go in without paying their entrance fee.'

I said, 'So you have never paid a membership or entrance fee and yet you were in there nearly every night.'

He said, 'Yes that's right, the club wanted me there.'

I said to him, 'What has been your financial position over the last 18 months.'

He said, 'My club is not worth a light and I have not got a pot to piss in. I have got 3 mortgages on the house. I am in debt all around and have been for a long time now.'

I said, 'If that is the case, how have you been able to gamble heavily at the Craywood during this period without money.'

He made no reply.

I said, 'You told Bruce that the police had an interview with the directors of the Craywood Clubs blaming you for the fire. How did you know whether they had been to see the Directors.'

He said, 'Sammy told me. He said "Watch how you go, Billy, the law have been to see the directors of Craywood about the fire and other matters."'

I said, 'What other matters.'

He said, 'He didn't say.'

I said, 'If you have been doing nothing wrong why did he tell you to watch it.'

Howard said, 'Well, Sammy seemed to think I had something to worry about, but I had nothing to do with the fire and I haven't blagged anybody.'

I said to him, 'I am not satisfied with your answers and you will be charged with demanding money with menaces.'

I further cautioned Howard and he made no reply. He then telephoned his solicitors.

The interview with Bill was terminated and he was returned to the cells. Others were interviewed later and cross-referenced with statements taken from members of the club staff earlier in the investigation.

* * *

'This is a proper protection case,' Mr L. Winston, for the Prosecution, said to the Court in Balham. Standing in the dock were 5 defendants: William Howard (51) of Battersea, Anthony Sams (33) of Clapham, John Charles Clarke (39) of South Lambeth, Brian Lake (31) of Battersea and Henry Thomas Wagland (47) of Brixton. William Howard, Anthony Sams and John Clarke stood before the Court charged with demanding money with menaces from The Craywood Club in Streatham High Road, south London, in January. Brian Lake was accused of demanding £2 from the club on 17 August 1967, and Henry Wagland was charged with demanding £20 with menaces from two men at The Craywood Club and stealing gambling chips belonging to the club.

'Witnesses in this case are very frightened. They have only come forward because they know the defendants are now in custody,' Detective Chief Inspector Reginald Davis told the Court. 'A police officer has received a threat that he would be crippled if he did not lay off,' he further alleged.

The hearing was an application for bail, which was refused and the defendants were remanded in custody until 18 November 1967. The committal hearing took place in December at Marylebone Magistrates Court. Mr John Hazan, counsel for the prosecution, told the Court that William Howard had warned a Detective Sergeant investigating the case that if he did not desist, he would be crippled and that he should understand that he was dealing with another Richardson affair. Hazan then added that three witnesses had complained that they had been warned of being beaten up, run over or having a bomb put in their car. He told the magistrate that a 24-hour police guard had been mounted on all the witnesses and he asked that their names and addresses should not be disclosed.

The defendants were committed for trial at the Central Criminal Court and an application for bail was refused.

* * *

'More peas. Can you ask Jan to give me more peas in future?' Billy Howard asked his brother during a prison visit.

On remand, prisoners are permitted to wear their own clothes and to have meals sent in. Each day without fail, Jan delivered a tray of hot food and a half-bottle of red wine, the maximum amount of alcohol permitted. This did not prevent private arrangements with corruptible prison warders, who could be bribed or otherwise persuaded to smuggle in luxury items for influential prisoners, often referred to as 'barons'.

Bill was held over the Christmas period of 1967, but his incarceration did not prevent him making the most of the Christmas spirit. Although a gin drinker, it would have been a bit cheeky to persuade a screw to smuggle in bottles of gin and a crate of tonic waters, not to mention the lemons. So, during those weeks Bill switched his tipple to Remy Martin, a drink that was later to prove to be a frequent friend and powerful enemy. The same warder also regularly brought in small quantities of 'blow', which many of the prisoners felt took the edge off being banged up with hundreds of other blokes, sharing overcrowded cells, slopping out and having no real way of working off the considerable frustrations of being isolated from what was going on in the outside world. Business ventures, children's welfare and potential female infidelity were causes for concern amongst most prisoners, particularly those held on remand for long periods, only to be found not guilty when their cases came to court. Much of it was more paranoia than fact, but that did not lessen the irritation and anger. Maintaining good communications with the outside was essential, especially for gang leaders whose interests could be devoured by young, up-and-coming tearaways eager to make a name for themselves. The Kray Twins were one firm where the control remained strongly in place and many would say that they proved to be more financially successful during their long years behind bars than they ever were when left to their own devices during their relatively short tenure as gang leaders in their own manor.

Directives and messages could be passed through visitors and by prisoners being released. However, on many occasions, it was advantageous to discuss matters arising with other incarcerated gang bosses. This posed certain difficulties, even when they were banged up in the same nick, being celled on different landings. It became necessary for a meeting to take place between the Krays and various other members of the criminal fraternity held on remand in Brixton. Despite being in the same prison, it was not easy for them all to get together. There was only one way. Each told a friend on the outside to arrange a visit on a particular day at a particular time. All the same day and all at the same time. It worked like a charm. All the visitors chatted amongst themselves. All the prisoners discussed critical matters that could only be hammered out face to face.

Previously, Bill had brought pressure to bear on witnesses, police, the judiciary and members of the public chosen at random to be 12 good men and true – the jury. On these occasions it had usually been for the benefit of those enjoying his patronage. Now in serious need to bring pressure to bear in his own favour, major difficulties barred the way. Threats, promises and blackmail brought into play by those close to Bill would not carry sufficient weight. These could not be relied upon under the present conditions. On the other hand, promises, reassurance, blackmail, deals and threats offered up by the police to secure a conviction were plausible to any slightly shaky person involved in the prosecution.

The police might well have felt that pressure could be directed from the Knight firm on Bill's behalf, so that was out of the question. Dimes carried weight with the Italians, but not with the broader public. Hill was out of the country and, Bill believed, no longer commanded the necessary power, and the Richardsons had received long sentences only months earlier, despite financial incentives and the threat of violent retribution. It looked as if it would have to be payback time for the Twins. Bill felt he could now only rely upon the Twins to handle the money, violence and blackmail delivery successfully.

There was one problem. Well, two really. The Twins were unstable and lacked subtlety, and Bill was of the opinion privately that they were going down for a long time. But they still commanded respect. This status was fine when dealing with other villains, even jurors, but was less appropriate when making overtures to members of the Prosecution team, the Bench and senior police officers who may be required to give evidence. Their instability also made it difficult to advise them how best to approach a situation, particularly if the advice was being relayed via a third party.

The Prosecution were looking for a term of 12 years, Bill had been advised by his defence team. There was little other choice. Within weeks, the Krays of course were looking to achieve the same successful nobbling on their own behalf, but as far as he was concerned, they owed him. The fly in the ointment was the jury. Where witnesses and those involved with the actual prosecution could be intimidated, bought or influenced at an early stage, the jury could only be nobbled after the court case had started, and the later the better. Ten days before the jury gave their verdict, the Krays were off the streets. Had enough been done? Bill could not be sure. Bill's thoughts went back to his meeting, if meeting was what you could call it, at the gentlemen's club. Somewhere there he believed there was a lever. What he could not make up his mind about was whether pulling it would see him get a long drop, or whether it would open some doors. Were the Krays the only ones who owed him a favour?

* * *

The case was held at the Old Bailey and came to a close on 18 May 1968. All four men were found not guilty of conspiring to rob.

The court had been presented with a catalogue of evidence by Mr John Hazan for the Prosecution. Hazan claimed that William Howard, aged 51, of Battersea, was the ringleader and that John Clarke and Anthony Sams were very able lieutenants. All four defendants had pleaded not guilty.

'Members of the jury, I should advise you that you will all be under police surveillance throughout the period of this trial which is estimated to last for a period of five weeks, as it was felt that people might try to get in touch with you to influence your verdict,' Sir Carl Aarvoid stated before the proceeding commenced.

'The four accused operated a subtle and insidious form of protection racket. After Mr Howard and Mr Wagland created disturbances, the manager was persuaded to employ Mr Sams and Mr Clarke as doormen. Howard was the prime mover and for months they virtually took over The Craywood Club.' These accusations were made by the Prosecution.

It was in this atmosphere, Hazan stated, that the defendants conspired to rob and steal. Some were also accused of assault on employees and of blackmail.

'There was frequent talk of bombs being placed in cars and the managers were warned that their wives and children would be blown up,' Hazan had added. 'Employees were threatened that they would be knifed or blasted with shotguns,' he had continued.

Shortly after Bill's arrest the police had called to see Jan, she believed, to take her into custody for questioning. This would have left young Billy and Jan's elder daughter without parental care, and would have automatically required the children to be placed with social services – a tactic not uncommon with the police at that time, to put pressure on the defendant. If the accused admitted guilt and signed a statement making a full admission, the wife would be released and the children allowed to return to their mother. Jan did not want to place Bill in this position. When the police called, Jan was already on her toes, long gone. One child hid under the dining-room table, the other was said to be the baby of a visiting friend who had called round the moment news of Bill's arrest was broken. Jan took refuge in a suite at the luxurious Claridges Hotel and the children were well taken care of by other members of her family.

Once solicitors had been instructed, it was safe for Jan and her children to return home, and plans were put into place to ensure that a top legal team began to prepare a costly defence. Jan took responsibility for funding the defence and began to make arrangements for her properties to be placed on the market should the need arise. It was then a question of obtaining character references, one of which was naturally required from Ted Bland.

Whilst many people, including Bill's best friend Harry H. Corbett, looked to distance themselves, many in the police and other government agencies were prepared to rally round and provide support, albeit in a covert manner. At the time of the arrest, Bill had passed a pistol to a young officer to lose. He quickly passed it to one of the barmaids, but not to one of his superiors. Being arrested in the possession of a firearm would have been extremely difficult to defend. Then there was a letter from a police officer's wife, offering to provide Jan with any help that she might need. Both were highly unusual occurrences.

The convoy, with klaxons blaring, escorted by police outriders, left Brixton Prison at the same time each day for the Bailey. Jan, still with the children to look after, attended court each day without fail. Although she did not have the luxury of the traffic moving aside as she approached, if she heard the klaxons she knew she was late and needed to hurry.

Having all been found not guilty of the most serious charges, the guilty verdicts on the lesser counts did not come as too much of a surprise. Justice must be seen to have been done! Bill was sentenced to 12 months, most of which had been served while on remand. Clarke and Sams received 12 months each, suspended for two years, and Wagland received a 12-month conditional discharge.

Bill had received a severe kick in the crotch some time prior to his arrest and this had caused a badly swollen rupture. The Brixton car dealer responsible paid a heavy price, but the injury allowed Bill the opportunity to avoid spending the remainder of his sentence in prison. A doctor kindly agreed to confirm that surgery was necessary and arrangements were immediately made for Bill to be treated at a clinic in Highgate. He apparently healed slowly. Convalescence at the hospital was required right up to the time of his release.

CHAPTER SIX

Walking In and Walking Out

Michael Howard stood in the centre of the rear section of the foyer at the Regent Palace Hotel, a three-star corner site fronting the edge of Piccadilly Circus, its ship-like shape noticeable, bow protruding towards the flotsam and jetsam that cruised the 'meat-rack', port and starboard escape hatches and a stern that stretched back into Soho.

He stood waiting, moving his weight first from one foot and then to the other. He was nervous, not so much of the person he was expecting to see, but of the wait. Would he recognise him? Would he be recognised? How would they know each other? He searched every face, studied every walk criss-crossing the expanse of marble floor that stretched out before him. They were there by the score, probably by the hundred. The older ones, the Americans, wrinkled red necks, had bought life insurance policies at the end of the war, 25 years earlier, bribed to do so with the offer of the trip to Europe when it matured. Now they both had. Most had not been out of their home county previously, let alone their state or across the Atlantic. The multiple glass front doors were hand-smeared but still allowed a view of the street and passers-by as Michael watched. More faces, although not part of the hotel activity, still seemed to swell the numbers needing scrutiny. This was ridiculous, of course. He was concerned that he would not recognise him face to face, let alone in a crowd.

The passage of people crossing the foyer was equally frenetic. No porters here. Guests carried or dragged their own cases from the lifts to the reception cash desk to settle their accounts. The same quantity showed their passports – most were foreigners, many American. They filled in the hotel registration forms and provided the prerequisite signature, before heading for the upper-floor bedrooms. Old-fashioned with lumpy beds and bathroom facilities down the hall. Bathroom maids in attendance to run the water, provide towels and clean up. A constant scurry of robed figures to-ing and fro-ing. Michael could not see them, but he knew they were there. He had stayed in the hotel and been one of the bathroom rats on various occasions over previous years.

Still no sign. Had they missed each other? Was it the right day? He checked his Rolex Sub-mariner. The bevel had already started to fray the folded edge of his cuff, despite the shirt being almost new. All his shirts had that wear, but the watch meant more to him than the shirts. It was still only a few minutes past the time agreed, but he had arrived ridiculously early and now he was feeling self-conscious, standing there, almost on guard. He put his hand in his pocket and tried to look more casual. Two hotel security men, big, over-indulged, ex-Met, probably ex-Vine Street or West End Central, knew all the faces, had already been over to reception a couple of times and now they were back. Michael knew they must have clocked him on each excursion. They wouldn't know his face, but they would be curious. At some point, he was sure they would approach him.

Suddenly he was desperate to go to the loo. The toilets were across the foyer, past the entrance to the cocktail bar and down the stairs, by the conference suites. If he went, he was sure his father would turn up the moment he was out of sight. With hotel security sniffing about, he was equally sure his father would not want to hang around. If he went he would miss him, if he didn't he'd pee on the floor. The embarrassment.

It was no good, he had to go. Having taken the decision, Michael glanced around to ensure nobody resembling his father, whatever he looked like, was heading in his direction. No potential recognition, he moved his weight on to the balls of his feet and made to step forward at exactly the same moment as one of the ex-Met men positioned himself at the top of the stairs Michael was going to have to go down. 'Christ,' he thought, 'that's all I need, if he sees me going down to the gents, he'll pull me as "rent".'

'Michael.'

The voice spoken from his left made Michael jump. He half-turned and took the hand that was being outstretched in his direction. This had to be the person he was waiting for. The word 'Dad' did not easily roll off his tongue. It did not roll off at all. 'Bill' seemed easier, more appropriate, and this would set the tone of their relationship in the future.

Michael was surprised to be taller than his father. Boys always expect to be looking up at their fathers, but that time had long passed. Bill was not short, but average height with a broad chest and slicked back, grey, thinning hair. He was wearing a blue serge suit, white shirt and a silver and dark-blue striped tie. Smart, well turned out. But it was the handshake that really caught Michael's attention. It was not the fact that it was crushing, because it wasn't. It was not the fact that it was limp because it wasn't that either. Michael knew his father's reputation and for some reason he had expected it to be hard, rough, powerful. It was none of those things. It was a soft, smooth palm. Almost feminine. Possibly manicured. What it actually was, Michael realised, was the hand of a person that had never done a stroke of work in his life. They were the hands of a gambler.

They smiled at each other, grinned and laughed at nothing. Michael cast an eye back at the ex-Met, now more out of curiosity than paranoia, as they headed off in the direction of the side exit and Soho. No one was taking a blind bit of notice.

'So how did you recognise me?' Michael asked.

'Couldn't miss you. You've got your mother's nose!'

Talking about the weather, a bright, dry, sunny day, and the drive into London, they walked side by side along the narrow pavement, turning right into Brewer Street and heading off in the direction of Wardour Street.

For the Soho low-life, it was still early. Most of the people on the street were office types, admin to the film industry, restaurant deliverymen and the shoppers and sellers in the bustling Berwick Street market. Bill stopped outside The House of Floris, its windows filled with the highly decorated gateaux and elaborate wedding cakes that had turned this patisserie into a local landmark. Bill hesitated a moment and then decided not to go in, not wishing to carry a boxed cake around the streets.

'We'll get something on the way back,' he said, and crossed.

Isow's stands on the corner of the alleyway that splits the two sections of the market. Michael followed his father in through its door. It was a restaurant he knew, but had not eaten in previously. The lobster and trout swimming in the tank that formed most of the front window was a good attention grabber. It was not yet noon. All the tables were laid, but not filled. White linen and the glint of silver and glass awaited lunchtime expense account diners. Bill did not know the waiter and the waiter did not recognise him. He showed the guests to a window table and left them to view the menu while he continued preparing Melba toast and butters. His *mise en place* had been interrupted and it was noticeable that he was showing a lack of enthusiasm.

The awkward silences between Bill and his son were glazed over by excessive studying of the extensive menu, glancing out of the window and back around the unoccupied room. Bill told his son about Isow's, but it was nothing Michael did not know already. Michael knew a lot about this enclave of the West End — not the people nor the intimate details of club, pub and restaurant interiors, but he knew the streets, the smells, the outside of the buildings and the type of people that came and went through the doorways. He also recognised the faces of many of the prostitutes, pimps and hustlers that formed the furniture on a daily basis. Isow's he knew was famous, a celebrity hangout, a place packed on first nights from the shows around the corner in Shaftesbury Avenue, Cambridge Circus and the Haymarket. The casts, friends and hangers-on would crowd into the place and wait for the nationals to hit the street. If the critics gave praise they would also receive praise, and the party would go on until the early hours. If they slated the performance, their views would be brushed aside as comments from failed actors and the champagne corks would still pop, if with less fizz.

Bill stopped talking about the restaurant and Michael stopped nodding in the right places. As it became silent again, Bill caught the attention of the waiter.

'Do you like lobster?' Bill asked, as the waiter, pad in hand, headed in their direction.

'Yes.'

'Two lobster thermidors to start and two fillet steaks and a bottle of Moët,' Bill told the waiter.

This seemed to inject a little life into the clapped out, black-and-white-clad body who, round the corner in Wardour Street, they would probably have cast as an old retainer. The check deposited in the kitchen, he bustled back to clear the two unwanted covers from the table and replace the other cutlery with the appropriate lobster and steak settings. Water from the ice bucket and stand slopped as it was manoeuvred into position. Moments later the cork was eased out of the bottle, without loss of liquid, and the two strangers touched their glasses together with a simple 'Cheers'.

Halfway through the thermidor, which had been punctuated with shallow chit-chat centred on the taste of the food, the refilling of glasses and a couple of lame humorous comments about people walking past along the alleyway on the other side of the net curtain, a preoccupied figure came in through the front doors. He was well on his way across the floor in the direction of the kitchen entrance before he caught sight of the two lone customers. He slowed and took a second glance before recognition stopped him. He turned and walked over, hand outstretched. 'Mr Howard, it's very nice to see you. It's been a while.'

Bill took the outstretched hand and made to rise, but was motioned to sit. As he did so, he indicated across the table. 'This is my son, Michael.'

Mr Isow looked surprised as he took Michael's hand. 'I didn't know you had a grown-up son. Are you back in Soho?'

Bill explained that he had interests in south London that kept him busy but he came up to the West End when necessary. Mr Isow wished them both bon appétit and hoped that they would not leave it so long before coming into his restaurant again.

By the time the two had finished, other customers had started to fill the tables and a full brigade of waiters was now busily taking orders and serving drinks.

'Are you getting this?' Bill asked as they got up to leave.

Michael made to get a wallet from his hip pocket. Bill slapped him on the shoulder and winked. No bill was requested and none presented. As they neared the door, the old waiter moved to open it. 'I'm sorry I didn't recognise you, Mr Howard, when you first came in,' he apologised.

Bill smiled, assured him it was not a problem and, stuffing some notes into the old, scrawny hand, told him they had enjoyed their meal.

Out on the street, office workers had left their buildings and many were hastily dashing in the direction of Oxford Street and the shops, or buying fruit and veg from the well-stocked market stalls, wrapped and weighed by fast-talking barrow boys with cheeky grins.

Bill was carrying his own brown paper bag, which Michael had not really noticed earlier. He changed his grip from one hand to the other and pointed up at the neon-lit entrance of Raymond's Revue Bar. Either side of the glass doors, coloured photos displayed the attractive show girls, scantily clad in feathers and sequins.

'Made millions out of standing orders,' Bill said. 'To get in you have to be a member. Most of the customers have got a few bob, they're down here for conferences or meetings, they have a few drinks and end up here. Fill in the membership form with their bank details and every year out it comes. Most of them only ever go in the place once, but they just keep on paying.'

'Don't they cancel it when they see it on their bank statement?'

'It's not that much and they either think that they might use it next time they're up or they decide to cancel it and then forget until they see it again the following year. They're busy people and it's not a priority, so it just keeps running and running.'

How true the extent of the earnings really were, Michael could not be sure but from Bill's tone it was clear that they were substantial, and Bill obviously thought the way Paul Raymond had achieved this cash flow was a clever angle. The operation itself, Michael knew, was stylish. Not only were the sets a talking point; Mickey Spillane, the American thriller writer, had remarked that the Girl in the Golden Fish Tank was the sexiest girl he had ever seen. It offered several comfortably fitted bars serviced by well-trained, persistent hostesses, and an expensive restaurant. All in all, a costly operation.

Raymond's previous club experience had not been quite so successful. The Tabarin in Hanover Square was in direct competition with Churchill's and Winston's and no matter how Raymond organised things there, it did not seem to have the same sparkle and public appeal. Eventually he saw the light and sold the premises to Danny La Rue, who with some friends with good experience in the entertainment industry began to see some success. Staff also came from Winston's and eventually almost the whole of the show moved over. In many respects, Churchill's had lost to Winston's and Winston's had in turn lost to Dan's place, although the hostess operation that was very much part of the Winston's product did not last long with Dan. The emphasis was very much on cabaret. At Winston's, fights involving much of the furniture being wrecked became a regular feature. With the loss of staff and the unruly atmosphere at Winston's, Dan's place really took off. What Bill had helped create at the start of Winston's now no longer remained. The magic was gone.

Paul Raymond, relocating in Soho and developing his theme, experienced success which continues today, but at a cost. His daughter, who at one point ran much of the Raymond empire, committed suicide. Dan went from success to failure to financial ruin before finding God and getting his life back on to an even keel.

'Bill, 'ow ya doing?'

They had crossed Wardour Street and were walking along Old Compton Street. Out of the doorway of a strip club stepped a tall, slim man in his late 40s, his white face and chocolate brown overcoat unseasonal in the warm weather. It was not difficult to believe that daylight and sunshine were not his natural environment. Black hair, slicked back straight, gave him the appearance of a Maltese or Greek. Bill had his hand shaken with enthusiasm and was invited in for a drink, almost pulled, but he held his ground and declined the offer, using his son as an excuse. Michael had been referred to, but not formally introduced. While the two men chatted, Michael stood casually taking in the pictures of the heavy-breasted semi-naked women displayed in the glass cabinet. The corners of the black-and-white pictures were curled and discoloured where rain had penetrated. They were the same photos that had been pinned there more than ten years earlier, and had the women even worked in the club at the time the pictures were taken, it was unlikely they worked there now. If they did, it was certain they no longer resembled the likeness now being used to lure in expectant tourists, harbouring the belief they were about to taste the erotic pleasures advertised. The Soho sex trade was a far and disappointing cry from the likes of Amsterdam and Frankfurt. Soho, in truth, was more scam than sleaze. Although not party to the conversation, Michael could hear the offer of drinks again being extended. He hoped his father would continue to refuse. He did not doubt they would be offered the 'near' beer, a watered-down version that kept the alcohol content below that required to demand a liquor licence. Mug punters either received a half-pint as part of their pricy entrance ticket or were forced into purchasing a pint at extortionately inflated prices.

The smell of the bleach used to mop up the spilt beer and the gents toilets, constantly pungent with urine and the stench of old men masturbating, wafted across the pavement. The smell of sweat mingled in as a middle-aged woman, wearing a short green dress and grey T-shirt and carrying a small case, rushed out through plastic, brightly coloured ribbon curtains. The man talking to Bill stopped just long enough to slap her arse as she passed and point to his watch. Her sweat was from rushing between the numerous strip clubs rather than any energetic stage routine. A disgruntled member of the audience deciding to go elsewhere, feeling he had received a raw deal, or not as the case may be, would more than likely be treated to exactly the same performance down the road. The little cases made the strippers on the merry-go-round easy to spot. As easy as the groups of men being led along the street by a spiv that had taken their money earlier. It was not unusual for strip clubs to be nothing more than staging posts. They had all the signs, photos and come-ons, but after the punter had parted with his cash, he would be told to wait in the room at the back. There was no show here. When sufficient punters had paid, which could take a half an hour or more, the lot would be herded on to the next supposed club, another group would be collected and so it would go on, until finally they reached the seedy little club they had walked past and rejected an hour previously. Many just gave up, gave up their money and gave up waiting. Disgruntled customers would be told by a heavy to button it, and he would not be talking about their fly. Few tourists wanted to risk getting their face punched in, so they either did as they were told or quietly wandered off.

Finally the man shook hands with Bill again, wished him well and ducked back into the darkness.

'He used to pimp for the Messinas,' Bill said.

Michael knew the Messina brothers' reputation from reading exposés in the *News of the World*, but before the conversation could advance and Bill could speak of his connection with them, they had been accosted. A woman in scuffed red shoes, a red leather mini skirt, a black belt of almost the same width and a white frilly low-cut blouse, who could have been someone's grandmother, descended steep wooden stairs into a doorway only a few yards beyond the strip club and grabbed Bill's arm.

'Billy, darling!' she exploded, and threw her arms around his neck. Caked make-up coated Bill's jacket, which upon release he brushed off and introduced Michael, who immediately got the same treatment. If she had been using the name Miss Lash, it could as easily have referred to the long, thick, black, false wings glued to her eyes, as any sexual extra she was prepared to offer. The smell of strong sweet perfume, which was as successful a mask as the bleach had been a few doors earlier and equally pleasant, filled Michael's nostrils. Bill discreetly removed some folded notes from his pocket and screwing them up in his fist, pushed them into the woman's hand as he kissed it and said goodbye.

'When she was first on the game here her clients used to arrive in a horse and carriage,' Bill said with a grin.

'I thought girls loitering in doorways and approaching passers-by on the pavement had been stopped?' Michael said.

'1959 Street Offences Act, but you can't stop people walking in and out of their own property.'

'Not even dressed like that?' Michael said.

Bill grinned. 'She's still got her regulars. Mind you, some of them are older than she is. Paid for her daughter to go to one of the top girls' schools in the country.'

Michael glanced back just in time to see her waving down a taxi.

'We'll have a drink in there and then walk over to the A&R.'

They had reached the corner of Dean Street. Across the road was a small pub.

'The French,' Michael said.

Bill gave him a sideways glance, but did not say anything.

The sign across the front clearly said The York Minster, but the regulars always referred to it as The French House. It had gained its nom de plume from being run by Gaston Berllemont. It had been the meeting-place for many of the Free French in London during the Second World War, including General Charles de Gaulle, and had since become the haunt of artists and writers as well as many of the notable Soho reprobates. Gaston refused to serve pints and, if asked, would simply serve a half without explanation. Watney's Red Barrel was the only beer and he personally selected the wine and the legion of aperitifs that filled the shelves.

Many people were eating in restaurants in Soho but the restaurant at The French had closed down, so the bar wasn't as busy as it might have been. A small crowd of recognisable faces, small parts on TV, scriptwriters and the like, were standing at one end drinking rounds of champagne. Bill walked to the other end, by the staircase, and approached a table occupied by a lone man hidden behind the newspaper he was reading. Realising he had been approached, the man lowered the paper. Michael, standing behind his father, knew the face immediately. He was another gangland figure, not as widely publicised in the tabloids as the Messinas, but easily recognisable.

Albert Dimes made to rise but Bill waved him down. Dimes' six-foot-two stature and his thick dark Italian hair were imposing enough, but Michael could also sense that he had the air of a leader. The man sitting opposite was lean, sharp-featured and smartly dressed. He seemed to fit the look one immediately associated with the place. Michael knew many Italians and Dimes' reputation went way beyond Soho, way beyond London. Only the foolish did not realise that his charm and good looks veiled a man prepared to mete out violence, and it was unusual not to be measured; rarely did he issue a command in a voice louder than his normal soft tone, and like Bill he did not have the background of a thief.

Bill made the introduction and then ordered the drinks. Michael, sitting at the table, looked around him. The bar had an atmosphere you could almost taste – it was probably the noticeable smell of cigar smoke or, more likely, French cigarettes, Gauloise or Disc Bleu. There were people smoking but it was not a fog. Years of smoke had dried the wood; the floors, the chairs and the tables all retained the deep pungent French aromas – 25 years, longer, of the distinct smell that would probably never leave.

It was clear to Michael that the meeting with Dimes had not been by chance, although the talk seemed to have little purpose. Talk about how different businesses were doing, what was new on the street, some racing jargon, and from time to time Bill brought Michael into the conversation by explaining to

Dimes that his son had trained in the hotel industry and was doing well. Dimes confirmed that the catering trade was a good business to be in.

'Catering and Campari! A real Soho chap,' Dimes smiled to Bill, nodding in Michael's direction.

Michael was drinking Campari, but what that had to do with Soho or catering, he didn't know. He thought maybe he had missed something, having been watching the far door. A young man, about his own age, wearing old jeans and a dark T-shirt, and carrying a holdall, had entered and approached the bar, only to be refused a drink and told to leave. Five minutes later he had made a second attempt, only to receive the same response. Now he was trying to sneak in via the other door. This time his success was even less, he had hardly got both feet on to the stained wooden floor before he was signalled to get out.

Michael knew that it was not unusual for the landlord to refuse to serve someone on the basis that he did not like their face, or even because he did not know their face. Either way, it seemed to be taking on an almost theatrical flavour which did not seem too out of place. Each side being equally persistent, it seemed to become a test of wills. On the sixth sortie, Dimes seemed to become aware of what was going on and signalled to the landlord that it was all right. A relieved look spread across the young man's face and, without pausing to order a drink, he approached the table. Dimes excused himself, nodding to the landlord that he was just popping upstairs with his guest. A few minutes after that, obviously pleased and swinging a lighter bag, the man bounced down the stairs and out through the door. Dimes descended a few minutes later and, after wishing Bill and his son all the best, picked up his trilby and left. Bill did not comment on the incident and Michael concluded that whatever had been in the bag must have been stashed upstairs, as Dimes showed no sign of carrying anything bulky. The meeting had in some ways seemed pointless, but it was a mark of mutual respect. In Italy, the family is important.

The two finished their drinks and headed off across Soho to the Charing Cross Road and the A&R Club. The walk was short, but took longer than necessary as it was punctuated with stops to chat, shake hands and exchange greetings at every turn. The club was housed on the first floor of a scruffy, stone-fronted building a few yards from Centre Point and the crossroads of the Tottenham Court Road and New Oxford Street. A bare light bulb lit the stone stairs whose edges were worn round by years of use. This was not a plush entrance to a fashionable West End club, simply a climb to an afternoon drinker favoured by many of London's notorious gangland figures and owned by two of its most powerful leaders, Ronnie Knight and his partner Mickey Regan. Here, Bill's arrival had not been pre-announced.

From the door, the bar ran along the wall, to where Regan sat talking to an attractive black barmaid. Further across the room, a group of people were standing drinking and laughing. Regan gave Bill what was the standard

greeting of the day and ordered drinks. Before they had been served Ronnie
Knight arrived, looking more Italian than English, with a topcoat draped cape-
like across his shoulders. There was no question of the warmth between the
two men. Knight clearly commanded a presence, but in his welcoming of Bill
there was the greeting of a father and son. Certainly far more so than between
himself and Bill, Michael thought. After the usual pleasantries, Bill directed
Michael to a table at the end of the bar. The long windows that ran down one
wall overlooked the swell of the afternoon flowing up and down the popular
shopping streets and in and out of the corner entrance of the Underground.
Bus and taxi roofs flashed slowly, red and black in a variety of configurations,
filling the street below. Regan and Knight took their drinks over to join the
group still enjoying a joke, and other potential drinkers drifted in with only
the slightest notice being taken. Slowly the room was filling. Bill and Michael
sat and drinks were sent over from unidentifiable sources. First one and then
several. From the brown paper bag Bill had been carrying he removed a blue,
leather-look, A4-sized photo album.

'I brought some photos,' Bill said, opening the cover to the first group of
black-and-white pictures.

Michael smiled. 'Mum has got an identical one,' he said, knowing they had
both held on to their individual copies for what could have been more than 20
years.

Bill turned the grey pages, pointing out different people, but it quickly
became apparent that in most cases it was not necessary. The majority of
photos Michael had seen before, many were even in the same order as those
pasted in by his mother. In both albums there were few of his father. The ones
that were there seemed to show him in a bad light, drawing back into the
shadows so as not to be easily distinguishable. Michael could not decide whose
retention of the album surprised him the greater. For one person to have kept
it was amazing, but for them both, separately, over many years, to have
treasured these mementoes said something.

From the time Michael had moved from London at the age of eight, with his
mother, new stepfather, grandmother and stepbrother, to the Cotswolds, the
name Billy Howard had become unmentionable. The slate had been wiped
clean. New name, new school, new friends. Hosed down and washed away
without trace. Decontaminated. A new beginning, far from his father's evil
influence. The quiet, leafy roads, the rolling hills and the elegant Cheltenham
Promenade only coming to life during the Gold Cup and other occasional race
weeks, failed to replace the excitement his mother had enjoyed in the capital.
Michael's stepfather had been totally immersed in the 'Dad' role, both in name
and propaganda. Michael's history was a secret. But in the privacy of his dad's
absence, his mother and grandmother had exposed Michael to the secrets.
Quiet afternoons leafing through that identical album, the recounting of
escapades, the occasional unfolding of hastily torn Sunday newspaper articles,

removed before her husband could find the story featuring Michael's father in one of his constantly changing personas. Villain, playboy, club owner, accused, prisoner.

Michael now felt that this was in some way déja vu. As they were coming to the end of memory lane, Bill was asked to speak to someone on the far side of the room. Michael passed the time talking to the barmaid about nothing and, half an hour later, they said their goodbyes and left, taking a mini-cab to the underground parking below Hyde Park. Pulling out into the flow of vehicles, Michael remembered they had both forgotten to stop back at Floris to pick up a cake. He also had the feeling the photo album had gone missing. In some respects he guessed that now they had met, it was not such an important piece of memorabilia. If it were lost, it would return. Its last known whereabouts had been the A&R and that seemed like a second home to his father. The traffic had built up and, driving down past the Grosvenor House Hotel, the Playboy Club and the Hilton on a warm late afternoon, in the direction of the river, the fumes from buses and trucks was unbearable. Bill coughed to the point of choking for almost the entire length of the road. Michael had offered to pull over and close the soft-top of the Vitesse. Bill, recognising the difficulty of finding anywhere to park, waved his son on. It was a cough Michael came to know well.

* * *

The Ellerslie Hotel stands on the outer edge of Crystal Palace, in south London. It is a large Victorian building, in its own grounds on a strategic corner. With the two children growing up, the property in Albert Bridge Road, Battersea, was quickly becoming too small. The Ellerslie provided a good opportunity to move to a large family home and benefit from operating a hotel.

The intention was to also open a bar in the basement, which with Bill's contacts had the potential to provide the chaps with a secure watering-hole on their Monday boozing sessions, Monday being the traditional day each week in most criminal fraternities in Britain for everyone to meet up, celebrate, commiserate and discuss future ventures with other faces.

Bill, very out of character, took on much of the DIY required to refurbish the hotel, and oversaw the tradesmen undertaking the more skilled work. Much to his surprise this included a tender from a group of lads who had caused a bit of trouble previously in The Beehive. One of the things that really got up Bill's nose was someone pointing their finger at him, and one night at The Beehive this is exactly what had happened. Bill suggested the lads stopped taking liberties and urged them to go home before they got into trouble. But they knew best and continued to point the finger. Bill, without further warning, grabbed one man's hand and, with one good bite, removed the offending digit. Sober, stitched and having seen the error of his ways, the man did not hold a grudge – well, not as much as he would have previously.

The bar boomed. Bill played his part as the generous host in much the same way as he had when the *Alfie* crew were at The Beehive and steadily increased his alcohol intake to match. His spell at Highgate had been a blessing in disguise, breaking the binge drinking that had previously been habitual. His accounting system was also reignited. Till takings were profits and Jan funded the restocking from the hotel revenue. She no longer had the financial safety-net of her legacy. All the money from the sale of her properties Jan put into the purchase of the hotel, and she had to obtain a bank guarantee from a major player in the nationwide shoe firm, Startrite, based in Norwich, whom she had known since her youth. The hotel business requires a high occupancy level to make good profits and while The Ellerslie was popular with its regulars, it failed to generate the high percentages necessary to pay all the bills, the mortgage and have sufficient left over to subsidise the bar. Jan having to shell out cash for everything soon became a source of argument. Bill, rarely sober, was not the easiest person to remonstrate with and quickly the disagreements became more and more violent. Valued customers were only returning out of loyalty to Jan, who they could see was grafting from breakfast to dinner. Bill was either out and about, in Brixton, Soho and the West End, or in the basement bar drinking or sleeping it off.

On one occasion, when Bill was drunk and in a foul temper, he locked and bolted the door, denying Jan access. What happened next, like in most bedroom farces, is not quite clear, but after some manoeuvring one ended up outside and the other inside. In an effort to gain entry, the exterior fire exit ladder was used and access was achieved through the window of a bedroom prepared for a very valued guest who had taken his young lady out for dinner and was soon to return. Bottles of spirits that had been arranged on the sideboard were drunk, and in the fracas that followed Jan clouted Bill with a heavy object, felling him where he stood. He was clearly dead. Jan climbed out of the window, unable to open the internal door, scaled the outside of the building and in a state of panic phoned an old friend to assist her in disposing of the body. When he arrived, having climbed in what by now had become the main entrance, Bill was gone and the room wrecked. Jan then proceeded to pull the bedding out of the window and drag a clean duvet back in. As they attempted to refill the bottles, the guest returned, suitably mellow and ready for a seductive night in his prepared room. Jan, never short of the right words, explained a mythical situation and saved the day.

Things had to change. The opportunity arose when a friend at the council offered to place homeless families in the hotel. This appealed to Jan, as it provided 100 per cent occupancy and a guaranteed income. She also enjoyed working with the women and children who formed most of the lettings. Bill was less charmed by the social status of his new clientele, although he did seem to find some pleasure in encouraging the young mothers into private drinking sessions at every opportunity. He was caught in the act and Jan finally handed over the keys, took the children and left for an apartment she had leased a short distance from the hotel. Bill took charge and loudly trumpeted how he would demonstrate his ability to run The Ellerslie as it should be run. This apparently lasted weeks, not even months. He didn't like the homeless families and had no intention of dealing with them. Jan moved back and Bill took up residence in the apartment, Jan paying the rent and providing a not insignificant amount of pocket money. At this point Bill had little to keep him occupied. Left to his own devices, his drinking reached unparalleled levels.

'Jan. Can you come over? I can't remember things. I keep blacking out,' Bill sat in the chair, disorientated, talking to his wife. 'And can you bring a bottle of brandy with you?' he added.

Jan discussed Bill's state with a doctor, who advised her that Bill was suffering from low blood sugar and that she either had to get him into a clinic to dry out or give him the brandy. Bill had no intention of going into any clinic – he took the brandy. And shortly afterwards he disappeared.

When Jan found him again, he was in the Brixton area, staying with a woman he told Jan he had known for many years. The freeholder of the building he had left wanted the flat back and had apparently offered Bill a few thousand pounds for the return of the lease. Bill had forged Jan's signature, taken the money and packed his bags. Now long bouts of heavy drinking followed by short recesses were forming a pattern. When the darkness closed in and the pain became unbearable, he either drank or he didn't, depending on what part of the cycle he was currently in.

Freddie Foreman moved in once Bill was out of the way. With his brother George, and Brian Gifford, he arranged with Jan to take over the running of the basement bar. But Ronnie Knight and Micky Regan were the money men funding the Foremans, and they were in a position to pull the plug if things were not being run the way they thought right. To ensure that Jan was happy with the arrangement, regular inspections were not unusual, sending all the staff into a bit of a spin.

'Is there going to be any trouble over your place?' The question was asked by a local Chief Inspector. He was worried that the whole thing would blow up into a gang war and regardless of the fact that Bill was in bad shape, the force was not unaware that Bill could still put some muscle together if required. Furthermore, he seemed to have a death wish and anyone with nothing to lose could make a fearsome enemy.

'You don't have to worry. Foreman can have it. You can have it if you want it. I was giving most of the booze away anyway,' Bill said.

Bill was approached by another old friend, who was also worried about the turn of events at The Ellerslie and the possible repercussions. Bill gave the same assurances.

'I not only lose the whole place, but I end up having to pay £25,000 tax on the transfer,' Bill was standing outside the cafe in Coldharbour Lane telling Michael his tale of woe. 'To be honest I'd just as soon put my head in the oven and finish it,' he added, as they crossed the road and headed for the Prince Albert.

'Everything always looks worse than it is,' Michael assured him and bought the first drinks of the day. A view of the world through the bottom of a glass was always less depressing at the start of the day. Later there were no guarantees. The barman handed the receiver to Bill before he had time to order a second.

'Tony. Yes, unfortunately. But don't worry, your money's safe,' Bill said into the mouthpiece. By his tone, Michael knew that he was talking to a friend but had no idea what the friend was telling his father. 'No, there's not going to be any problem and you're the third person to ask that question,' Bill said, with almost a laugh back in his voice.

The conversation became a little one-sided for a while and then Bill spoke. 'No. But if he ever asks you for a favour . . . Do me a favour. Don't do him any favours.'

After the conversation came to an end Bill was altogether perkier.

'Everyone seems to think I'm annoyed,' Bill said but did not explain who the person on the other end was or what the gist of the chat had been about. Michael guessed from his father's tone that it was a police officer, solicitor or even someone on the council. Maybe even a planning officer.

Michael stayed most of the day, they ate, drank, moved from place to place. Not Soho. Not the West End. Mainly pubs and drinkers around Brixton, Camberwell, Walworth and the Elephant. Early in the evening, Bill climbed into a cab and promised his next stop was back to where he was staying, and bed.

CHAPTER SEVEN

My Little Boy

For a long time Albert Dimes had been happy with the Soho arrangement that allowed the numerous power figures to control their own specific interests. The Spot affair was a minor disruption very early on and had been quickly resolved. It was now well documented in the history books as 'The Fight That Never Was'. But it had shown, before the trouble, how things could work well if everyone kept to their agreed patch, even within the tight confines of Soho.

However, in the early 1970s it became clear to Dimes that the English firm, headed by Ronnie Knight, was seeking to exploit opportunities in and around Soho that Dimes considered were traditionally controlled by the Italians. Dimes was not looking to launch a war against the Knight firm, he simply wished to maintain the status quo. He continued to remain on good terms with them and sought to develop a plan of how the established boundaries could be continued. The Knight firm were far from stupid. It was common knowledge that Dimes had been grooming his successor, Alfredo Zomparelli, and Dimes believed that the Knights would wait until after Zomparelli took over the business before making their move.

One possibility was to talk the matter over with Billy Howard, but Dimes knew this approach had its drawbacks. He believed Howard could settle things but if that were to happen, it would have to be now. An approach later, made by Zomparelli or by himself after he had stepped down, would not carry the same weight. It was equally common knowledge that in the same way he had nominated Zomparelli as his successor, Billy Howard had for a long time considered Ronnie Knight his own godson. The other drawback was that asking Howard to speak to the Knights would be tantamount to an admission that Zomparelli did not have the power to stand up to them. This could lead the Knights to aim for control of the whole of the Italian firm's sphere of influence instead of simply poaching lucrative areas. If this happened and developments went badly there would be no power base from which to return. It was a matter of strategy. After careful consideration, Dimes decided to allow matters to take their course, to spend more time bringing Zomparelli on and, if necessary, not to step down as early as he had anticipated.

'So,' he said to himself, 'I'll work a few extra years.' He loved Soho. It was no real hardship. Brighton, Scotland, Morocco or Italy, wherever he finally decided to retire, could wait a little while longer.

* * *

Unlike Albert Dimes, Alfredo Zomparelli was born in Italy, in the small town of Frosinone, 80 miles south of Rome in the province of Latium. In the year of his birth, 1937, Italy was already in the grip of the fascist leader and close friend of Adolf Hitler, Mussolini. By the age of three, his motherland had been plunged into war, leaving his parents, as with most other families, to bring up their children lacking the economic means to do so. But despite this, Alfredo grew into a strong, good-looking lad who, when the war ended, was sent to relatives in England where his parents hoped he would receive a good education. However, the discipline of the school day did not appeal to the boy, who preferred to roam the streets, dodging trouble.

By the age of 17, he had become a regular face in Soho, where his prowess as a street fighter quickly caught the attention of Albert Dimes. Knowing there was little fun around the West End with no money to spend, Dimes started giving Alfredo errands to run in return for a few pounds. If difficulties arose that could not be resolved with a few words, Alfredo, who had by now picked up the nickname Italian Tony, would not be averse to using violence. Where he found himself outnumbered or his strength looked as though it might not win the day, he was quick to pull a knife. By the late 1950s, Italian Tony had started to achieve the makings of a small reputation for himself. When there was little else to do and the streets seemed to hold no possibility of violence, it would not be unusual for Italian Tony and his small group of young friends to fight amongst themselves. Where others may have pulled a few punches for fun, Zomparelli always fought hard enough to ensure that he emerged the winner. His reputation was further enhanced when he slashed the throat of his best friend to prove a point. His friend was lucky that the cut did not prove fatal, and this action earned his assailant the name Tony Ilmato – Mad Tony. Following incidents like these, people started to steer clear of the cold-blooded Italian Tony and Dimes realised his potential for collecting protection money.

Collection of dues from the Italian restaurant owners and shopkeepers was the prerogative of the Italian gang. Dimes was considered a fair man and although a thriving business enjoying a good week was expected to give a little extra, a small business experiencing difficulties was allowed to pay less. However, good or bad, everyone was expected to pay tribute. So Dimes had not been amused when Augustine, a Soho tailor, pleaded poverty and refused to pay. With a couple of his young friends, Tony was dispatched to bring the poverty-stricken shopkeeper before the court. Dragged roughly through the Old Compton Street patisserie that Dimes often used as his office and to regularly hold court, he was pushed down into a chair. Augustine sat crouched and shaking, with one eye on Dimes and the other on Tony, fearing that some sign would be given and his sentence would be severely inflicted before he had been given time to plead his case. Dimes proved to be in a charitable mood. Tony was of the opinion that they should have made an example of him. Augustine was told that he must either pay or go. He did not need telling twice. Within days he had sold his business and emigrated to Australia, never to return. It was not too many months later that an old villain took one too many liberties with Dimes. On this occasion Dimes was not so forgiving and Tony was told to take him for a walk. The body was found the following day in a Soho gutter. The murder remained unsolved and Dimes started referring to Tony as 'my little boy', a title that was to prove fatal.

Tony and his young group of friends now had a little money in their pockets and were looking to make more. Fake goods, imported from counterfeiters in Northern Italy, proved to be a good source of funds. Good-looking fake Omega and Rolex watches, with low-grade movements, which would be unlikely to tick for longer than a week or two, could be purchased for two pounds. Sold in London betting shops, pubs and factories, they could fetch a pony and, on occasions, the odd mug punter could be enticed into parting with £100. The real thing at that time would have been on sale in West End stores for upwards of £200. Easy money bought Tony a lifestyle he found attractive. As time moved on and Tony grew into manhood, he was rarely away from Dimes' side. When Dimes was collecting large amounts of cash from clubs or racecourses, it was always Tony that acted as his bag man and bodyguard. He had not only proved himself, but he had also become trusted.

Situated in the heart of Soho, The Latin Quarter Club was a traditional haunt of many of London's top gangsters and also attracted a wide-ranging celebrity clientele. Tony began to use the place regularly, liking to be seen on a par with the other notorious faces. Heavy drinking and good-natured banter was not out of the ordinary, but the club was not noted for trouble. The Tolaini family from Stoke Newington, who owned the club, paid Dimes a substantial amount each week to ensure that everyone not only understood the rules, but also complied with them.

On an evening towards the end of 1969, members of the Knight firm had arrived in The Latin Quarter intent on celebrating some business or personal success. The atmosphere was again boisterous, but good-natured. David, the youngest and cheekiest of the Knight brothers, spent a great deal of the evening kidding and jibing at Tony, who had arrived sober with a group of his friends. David continually baited Tony with the 'my little boy' phrase.

'It'll take more than a little boy to take over Dimes' interests, when he
retires,' David repeated time and time again.

Tony did not rise to the bait and laughed it off, which surprised many of the
people in the club who knew of his quick temper.

The next time the two young men met was in Ronnie Knight's A&R Club,
the afternoon drinker on the Charing Cross Road. David appeared to have been
drinking since before lunch and was not looking at stopping. On seeing Tony,
his repertoire was a continuation of their previous exchange at The Latin
Quarter. On this day, Tony did not find the humour that would have allowed
things to pass off as quietly as they had done previously.

It is not clear who threw the first punch, but David was quickly downed, bar
stools, tables and chairs were scattered, and Tony was bludgeoned to the floor
by others who raced forward in David's defence. Whether it was during the
time fists and feet pounded into Tony's head and body, or when the victors
threw him down the stone stairs, he had sustained a broken arm by the time
he stumbled out on to the street. The beating was serious enough for him to be
hospitalised, but its seriousness was greater than that. When Dimes visited
'his little boy', he sat quietly by the hospital bed and spelled it out. Previously,
Dimes knew that Tony would be required to prove to the Knight firm that he
was capable of taking over the responsibility of the Italian interests in Soho,
but now he would also find it necessary to win the support of the Italians.
Members of the Italian firm would want to be sure that the man at the head of
their business interests was capable of operating in a manner that would
provide them with a good living. Members of the Italian business community
would need to believe that the person to whom they paid tribute could look
after their interests. They would not wish to support Tony and then find they
were receiving demands from elsewhere.

The conversation that took place between Dimes and Zomparelli was in
private. It is not possible to know exactly what was said. Some people believe
that Dimes told his little boy that if he were to maintain any chance of taking
over, he would have to kill David Knight. The other version favoured by many
of Zomparelli's closest friends is that Dimes told him to forget what had
happened the previous night and that he, Dimes, would handle the matter. If
this is the true account, it is believed that for the first time in his life
Zomparelli refused the directive of his godfather, insisting that the revenge
must be personal and inflicted by his own hand. This would seem to fit in with
what is known of the vendetta, the Mafia code of revenge. If this were the line
taken by Zomparelli, Dimes must have known it would have been difficult to
dissuade him from the strong traditional course. His fear, correctly founded,
was that Zomparelli would find it difficult to distance himself from any action
taken, and although the result would strengthen his position, he would need
to go into hiding for a long period, thereby still preventing him from taking
control of the business when the time came.

Over the weeks and months that followed, Zomparelli's arm healed and life in Soho continued much as before. Protection money changed hands, disputes were settled in back alleys and gangland leaders from across London frequented the clubs and restaurants, rubbing shoulders with celebrities. The fight at the A&R faded from most people's minds. Most people's, but not Zomparelli's. The blows that had rained down on him became more painful, not less, and his shame festered. But he was biding his time, waiting for the right opportunity.

The moment presented itself on the evening of 7 May 1970. Ronnie Knight, his elder brother Johnnie and the younger David were once again in The Latin Quarter Club. It would be wrong to say that the guests, staff and the Knights did not sense the hostility surrounding Zomparelli when he entered the club, stood at the bar and continually eyed the Knights' table. But no one envisaged how the evening would end. A few sarcastic comments originating from the Knights' table were directed at Zomparelli, but as time passed this source of amusement lapsed. So no attention was paid when David rose from the table and headed off in the direction of the toilet. Without a second thought, Zomparelli seized the moment. Taking a knife from the kitchen, he followed David. Confronting him and barring the exit with his own body, Zomparelli lunged forward, plunging the blade deep into David's upper body.

David's absence went unnoticed until eventually his brothers became uneasy and someone was dispatched to locate him. When the shout went up that David had been stabbed, tables and chairs were overturned, sending glasses and bottles crashing to the floor as the brothers and their friends rushed across the room. At the age of 23, David Knight was dead.

By the time the police arrived on the murder scene, Zomparelli was long gone and from the information provided to them, no time was wasted issuing a warrant for his arrest on a charge of murder. At that moment Dimes knew what had taken place, he knew that his worst fears had come true. The only outcome that could have angered him more was if it had been his little boy whose lifeblood had drained on to the toilet floor. Arrangements had to be made quickly. Dimes knew that if anything was to be done to save the situation, it had to be done without delay. The priority was to get his little boy somewhere safe, preferably out of the country. Through the Italian societa, Dimes organised with a restaurateur on the south coast for Zomparelli to hide up in his establishment for 24 hours, during which time an Italian passport, in a false name, was obtained and transport across the Channel arranged.

Any meaningful discussions with the Knight family were now out of the question. But Dimes realised the necessity of dialogue. What he had in mind, in all probability, would not be a suggestion the Knight family would be prepared to consider now, but he believed, if put to a member of the firm by someone they trusted, it just might have a chance of success. Dimes telephoned Billy Howard.

The following night a privately owned yacht slipped out of Ramsgate harbour. Before dawn it had dropped anchor. Zomparelli was quickly ashore and safe, for the time being, in a continental port.

Now, Dimes knew, the real work would begin. If his protégé was ever to return to England without facing a lengthy prison sentence, many strings would have to be pulled and much money spent. The strategy was to be three-pronged. Firstly, it was important to instruct the right firm of solicitors and obtain the services of an appropriate barrister. Secondly, he had to obtain the names and addresses of all the guests and members of staff who were at The Latin Quarter on the night of the killing, so many could be contacted and persuaded not to make damaging statements; many people in the club at the time had left quickly before the police had arrived, not wishing to become involved. Thirdly, it would be necessary for the police to tread lightly. This could be achieved in a variety of ways – a large payment to a senior officer in the investigation, smaller amounts of money spread thinner through the investigating team, or finding one detective who was prepared to bury evidence and to encourage his colleagues not to enquire too thoroughly. All this had to be arranged within hours. What could not be settled within the first few days of the killing would be forever out of reach.

What Dimes was seeking to achieve was to have the charge of murder reduced to one of manslaughter. Sentencing before an understanding judge could result in Zomparelli being banged up for as little as two or three years. The meeting between Dimes and Billy Howard took place outside Soho. Dimes travelled over the river to a spieler off Coldharbour Lane, Brixton. There, in a back room, he handed Howard a package containing £10,000, plus a list of names and addresses of people he thought should be contacted. Within a few days, Zomparelli had received word that he should give himself up. So, trusting Dimes completely, he surrendered to the police and was duly charged with the murder of David Knight. Shortly prior to the date fixed for the trial, due to be heard before a jury at the Old Bailey, Billy Howard received a further payment of £2,000. The final attempt to influence the outcome of the trial was to bring pressure to bear on the jury, but this could only be done once they had been sworn in. Jury nobbling, through financial inducement or threat of physical violence, had become Bill's stock in trade. He was reputed by many to be the most successful organiser of predicting court proceedings of any person in southern England. Dimes had believed Billy Howard was the only person with the power and influence to bring about the desired verdict. Had his belief been misplaced? Had he parted with a large sum of money and received nothing in return?

As the judge passed sentence, Zomparelli looked impassively ahead, giving no sign of emotion when it was handed down. As the officers led him from the dock, a voice belonging to one of the Knight family in the public gallery called out, 'Oi, Tony, don't worry. That's the easy part.' The meaning of the comment was not lost on anyone in the court and must have caused Zomparelli some concern. The case had lasted for less than one week. The jury had returned a verdict of manslaughter on Alfredo Zomparelli and he was sentenced to four years' imprisonment. Both Dimes and his little boy, now 33 years of age, considered this to be a result. Unfortunately, Dimes was to die of cancer within two years of the sentence being passed.

* * *

On a hot summer's day, Soho can be stifling. A light afternoon breeze on the wide boulevards of The Mall, Park Lane or The Strand does not penetrate the confines of Soho's alleys and narrow streets. Berwick Street Market, earlier teeming with people from Shaftesbury Avenue at one end and Oxford Street at the other, had lost its urgency. Wooden barrows were boarded up and wheeled off to cobbled cul-de-sacs for the night. Rotting fruit and vegetables, dumped in the gutter, soured the air. But on an early September evening in 1974, it was not hot. The 4th of September is one of those dates that should still be summer – a swim in the Serpentine after work or a pleasant stroll along the Embankment before dinner – but this Wednesday it was depressingly cool and cloudy. Tourists stayed in their hotel bars, or ventured out in creased plastic macs. Unlicensed street traders operating from suitcases hovered on street corners, a left-over from the 1950s spivs, waiting for the rain to return and a quick turnover from fire-damaged umbrellas.

At 4 p.m., light showers have driven people off the pavements, looking for shelter in shops, coffee houses and arcades. Scavengers, some quite well dressed, others a little less so, forage through the rubbish in Berwick Street. Before long the dustmen will walk in slow procession behind the cart, like mourners at a funeral. A man in a trenchcoat sorts through a pile of soft tomatoes, wiping some with a tea towel and popping them into his briefcase. Others, after careful inspection, he discards, too bad even for him. Shortly before 7 p.m., although still daylight, the sky has darkened, threatening heavy rain later. Soho prepares for a quiet night.

Police in unmarked cars, on foot, in vans with blue flashing lights, klaxons blaring, all answer the shout and within minutes Old Compton Street is sealed off. Theatregoers outside the Casino forsake the queue, and the prospect of Twiggy live on stage, for the unknown drama. Customers from the Helvetia public house spill onto the pavement, pints of bitter, a glass of stout, a large gin and tonic grasped firmly in hand. Some glasses still half-full remain, along with half-eaten sandwiches and a small stack of change. Waiters in black bowties eagerly exchange information in rapid Italian with their counterparts from across the street. Uniformed constables quickly erect tapes and barriers that are the only reason the morbid curiosity remains unquenched.

Situated halfway along Old Compton Street, the Golden Goose Amusement Arcade is normally crowded: tourists turning coins in their fingers, closely inspecting the currency and wondering whether a five-pence piece is the same as a shilling; barmen and doormen enjoying an hour's entertainment amongst the bright lights before six hours' work in the darkness of a basement night-club; among them circulate the permanent collection of pimps, dope pushers, hustlers and Social Security fiddlers, who all know the machines as well as a tradesman knows his tools. Cherries, bells and oranges spin at the pull of a handle, scores mount on brightly flashing pintables and gangsters wearing trilby hats and carrying machine-guns are shot down by a continuing hail of bullets on video gun ranges. Cash continually pumped into chrome slots makes this world go round.

By 7.05 p.m. the body of an unidentified man lies on a stretcher covered with a police blanket, stained brown with blood. He appears to be in his early 40s, tall, heavily built and wearing an expensive dark-blue suit. Outside the street is crowded and noisy. A short, heavily built figure wearing a cap pushes his way to the front of the crowd and tries to pass through the barrier. He is stopped by the police and after a lengthy argument and much waving of hands is allowed through, but told to wait to one side. In the arcade, its glass doors closed to the public, it is quiet. A young overweight detective, wearing an ill-fitting sports jacket and trousers, idly plays the last ball of an unfinished game on a pintable at the rear of the room. Showing little reverence he shakes the machine in an attempt to persuade the silver ball into a high-scoring hole. He is successful – the bells ring, the ball is ejected and 100 is added to the score. A uniformed inspector, standing near the body, gives a disapproving stare. 'TILT' lights up on the machine. The game is over!

CID and uniformed officers settled down to questioning and preparing statements, a possibly lengthy task involving hundreds of eye-witnesses, but many close to the killing were locals who had already slipped quietly away into the swelling crowds of sightseers. The Sicilian code of silence in this still predominantly Italian enclave would prevent police from obtaining a clear picture of what actually happened.

'What have you got?' one of the detectives asked a uniformed constable who was flicking through his notebook.

'Quite a lot. But it's just a question of sorting it out. And there are a few tourists who don't speak English, so it's difficult to get what they're saying straight,' he replied.

'In other words, you've got nothing.' The detective didn't sound too surprised, or maybe not even too interested.

'No, there's a few bits,' the constable added, not wanting the work he had done to be dismissed so lightly.

At the end of the conversation, the detective wandered round the other wooden tops to see if they had done any better, and then spoke to some of his plain-clothes colleagues. Then, sitting on a plastic seat in the back of the arcade, he made some effort to sort out what information he had collected.

First reports indicated a dark-coloured 3.4 Jaguar – registration unknown – pulling up directly outside the Golden Goose in contravention of the No Parking restriction. As the car pulled to a halt, two men were said to have left the car, entered the arcade and, from handguns, fired a number of shots into the back of the man playing a Big Shot pinball machine. The killers returned to the car where the driver, who had kept the engine running, drove off at high speed in the direction of the Charing Cross Road. Only vague descriptions of the gunmen and the driver could be obtained, so this was of little use in advancing the police enquiries. A number of conflicting reports were also circulating.

An old man thought to be the local newsvendor had made a statement to the fact that he remembered seeing a car with foreign number plates parked a short distance from the arcade earlier in the day, although when one considered the vast number of cars with foreign number plates in London on legitimate business at any one time, the possibility of the vehicle being connected with the killing was remote. Nevertheless, not wishing to leave any stone unturned or avenue unexplored, this would certainly be followed up as a serious line of enquiry.

A third report suggested that the shooting was carried out by four heavily built, aggressive men, who shouldered their way through the crowd. Without speaking they pulled guns and fired into the back of their unsuspecting victim. Two men were said to have been seen leaving the Golden Goose only moments after the killing, running off in a northerly direction.

As he had said to the first constable at the outset – 'Sweet Fanny Adams'. He guessed that if this case were going anywhere, it would not be on evidence collected, but on information received or obtained by twisting a few arms, making a few threats and then, if it came to it, fitting up the right person. He moved back on to the street, looking around for a face that he recognised, someone to start the process.

The earlier promise of a quiet night in Soho turned out to be surprisingly correct. Although on this Wednesday night there were more people on the street than usual, action was slow and business was not good. The body was removed to the mortuary for a police surgeon to carry out the autopsy and write a report telling the investigating officers basically what they already knew. The victim had been shot, the weapon was likely to be a 9mm pistol.

The arcade remained closed. Outside, a dark blue caravan was parked and manned for the duration of the investigation. The Old Bill were everywhere, stopping, watching, questioning and pestering locals and punters alike. Beneath the apparently busy exterior, the street was quiet. The Italian community was stunned. The dark sky also kept its promise – a cool, dreary, damp day turned into a cold, wet and windy night. In summation, the people of Soho considered Wednesday, 4 September 1974, a black day.

For Alfredo Zomparelli, described as a Soho travel agency owner, it was also not a good day – he was identified by the Murder Squad detectives as the dead man. The police hoped once the identity of the body had been established, a motive would become apparent, leading to a quick arrest. But this was not to be the case. Like the eye-witness reports, motives for the killing were equally numerous and varied. Detectives settled in for what promised to be a long inquiry in which fact and fiction seemed to travel happily hand in hand. One theory put forward was that Zomparelli was the English connection of an Italian crime syndicate, operating illegal currency dealings between Europe and the UK, a profitable business at a time when the dollar was at a premium and there were exchange control regulations in force. The unauthorised export of cash could be a lucrative pastime, although the transportation of black money and forged notes in hard cash had always been risky. There was speculation that Italian Tony had failed to deliver the appropriate sums, resulting in a Mafia-style contract killing. The police believed this could tie in with the sighting of the foreign car. Other motives included a power struggle between rival gangs for control of the highly profitable fruit machine sites and the satisfaction of a vendetta.

The basis for a vendetta could have rested on either of two earlier killings, both administered by Zomparelli. The killing of David Knight was an obvious possibility, and as a result his older brother, Ronald John Knight, husband of actress Barbara Windsor and owner of the New Artists and Repertory Club in the Charing Cross Road, was questioned by senior detectives. The other killing, in 1972, was that of Joe Williams, who had his escort agency premises in the same building as the A&R Club owned by Ronnie Knight, on the outskirts of Soho. While the police mulled over the various possibilities of the Zomparelli murder, Bill and those Italians who had been close to Italian Tony had only one name on their lips: Ronnie Knight.

If Bill's protégé was to become the don of dons in the future, Ronnie had to remain alive. The vendetta rarely stopped when the first killing had been revenged. For Italian families, the tit for tat could go on for generations. The word on the street was the same as the word Bill was able to get from the Italians still with strong connections in Italy. If Ronnie Knight went down for the killing of Zomparelli, everyone would wipe their mouths. But if the Zomparelli murderer was not caught and punished by law, the Italians would have no alternative but to take revenge themselves. Bill knew if he was seen plotting with any of the Knight family it would be the kiss of death for Ronnie in any court case. Bill's sheet for jury nobbling was long and well marked. Bill realised any action would have to be undertaken quietly and without assistance, which almost certainly ruled out violence. What remained on the cards – blackmail or money? To take the pressure off his little boy, it had cost Dimes in excess of £40,000. The cost of keeping Ronnie out of prison, and out of the ground, would reduce that figure to pocket change. Blackmailing the

Italians would be a waste of time – only money would talk. The difficulty was to place the funds appropriately – to provide greatest effect. Money to the immediate family was unlikely to provide the desired result. A more compelling argument was made to contact someone higher in the Italian hierarchy, someone more likely to be asked to make the arrangements to settle the vendetta. If this person could be encouraged to speak sensibly to the relatives, the retaliation might be diverted. It was not likely that any request would be made from within the UK. Zomparelli had failed to gather the community around him, even many of his own countrymen would not be sorry that he was no longer a burden on their businesses. Sorry to see him killed, yes, but not sorry to have his unreasonable attitude and demands off their backs. Bill concluded that the most effective conduit for dispersal of funds would be through Italians he had met courtesy of Lansky and Raft.

Although the police involved in the case were many, Bill would have been surprised if the reminder of previous misdeeds, or the promise of a substantial bung, would not encourage a softly, softly approach. Bill believed the judiciary were similarly accessible. What many people failed to remember, but Bill always knew, was that members of the judiciary had once been young barristers, some of whom had fallen prey to offers which at the time had seemed hardly treasonable. From high places, the fall can be fatal and careers could be ruined from the embarrassment of public exposure.

This episode would remain in the back of Bill's mind for the remainder of his life. Over the coming years it would enter the public domain on numerous occasions, including the high profile trial of Ronnie Knight at the Old Bailey.

CHAPTER EIGHT

Down But Not Out

Bill walked slowly out of the greasy spoon cafe. His shoes were tight and his feet hurt. Earlier he had used a Stanley knife to cut the leather in the worn uppers of his right shoe, to release the pressure on his badly swollen toe joint. Unsteady on his feet, he swayed at the pavement edge as white van men raced through Brixton, along Coldharbour Lane, punctuated by big cars that had seen better days and kinder owners. He turned up the velvet collar of his overcoat against the light breeze that chilled his bones. He waited patiently, feeling old age creeping, feeling it stealing the lubricant from every joint, the power from every muscle and the very oxygen from his burning lungs. He coughed into his broken fist, the shudder sending sharp pain up through his legs.

A gap presented itself and he stepped out, moving from the ball of one foot to the ball of the other, his eyes firmly on the closing kerb opposite. Brakes screeched, a pick-up Transit with ladders and a cement mixer on the back, burned rubber. ''Ave you ever thought of looking both ways, ya stupid old bastard?'

Bill looked at the blonde dreadlocks and the podgy white face of the woman driver who had brought her vehicle to a stop less than a couple of feet from his path, her head shoved partially out of a half-open window. Ignoring her, he continued on his journey. Reaching the other side he slipped his hand into his pocket and removed an off-white folded linen handkerchief. Dabbing the side of his mouth, he dried the slight dribble and headed for the pub. It was a routine that would carry him through into the '80s, the same time every day. Well, most days, give or take an hour. The same stool, the landlord would put a drink and newspaper on the bar and pass on any messages that had been left by people wanting to get in contact. This was the main point of communication with his son Michael. He wondered where Michael was. He had not been in touch for more than two months. Bill had thought of telephoning him but somehow didn't like to intrude. Michael didn't show that day, or any other day for the next week or more.

Bill sat, read and drank three halves of bitter, and then had a brandy. Drinkers, mainly old-time drinkers, drifted in, spoke, nodded or ignored each other. Each seemed to have, if not a set position, certainly a preferred seat. By lunchtime it started to get busy, lads off the market and others. Most found seats at the other end of the dogleg lounge. A skinny black geezer, with nervous speed, was beginning to annoy Bill as he dodged backwards and forwards, feet almost still, his head and shoulders making all the movement, along a small length of bar. Every time the landlord finished serving one round of drinks, the jumpy movements would intensify, without achieving recognition. When there was nobody else to serve in the lounge bar, the landlord slipped through into the public bar.

Bill looked over the top of the racing page. 'You'd get served quicker in the other bar. The service round this side is awful.'

The black geezer dashed out of the door and moments later reappeared facing Bill through the archway. A couple of seconds later he was raising a pint of lager to his mouth.

'They all catch on eventually,' the landlord said with a cynical smile.

'I thought I better set him straight.'

'Brandy?' the landlord asked, picking up Bill's empty glass.

Bill nodded. He was not bothered one way or another about drinking with blacks, but it was a house rule. Blacks were welcome, but not in the lounge bar.

At two o'clock, feeling better, fed and watered, Bill walked round the corner into Electric Avenue. He spoke to the white-coated lad behind the eel shop counter as he passed, crossed on to the other pavement and headed down to the last shop in the street. The shop was empty and had been for months, probably years. A side door, chipped and old, hung slightly ajar. Bill pushed through into the 60-watt bare bulb light and climbed up the bare board stairs. The effort required the use of the banister and caused his lungs to wheeze in air. The door on the landing opened just as Bill's arm stretched to push it, almost taking his feet from under him.

'Hello, Bill. Just looked up to see what was going on. I'll be back later.' It was one of the many mini-cab drivers who played there.

'There's a warden about,' Bill lied, to wind him up, realising it was his car he had seen with two wheels parked on the pavement opposite. The cabby was down the stairs two and three at a time.

Inside, one man sat playing patience, another stood to his side, looking over his shoulder and pointing out opportunities as cards were laid. All the other tables were empty. There was a smell of cigarette smoke, bleach and air freshener. Two strip lights prevented the room being completely dark, as the heavy brocade curtains remained tightly closed, blocking out the little of the day that penetrated the thick coat of whitewash painted on the window-panes. The two men looked in Bill's direction, nodded and smiled. They were bored and they anticipated that Bill's arrival would prove to be a catalyst for the players. When Bill was not there, people would often drift in and slide off. Bill seemed to have the knack of generating an atmosphere and bringing games to life.

'Tea?' Scouse asked from behind the simply constructed snack bar in the corner.

'Go on then.'

Scouse looked after things for Bill, but mostly looked after Bill. Scouse needed money to live. Bill's financial needs were little, but he liked the social aspect. Something to do, somewhere to go, a purpose, somewhere he could meet the chaps. The spieler satisfied these needs all round. A dice table, faro and eight four-seater card tables, all covered with green baize. Players parted with a pound an hour table money. Curtains closed off another room reserved for poker players with serious money, spectators discouraged. There was no way of knowing how the day would go. Nothing all day and all evening, closed by eight. On other days the tables would be busy right through, and on rare occasions money would still be changing hands late into the following morning.

The property was a squat, the light and heat were gratis, courtesy of the Electricity Board and rewired by a friendly engineer. Takings averaged £150 a day, sometimes just a few pounds, other days anything between £300 and £500. The only outgoings were Scouse, punters that lost their wedge and needed the fare home and, of course, the filth. That was a regular £300 a week to the local nick, and less regular was a bung to the man at the council. An odd £50, which regularly found its way back across the tables. Neither were foolproof, or provided long-term guarantees. Scouse poured tea into two large chipped china mugs and handed one to Bill.

'I thought we might try and get a crap game going, if we get a few in,' Bill said thoughtfully.

'Someone's nicked the dice,' Scouse complained.

Bill slipped a note from his pocket and sent Scouse down to Woolworths to buy whatever they had. Rounded corners, he knew the punters didn't like toy dice. He decided to leave a message for Michael at the pub, to ask him to bring some clear, sharp-edged spots with him the next time he came.

In the short while Scouse was gone, the place started to fill. Mostly lads off the market who by now had closed down their stalls for the day and had the takings to speculate. No one showed any enthusiasm for dice, mainly poker and kalooki, and a game that looked as though it might go big in the back room folded shortly after eight. By eight-thirty the place was empty. Bill hobbled back to the pub, bought himself a drink and put one on the bar for Scouse, who had stayed behind to lock up. By nine, they had gone their separate ways, Scouse back to his small flat and Bill to put his feet up in front of the television with a bottle of wine and some fish and chips.

The remainder of the week was equally painful and uninteresting. On Sunday he did not open the spieler. There would always be the degenerates looking for a game, those with no homes to go to, but most of the punters had families and with the market boys not around, it was difficult to get very much going. Sunday, Bill liked to get down the Lane, but it depended on how he felt. On this Sunday, for no apparent reason, his foot was less painful and the swelling had reduced. He shaved, dressed and walked a few hundred yards to a mini-cab office. The weather was cold and bright, which he knew would bring them out.

His brother had worked the family stall in East Lane almost continuously since their father had died. Icy winter days, wet and windy days and in the hot summer sun. The wet fish stall stood a couple of stalls in from the Walworth Road, a couple of stalls away from the sarsaparilla vendor, and was well known. Many of the south London publicans bought boxes of prawns on a Sunday morning to provide bar snacks for early morning drinkers, as was the tradition. Bill was happy to don a white coat, rain or shine, and help shovel pints of large pink prawns, small brown shrimps, winkles and whelks into brown paper bags. Some were eaten there and then, sprinkled with malt or spiced vinegar, amongst the pushing and shoving, as people ploughed their way further into the Lane between the rows of traders. Or, as was often the case, particularly with the winkles, the brown paper bags were taken home and the flesh hooked from the small black, sea salt-smelling shells with pins, the flat eye discarded and the winkle eaten for Sunday tea.

The whole morning was an institution, which inevitably included a pint in the pub to socialise with the lads and moan over the weather, the lack of business and to spread general gossip. This would be followed by Sunday lunch with his brother and his family. Going down there and not working would not have been the same. The stall could, he knew, manage without him. But if you didn't work, you weren't one of the lads, and if you weren't one of the lads, you were a punter.

On Monday, Jan telephoned Bill and arranged for young Billy to come over the following Saturday. Scouse had picked up from somewhere some dice that were an improvement on the toys from Woolworth's. And one of the chaps Bill had not seen for a year or two rang, asking if there was any chance of Bill sorting out a bit of trouble he had got himself into. Bill arranged a meeting the next evening at a pub in Victoria. When the meeting took place Bill hardly recognised the bloke, who was a lot younger than him. He had spent three years in a prison in the Far East and had only been back in the UK for less than a month.

'I tell ya, porridge in England is like Butlin's compared with out there. The first two years wasn't too bad, I still had money and could buy food and medicines. I got malaria six months ago and nobody wanted to know. If you didn't have cash, the guards weren't interested. If you could persuade someone at the consulate to do something, it didn't make any difference. The guards would swap the tablets for aspirin and sell the good stuff to a prisoner that still had cash to pay with. I don't know how I didn't croak.'

Bill bought another round of drinks and downed a brandy at the bar while the barmaid was drawing a pint. 'So what's the trouble?' Bill asked when he sat back down. It was a big pub with tables spread out and a pool table at the other end away from them. Most of the trade would have been done at lunchtime. Apart from around the pool table, and a bloke pumping tokens into a fruit machine, the place was all but empty. Little chance of being overheard.

'Breathalysed. I got pulled over coming back from up north,' the man explained, stopping to gulp a mouthful of bitter.

'Might be able to do something. When was it?' Bill asked.

'Last week.'

'It's really difficult now. They've really tightened up, load of stuff in the papers a couple of years back about people getting it sorted. Once it's sent off, it's almost impossible. You should have phoned me straightaway. It's not a problem while it's still in a local station. I'll see what I can do, but I can't promise. The best bet might be to get someone to stand up and say you work for a charity and it would seriously affect your work if you lost your licence,' Bill explained.

'I'm not worried about the licence. They searched the motor and found a couple of guns in the boot,' he explained.

Bill was suddenly a bit wary. He glanced around the bar to see if there was any surveillance. A couple of shooters would usually preclude bail.

The weasel of a man looked at Bill with sharp eyes. He knew what had flashed through Bill's mind. 'It's all right,' he said, but not happy that Bill had questioned his motive. 'There's no filth. They were antiques, modified, but I said I didn't know anything about that. My brief got someone to verify it, but I'm not sure I'll stand up once they start poking around. I've got things to do. I can't afford to be banged up, not even on remand.'

Bill wasn't sure that he was getting the full SP. He guessed that he was either being set up, or the man sitting opposite him was eager to get even with someone that he thought had grassed him up. If faces were going to start disappearing, Bill did not want to find himself caught in the middle, the wrong side of the wrong firm, or involved in conspiracy to murder. Bill finished his drink and told the man to phone him in a few days. Bill did make a call to a detective inspector at West End Central early the following morning. Later that day he received a reply. The message was simple – anything concerning that individual would cost an arm and a leg, and the best advice was to steer well clear. Bill did not receive any contact from the individual concerned, and a year or so later he enquired as to the man's whereabouts from one of the chaps who Bill knew was acquainted with him.

'That's strange. He was not around for a long time and then all of a sudden he reappeared and then a few months later completely disappeared off the face of the earth. Strange really.'

As far as Bill was aware, he never appeared again.

On the Wednesday of that week, Bill was feeling good. He was walking better and he didn't seem to have the chill in his bones that had been getting him down for days. Weeks. The spieler was busy from early on and it looked as though it was going to be a profitable day. There was a lot of gossip about the cafe, Bill's local greasy spoon, having been bugged by the filth. A little team that had blagged the council offices had got themselves nicked, because that was where they had planned it. Bill walked across the street, peered through the steamed-up glass door and went in. He ordered a roast lunch and had a word with the owner, but he was not telling anything. He said he didn't know anything about any robbery or any bugging. Bill knew all the chaps involved and realised that it was unlikely he would be able to do anything anyway, as none of them had the sort of money it would take to speak to anyone.

Bill stood at the bar. He had wandered across to the Prince Albert later than usual so the few stools lining the bar were all occupied. He nursed his beer and read the paper. Half an hour passed before a stool became free and by the time he sat down his legs needed the respite. He bought a packet of cigarettes and ordered another drink. The lounge bar was beginning to empty. Bill pulled his stool into the corner, his favourite position, repositioned his paper, cigarettes and drink and then walked off to the gents. Coming back, he watched a heavy black guy step in off the street. The landlord also clocked the new customer and immediately ducked through to the other bar where a few black lads were playing pool, but did not need serving.

The black guy sat on Bill's stool and tapped a coin on the bar top to attract attention.

'Excuse me, that's my stool you're sitting on. I've just been to the gents,' Bill explained as he drew level, pointing a finger at his paraphernalia on the bar.

By now all the other stools were empty. The black guy looked at him in a dismissive manner. 'It's mine now. Sit on one of them,' he told Bill, nodding his head along the bar.

Bill knew that it did not make too much difference, the fella wasn't going to get served anyway. Give it five minutes and he'd be gone. A single left hook powered up from Bill's waistline. The broken knuckles crashed into the side of the black guy's face, just above his jaw. His body hit against the bar and fell back, upsetting the stool and toppling the man on to the floor. He lay there for a moment, stunned. Bill picked up the stool and replaced it where he had left it, but did not sit down. The black guy got to his knees and then to his feet. He half-looked in Bill's direction, but avoided eye contact with anyone. Steadying himself, he straightened his shoulder and walked out, the door closing quietly behind him. Bill knew that it had been a good punch, it would have hurt and his fist was still throbbing. The reason there had not been any retaliation might well have been that he didn't have the bottle, but Bill guessed that he was more embarrassed than scared. Bill finished his drink without sitting back down, leaned over the bar, tucked the paper between the glasses and picked up his cigarettes.

'Nice one, Bill,' said the old boy, wrapped in his equally old overcoat, sitting at a table by the door with an empty glass of Guinness in front of him. 'Any chance of a fag?' he added.

Bill smiled, took the packet of Rothmans he had just allowed to drop to the bottom of his pocket and gave him the lot.

At the spieler there were a few faces Bill had not seen for a while. It was good to see old faces, even young old faces. He wondered what they were doing south of the River. Bill acknowledged them but did not interrupt their play. Scouse said they had pitched up shortly after Bill had left. When they had arrived they had asked for Bill and decided to play a few hands while they waited for him to return, in preference to tracking him to the pub. As soon as they finished the game they left the table and came over and shook hands. Bill knew two of the three, but the third, who looked very young and self-assured, without being brash, he did not recall having seen before.

'Monday, Bill. Can you fix us up with a dealer? Probably all night.'

'Poker?'

'Yes. Someone that knows what they're doing, can keep their mouth shut and that can be trusted.'

'What sort of time?'

'Four. There'll be about eight of us, but only five playing. Oh yeah, and you'll need to get some skimmed milk. I'm told one of them only drinks that stuff.'

'Why can't he drink shampoo like everybody else?' the young lad butted in.

'I only do soft drinks here, no booze,' Bill said.

'That's one of the reasons I want to play here. I know you don't stand no fucking about,' the face said.

'Or bad language,' Bill added.

The face slapped him on the shoulder. 'Don't worry, you won't have any problem with us. It's going to be really heavy money and I want to be somewhere where I don't have to look over my shoulder every two minutes.'

Thursday, Bill was having problems with his breathing again. Being short of breath made even the smallest journey and the lightest task hard work. Outside the rain pounded the street and the dark clouds gave the morning the feel of a winter's evening. He panted, pulling on his overcoat, and slowly made his way out to the waiting cab. The damp air made his lungs feel like wet flannels. Most of the usuals were already at their tables, birdlike, wizened, pinched faces staring into wet newspapers. Nobody looked up when Bill entered. He hung his coat, settled on his stool and started the day with a brandy.

Parking in Brixton was difficult at the best of times. In the pouring rain everyone wanted to park outside wherever it was they were going. A double yellow line, with two wheels on the pavement, seemed to be the favourite option. The white Vitesse swung off the street and bounced across the rough ground. Reluctantly, a figure, hat pulled down and collar turned up, left the shelter of his glass-fronted shed to remonstrate with the driver. Then he recognised him.

'Is it all right if I tuck it in over there for a couple of hours? Just popping over to see Bill,' the driver asked.

'No problem. I think I saw him going into the pub when I was over at the cafe.'

With a soft-top, the driver knew it was wise to park where someone could keep an eye on it. Slicing through the roof was just so easy.

Jumping the puddles and trying to avoid the spray from passing cars sending fountains of dirty water high across the pavement, he darted from one dry doorway to another. Opposite the pub, he waited as narrow as possible against a wall, inspecting Caribbean and West African vegetables displayed on boxes and protected by flapping plastic sheeting. Ladies fingers were difficult to find in his local supermarket so he made a mental note to buy a couple of pounds on his way back. A space presented itself and without a moment's hesitation, he sprung forward.

The bar was quite full. He scanned the customers, but it didn't take a moment to recognise the back of Bill's head. He walked up and stood behind him. The landlord caught his stare at the same second Bill realised someone was looking over his shoulder. With a reflex that was beyond the state of his body that day, he spun on the stool to confront the presence.

'You better put a brandy in there,' Michael said to the landlord, nodding in the direction of Bill's still-full glass.

A broad smile spread across Bill's face. He stood up and shook hands with his son. For a while he felt good; his aches and pains had taken a backseat.

'Did you phone?' Bill asked, getting ready to ask the landlord to give the bar staff a dressing down for not passing on the message.

'No. I had a breakfast meeting in Piccadilly, so I thought I'd take a chance and look in,' Michael replied.

Bill wished he had made more of an effort before he left this morning. He hadn't bothered shaving and he hadn't picked up any cash. Later, while Michael was in the toilet, he borrowed a oner from the landlord.

Bill and his son talked about nothing. Bill pointed out Queenie Watts, one of the regulars at the end table, describing the less than elegant figure as a dipso, but one of the greatest shoplifters in London. The next round, Bill sent her over a drink.

'It's a shame it's not Saturday. Jan's bringing young Billy over. He likes coming in here and playing on the machine,' Bill said.

'Saturday is difficult, the casino gets really busy, so it's almost impossible to get time off.'

'Do they play dice?' Bill asked, suddenly remembering the lack of a decent set at the spieler.

'No, they don't even play French roulette. Just American and blackjack. Punto banco occasionally, oh yeah, and lots of kalooki.'

As people came and went, Bill would stop them and introduce them to his son. Michael often recognised them from previous visits, but it was difficult to remember everyone's names. Later, they walked across to the cafe and had some lunch. Bill always suggested eating somewhere more salubrious, but Michael knew his father liked to show all the cronies that his son had come up for the day. The next stop was usually the Prince of Wales public house on the corner; a large cavern of a place which Bill alleged was looked after by the IRA, who siphoned off money to fund arms deals. It was certainly a favourite haunt with Irish drinkers. After a drink there, the routine was to wander round to the spieler to see Scouse, and then Michael would be on his way back to the south coast, probably not to reappear for another two months or more.

This Thursday was no different. But on the walk to the cafe, then to the Prince of Wales and finally to see Scouse, Michael noticed the slowness of his father's pace and the uncertainty of his step. He had noticed it on other visits, but it was never quite as pronounced as on these short walks. It was the first time he almost instinctively moved to hold his father's arm to provide support. He stopped himself and checked his step. While Bill was talking to a table of players, Michael questioned Scouse over Bill's health.

'He's in a lot of pain sometimes, so he drinks. He breathes badly when it's damp and he won't stop smoking, won't even cut down. Sometimes he should be in hospital, but he'd have to be dying. I do what I can for him, but he's not interested.'

The conversation came to a stop as Bill returned.

'Listen, I've got to shoot off soon. The next time I come up why don't you come back with me and have a bit of a holiday down at my place for a couple of weeks?' Michael suggested.

Bill hummed and hawed.

'Come on, it'll do you good.'

'I was down that way a few weeks back,' Bill confessed.

'What? Why didn't you give me a ring?' Michael was slightly astounded. He was of the belief that it would take a team of white horses to drag his father out of London.

'Canterbury is near you, isn't it?' Bill said, as if he wasn't sure.

It suddenly dawned on Michael that he was probably visiting one of the chaps at Canterbury Prison.

'Yes. Just down the road. You should have called.'

'I thought about it, but then I couldn't find your number.'

'So what were you up to?'

'I had to visit a jungle,' Bill smiled.

'Well, now you know you don't need a passport, you could come down and stay for a couple of weeks. Scouse could look after things here and it'd do you good.'

'Wait until the weather's better and then we'll sort something out,' Bill promised.

Michael shook hands with Scouse and gave him a knowing smile, as much as to say keep an eye on him and give me a call if there are any problems. He knew Scouse had his number pencilled on the wall.

Michael shook hands with his father. 'As soon as the sun comes out, remember. And say hello to Billy for me.'

After Michael had left, Bill went and sat in the poker room, which was not in use, and pulled the curtains. Scouse brought him through a cup of tea. The day had drained the little energy he had in reserve. If life had been a game of poker, he would have folded.

'Filth.' Scouse had stuck his head through the curtains. Bill came to. He did not know how long he had been sitting there. He wasn't sure if he had been asleep or not.

'Filth,' Scouse repeated.

'I'll be out in a minute.'

Bill took a deep breath. It only seemed to fill half his lungs. Slowly, using the table, he pulled himself upright, wiped his mouth with his handkerchief and walked out to see what favour he was required to perform now. The mug of cold tea remained untouched on the table.

'It's someone at the council that's the problem. I keep putting them off. Last time they spoke to me, I told them the property was part of an undercover surveillance op, so it would not be possible to close the place down. But that was about four months ago and frankly it won't wash any more.' The voice was apologetic.

'Well, give it another couple of weeks and we'll organise a quiet evening. I'll find you half a dozen bodies and leave a few old tables in here. That should keep them quiet,' Bill said. 'I'll see there's double in the purse that week.'

'I'm sorry, Bill, but they want the place closed and boarded up. They are not happy that within a few days after every raid the place is open again. I'm sorry but you're going to have to find a new place somewhere else. The Chief Super's organising a raid here, at the bubbles place and a few of the joints that the niggers use, early next week. That's why I came over to let you know myself. I'm sorry, Bill, but there is nothing I can do about it.'

'Well, I'm telling you and you can tell the rest of the lads down there, I've got a big game on Monday night that might run into Tuesday, so I don't want any trouble.' Bill's voice had lost its shakiness. The extra power going through his vocal cords rattled his chest.

'I'm not sure that is going to be possible.'

'Well, I'm telling you, you had better make it possible, because too many people have had their noses too deep in the trough down at that nick to just think they can walk away.'

'Bill, you're asking the impossible.' The voice was angry but scared.

'I suggest that the whole of your relief goes down with a bad case of the shits, or you arrange a bomb scare at the Palace. I don't care what you do, but if any cozzers walk in here between now and Wednesday there'll be more rubber heels in Brixton nick than Brixton market.'

Bill followed the disgruntled officer out and called down the stairwell after him. 'I'll bring the lot of you down. Don't think I won't. There's a nice earner in this for everyone. Don't spoil it now. Nobody will thank you.'

Bill felt he should have made the effort to walk over to the council offices, but it was a real exertion just thinking about it. Instead he went round to the pub later and left a message.

Friday he woke late, having slept little. Gout had crept back and the slightest movement sent pain shooting high up his leg. His breath should have been a sharp intake, but there was little depth to draw on. He rolled to one side, trying not to cause movement over his swollen toe. From beside the bed he drank the remains from a glass of beer, flat but not warm, that he had been sipping through the night, lit a cigarette and tried to muster the enthusiasm, between deep rasping coughs, to bathe and shave. An hour passed before he was able to stand in front of the sink, lather his face and remove the two days' grey growth. Small cuts blooded his neck. He splashed on cold water and decided the bath would have to wait.

Getting out of the door and travelling to his destination was an unpleasant experience. His council contact did not show and there was no answer from the extension when Bill phoned. Everything needed pulling together and in his present state he realised this was something he could not do. By the end of the day he felt worse than he had all day. The thought of nothing more than walking down the stairs had become a hill that could not be climbed. He assured Scouse that he would be OK, that he would wait on his own for the mini-cab. He heard the horn, took an old, dust-laden curtain that was folded behind the snack bar, heaved himself on to the dice table, covered himself over and fell asleep before the cab had even given up.

He awoke screaming more than once, but by the time the market was coming to life, his gout-swollen foot had subsided and the horrors that had visited his sleep had left. That did not mean that he felt good. A night on a dice table can have its own casualties. It dawned on him that it was Saturday and Jan was bringing Billy over.

He went home, bathed, shaved and put on clean clothes. He pressed his trousers, spent too long finding his cuff links, but was back at the pub long before Jan and Billy arrived. Billy was lively, Bill could see he was growing into

164 THE SOHO DON

a good-looking lad. They did not shake hands or hug, but sparred, Bill getting in a couple of soft left hooks and laughing. Jan stayed for a drink and put some notes in Bill's hand, before arranging to pick her son up in the evening. The day was not that different from the day spent with Michael, Bill showing off his young son to friends at the café and the spieler, and bending to Billy's wish to spend as much time as possible in the pub so, as predicted, he could play the machines.

The whole of the following week it was business as usual. No further threats of immediate closure from either the police or the council. Bill's general health seemed to improve, a fact that he felt he had little control over. The Monday night game went off with fewer large pots than had originally been envisaged and the half-dozen cartons of skimmed milk remained unopened. All the tea and coffee served that week became the benefactor, despite many of the regulars' face-pulling.

'Hello, can I speak to Michael, please?'

'Who's speaking?'

'It's his father.'

A few moments later Michael's voice came on the line. 'Yes?'

Bill could tell Michael was not sure who was on the other end, but the moment he spoke, it was clear from Michael's tone that he realised it was not his stepfather and there was no sign that he was annoyed at being called to the phone.

'I thought I'd better give you a bell and let you know not to go to the spieler. The council have been complaining to the police, so the local nick have asked me to close it down and find somewhere else. So I'm not sure where it will be for the next few weeks. I thought I'd better let you know in case you were thinking of coming up.'

'I thought maybe you were phoning to say you were going to come down and stay for a while.'

'When the weather gets better.'

'Now would be a good time. Nothing to do all day.'

'I do other things, you know.'

'OK,' Michael said, realising he was wasting his breath.

'Phone the pub. I'll leave a message.'

Bill had Scouse and a few of the lads from the market store most of the tables in an old, disused garage. He paid the lads a tenner apiece and stuffed a oner into Scouse's pocket. In some respects he enjoyed the freedom of not having to go to the spieler every day. Getting a cab up to the West End and keeping in touch with people he had only spoken to on the phone for longer than he cared to recall was good, but it was clear things were changing. To maintain his position, to be able to continue to fix things and sort out the problems, he knew he had to keep himself aware of the movements in trends that were taking place. Soho was changing the same as everywhere else. New faces were hanging around street corners, places had closed and new owners had moved in. Many of the old faces and characters were looking thin on the ground.

* * *

The spieler at the end of Electric Avenue was raided by consent. A day was arranged when Bill paid a few unemployed, unemployable locals to sit around the few tables that had been left behind. A couple of old packs of cards, a kettle, milk, tea bags and the chipped mugs made up the remainder of the contingent. The arrangement was that the old boys would insist it was a private game, for matchsticks. Not illegal. The police would take them to the station but eventually release them without charge, the tables would be impounded and the property would be boarded up and sealed. Bill agreed not to reopen. On this basis it was believed that all interests had been satisfied.

Within a few weeks the luxury of freedom, the trips to the West End, days working on the stall in East Lane and evenings drinking in a variety of pubs and clubs across the whole of south London had lost its appeal. Bill felt that he needed a small village, everything within a short walk. Although his health had been better on more days than it had not, the good days by previous standards were poor. Off to the back of Sears Blok, a Camberwell-based firm of solicitors favoured by many of the chaps and with offices in the West End, Bill located two rooms with a kitchen and toilet. A month later, Scouse was back making the coffee and passing the hat hourly. Punters came and in many respects it attracted more gamblers and fewer time wasters than the Electric Avenue operation. They came to gamble. The trade was mainly in the evening, but it was not Electric Avenue and it was not Brixton. Most of all, it was not a social club, no one just popped in off the market for a few hands. By the spring, Bill was not bothering to open three days out of four, partly due to his lack of interest in the place, but equally as a result of his health that had suddenly and for no reason taken a dramatic turn for the worse. With the additional pain came an increase in drinking, and with the increased drinking came despair.

Setting up in Camberwell had not been a good move. Bill decided he should have opened again in Brixton, but he had agreed to operate a little further afield so the council could not complain that the police had closed the illegal gambling den down only to have it open a few doors away. One week, the Camberwell spieler did not open at all. That was the same week Bill did not get out of bed. Scouse called and was persuaded against his better judgement to visit the off-licence. He also visited the convenience store and purchased cans of soup, sliced bread and a packet of butter. Before leaving, Scouse tidied the mess, heated Bill some soup and buttered two slices of bread. Three days later when he returned, letting himself in using a spare key that he had always held, he found Bill where he had left him, the soup congealed and the bread untouched. Empty bottles were strewn at dropping distance from the bed. The air was heavy and foul. The light, dark. A small shaft from a dim bulb hanging in the toilet prevented it being pitch.

Bill was dead, Scouse was certain. He opened the curtain a small amount, just sufficient to allow him to take stock. At the same time he unlatched the window and dropped the top pane a few inches. The sun and fresh air attacked the elements held under siege and light streamed across Bill's face. Scouse touched him and could feel movement twitching from the muscles. Bill was not dead, but he was not asleep either. Using a dirty towel he wet under the tap, Scouse wiped Bill's face and neck and tried, in some small way, to make him comfortable. Then he covered him with coats and lit the gas fire. In the bathroom he searched and found a bottle of smelling salts. If they did not work, he had decided that he would call an ambulance, but knowing Bill's hatred of hospitals, it had to be an act of desperation. The sharp, pungent aroma could hardly have been absorbed, Bill's breathing was so shallow. But Scouse's persistent waving of the small brown bottle under Bill's nose finally forced his head to pull away in a semi-conscious state.

Bill did not know where he was and did not recognise the figure at his side. He looked at the shadow towering over him and demanded, in a voice that was little more than a whisper, to be given a drink.

Scouse washed a cup that he filled with water. Bill sipped a little, but it was not what he wanted. He needed a drink. Alcohol. The person's hand was clear, but he still could not make out more than a blurred vision of him or the room. With a vice-like grip he took the wrist and held it. He muttered one word. 'Brandy.'

And then he again slipped into unconsciousness. Scouse had less than a pound in his pocket and after searching around, looking in drawers and pockets of discarded clothing, was not able to increase the amount significantly.

Down the street, he purchased a newspaper, a bottle of milk and when he thought the shop assistant wasn't looking, he slipped a bottle of brandy under his coat. She grabbed his arm and screamed for him to give it back. As he tried to pull free, the bottle spun in the air and fell to the ground, smashing on contact, showering liquid and glass in all directions. Scouse was scared. The thought of being caught and banged up terrified him. He hit the woman low in the stomach and pushed her down the shop, away from him. Pain and fear flooded into her face as display stands and shelving came crashing down around her. Scouse leaned over the counter and snatched the money from the till.

'Call the police and I'll keel yee,' he shouted, picking up a can and throwing it at her from the door as he rushed out.

On the street, he caught a bus and then another, staying out of the way until after dark. When he got back, Bill was lying much as he had left him, neither conscious nor unconscious. The room was hot but, having left the window open, the air seemed breathable.

Scouse had shopped using the few pounds he had snatched. From the bag he took out a flask of cheap brandy and poured a little in a cup. Bill choked on the first sip and was unable to take a second for more than a minute. The amount of liquid was so small it was hardly sufficient to coat the inside of his throat. The third and fourth sips were large enough to drain the cup. For the next 48 hours Scouse and Bill remained alone. Scouse insisted that Bill ate a little food or drink sweet tea, in return for a small amount of alcohol. Bill's state did not seem to be improving. From time to time he slipped in and out of consciousness. Other times he lay, without moving, without speaking, simply staring. Scouse was even more reluctant to phone for an ambulance, now he was concerned that it might attract the attention of the police. If the woman in the shop had reported the blag, they would certainly have a good description.

Over the hours, during the times Bill was lucid, Scouse told Bill that he thought Bill should go to hospital. Bill was adamant and was no more in favour of allowing Scouse to call Jan or Bill's brother. All, he knew, would put pressure on him to be taken into hospital.

Finally, Scouse felt that he had to take some action.

During the night, when Bill was sleeping, Scouse went to the property in Electric Avenue. He removed the boards, entered and made his way to the area where the coffee bar had stood. Still pencilled on the wall was Michael's telephone number. The only problem was the code, which had deliberately been left off. This he got from directory enquiries. Scouse had not realised it was an office number and therefore only provided a recorded message. Telephoning in the morning, Scouse realised, could prove difficult. If he phoned from Bill's place there was a good chance Bill would hear and become uncontrollable. Going out still filled him with paranoia. At nine-thirty the next morning, Scouse left the building and, as unobtrusively as he was able, he made his way to the nearest phone box. It took three journeys before he was able to locate a box where all the equipment had not been vandalised. It took him another three before he found a phone in one piece that also worked. He did not like the way he was putting himself about, and then it occurred to him that maybe the woman in the shop had not reported him. A woman answered the phone and yes, Michael was there but he was just leaving, and he was already late. Scouse was persistent.

'Hello,' Michael said, eager to deal with whatever it was and get on his way.

'Michael. It's Scouse, ya Dad's . . .'

'Yes, Scouse. How's things? What's happening?' Michael butted in before Scouse could finish his explanation.

'It's Bill, he's sick and he won't let me call a doctor. I'm not sure what I should do.'

'Listen, Scouse, I'm just off to India and I should have left for the airport half an hour ago. What's wrong with him?'

'I don't know. He's been in bed for about a week. He seems to be unconscious a lot of the time. And he's drinking.'

'Is there anyone else you can speak to?'

'He says he's all right, he just wants to rest.'

'Who's been looking after him?'

'I have, the best I can.'

'You're on the ground, Scouse. You're going to have to take the decisions. Can you look after him for another few days? I should be back in five or six days.'

'I haven't got any wonga, and Bill's place is empty.'

'Hang on a minute,' Michael said and put his hand over the mouthpiece.

'How much cash is there in the safe?' Michael directed the question to the woman who had answered the phone.

'Two hundred and fifty pounds,' she replied.

'I'm sending some cash up with a lad that does some work here, Luke Sangster, £250. Don't let Bill spend it all on booze. As soon as I get back, tell him I'll come up and see him. And listen, if he gets really bad get him out on to the pavement and call an ambulance. Where do you want the cash delivered?'

Scouse gave him the address and was about to put the phone down. 'Why have I got to get him out on to the pavement?' Scouse asked as an afterthought, not sure whether Michael was joking or not.

'Ambulances are for emergencies. They will probably want him referred to the hospital by a doctor if he is in bed at home. Leave messages for me here if you need to and if you want Luke to do any running around for you, just tell him. I'll talk to you when I get back.' With that Michael replaced the receiver.

'Get hold of Luke, give him the address and tell him to get up there before lunch,' Michael instructed and left, hoping that he had made the right decision.

CHAPTER NINE

Bacon Sandwiches and a Trip to the Zoo

Ten days after flying out to India, Michael was back in the UK and sitting in the pub in Coldharbour Lane talking to Scouse. Michael had arrived early without telephoning first, and sat eating breakfast in the cafe waiting for a friendly face to show. Scouse had arrived shortly before pub opening time, looking his usual wiry self, with a drawn white face and his normal worried look. He refused Michael's offer of a cooked breakfast and when he had finished his tea, they walked across to the pub.

'Bill's a lot better,' Scouse told Michael. 'He's been up and about for about four or five days. He's still a bit slow, really he should be having a bit of a rest, but you know Bill. He went up West last night and must have stayed up there. I went to see him earlier and he wasn't in, so he can't have come back.'

'Did you get the money I sent OK?'

'Most of it.'

'How do you mean, most of it?' Michael asked.

'Luke had a lot of expenses. He's a hungry lad.'

'How much did he give you?'

'Two hundred and some change. He said there was the train fare, some sandwiches and then he bought a meal and a drink.'

'Did you have enough?'

'Yes, that was plenty. He's a good lad. He went and did all the shopping. Then he stayed the night and ate most of the scran he'd bought. The next day I sent him out shopping again and I think he'd have eaten that. I think he'd have moved in if I hadn't sent him on his way.'

'Luke is as good as gold, but he can be a bit over-enthusiastic.'

As Scouse made a move to leave, Michael thanked him and pushed some money into his hand, which Scouse refused.

'Look, if you won't take it for yourself, take it and keep it in case Bill's ill again. That way if there is no other cash around, you won't have to worry for a while.'

Scouse did not want to but with Michael's continued insistence he finally agreed. After Scouse had left to do whatever it was he had on his mind, Michael ordered another drink and helped himself to the newspaper tucked under the counter that was his father's daily read.

Bill showed as Michael was finishing a sandwich he had ordered for lunch, more to pass the time than out of hunger. Michael thought his father had aged ten years since he had last seen him a month or so back. He could have been 80.

'A large brandy,' Bill ordered. He paid with a note from a large bundle and told the barman to keep the change. When the landlord served him, he rarely seemed to pay or even offer. Michael watched his father down the liquid and order a second, almost immediately. He did not realise Bill had not noticed him, as his father had crossed the floor only a few feet in front of where he was sitting.

'Don't I get one then?'

Bill turned and looked at the person sitting a few feet from where he stood. For a moment he seemed not to be able to recognise his son. Then a smile formed on his face. An uncertain smile, almost childlike, a child that had been caught doing something naughty. Not bad, more cheeky.

'What would you like?' Bill asked, as Michael got up and stepped across to the bar.

'Half a shandy's fine. How are you feeling?'

'Better. Thanks.'

Michael was not sure Bill was thanking him for asking or for sending Luke up with funds or for coming up to see him. Michael gestured back to where he had been sitting but Bill did not want to sit at a table. Michael guessed that he did not want to be seen as one of the old fogeys. There were no free stools at the bar, so they both stood. Someone sitting further along, who obviously knew Bill by sight, offered Bill his stool. Bill thanked the young man but refused the offer.

When Michael suggested that his father come down to Kent to stay for a couple of weeks, he thought Bill would protest, but that was not the case. It was agreed that Bill would come down on Friday, on the train to Dover. Michael had intended to come and collect him but Bill was insistent. The slow train stopped in Brixton, so it was easier all round, Bill explained.

Bill did not arrive on Friday, as agreed. He telephoned his son and made an excuse. Twenty-four hours late, he walked out of Dover Priory station carrying a small battered suitcase. Michael was sitting in his car opposite. A few minutes later they were roaring to the outlying village of Whitfield. Michael's flat was the top floor of an old, large converted house that had been built by the local coalmine owner in the late 1800s.

Michael had a private agenda, although he was sure his father was fully aware of what was on his son's mind and that, as much as anything, was the reason Bill had been so reluctant to come and stay on earlier invitations. Rest. Good food. A reduction in booze.

Michael was up really early in the day, before five sometimes, so he tended to be in bed early. Bill would follow suit but then not get up till close to ten. A cooked brunch, with coffee and lots of fresh fruit. Sandwiches and cakes in the afternoon and then a large steak, salad and jacket potato for dinner. Michael thought that the rest and the food were working out OK, but the booze was the big test.

Day one, things did not go exactly to plan. Breakfast was way off the mark.

'Bacon sandwiches. My favourite,' Bill said. It was a statement, not in reply to any offer Michael had made.

Not wanting to be contentious straight off, Michael pulled rashers from the fridge. Having disappeared for a few moments, his father reappeared.

'Have you got any orange juice?' Bill asked.

'No, but I can squeeze some,' Michael replied, pleased that Bill was at least opting for that in preference to a brandy.

'Where're the glasses?' Bill asked, producing a bottle of Moet, and adding, 'Bacon sandwiches and Buck's Fizz. Best scran in the world.'

Michael took Bill with him to his office, showed him the casino training-room and the various operational bits and pieces that filled the day. Before the ferry that Michael was due to meet arrived, he would take Bill into a hotel bar and they would have a quick beer. As there was always work on the horizon, a second drink was not an option. In the evening, Michael opened a bottle of wine, which he shared slightly unevenly with his father, ensuring Bill always received a little less than half. On a trolley in the dining-room was a good selection of spirits, but each bottle was full and still sealed. Michael felt that if he was not around and his father felt desperate, he knew alcohol was readily available. Had the bottles already been opened, Michael knew a measure or two could be drunk without it being noticed. Starting a sealed bottle would be a statement. It said something. The strategy appeared to work for the first three days. On the fourth, Bill decided that he would not bother going with his son to the office. He thought he would make a start on one of the hundreds of books shelved in Michael's flat.

Michael understood that Dover was not a particularly exciting place. He had offered to get Bill a day passport or even sign him on as supernumerary crew, so that he could travel on one of the ferries and watch the gaming tables in operation. It would have been chancy, if any of the shipping company executives or the Harbour Police got wind of Bill's form. It would not have done Michael's contract to operate any good. In the event, Bill refused the offer, despite the opportunity of a duty-free bar. Michael needed to travel. Hopping from one vessel to another, immediately they first docked in Calais, it was possible to return again without enduring the turn-round time. Four hours tops. It was during this absence that Bill ventured out to investigate the local public house.

'How did the trip go?' Bill enquired while Michael prepared dinner.

'Quiet. Not much action. The whole thing is very bitty. It can rely on a few good punters who can be travelling regardless of whether the ship is packed out or almost empty. Usually it is the antique dealers. Dealers is probably the wrong word. Most of them are knockers. They take wagonloads over to sell to dealers in Belgium and Holland. Lots of ready cash and always looking to beat the system,' Michael explained.

'What did you get up to?' he added, having already scanned the drinks trolley to satisfy himself his father had not spent the afternoon boozing in front of the TV.

'I made a start on Adolf Hitler.' Bill was referring to the biography of Hitler, by John Toland.

'Any good?'

'I don't know. It was quite interesting.'

'Did you go out?' Michael asked, as casually as he could without seeming to be carrying out a cross-examination.

'I walked down the road to the pub, but it was closed,' Bill replied with a ring of disbelief in his tone. It sounded like the Sinatra at Sands joke, 'I went to the Grand Canyon and it was closed.'

'I think they sort of suit themselves. I have to say I've never actually been in the place,' Michael said.

'Neither have I,' Bill laughed.

The following day Bill set out earlier, shortly after Michael had cleared away their brunch and left for another trip across the Channel.

'How was it?' Bill asked from the lounge where he looked as though he had been sitting comfortably for the last few hours, deep in the pages of Hitler.

'About the same.'

This was the first time the two had been together for any length of time. Certainly in Michael's memory. Certainly in any domestic situation. Over dinner, Bill related his trip across to the pub, without waiting to be asked. This Michael felt was a good step. He was not looking to stop his father drinking, which he was fully aware would have been an impossible task, he was just trying to break the monotony, the routine of having to head for the pub.

'What's it like over there?' Michael asked.

'I couldn't believe it. They've got a sign on the door saying "No Gypsies". That's like putting a notice up in Brixton, "No Blacks". I don't know how they get away with it.'

'Were there many in there?'

'No, there was nobody in the place. Most of the time the publican wasn't even in there. I had to wait 15 minutes to get served.'

'Did you stay long?'

'I glanced at the paper. Got him to serve me a second drink when he came back behind the bar and left without seeing him again.'

'He's probably got a spy-hole somewhere. Sounds as though he could do with a few gypsies,' Michael said.

'Didn't look like the place they'd want to go into even if the booze was free. Don't think I've ever met such a miserable landlord.'

The following morning Bill asked if it would be all right if he made a few phone calls.

'What's here's yours,' Michael told him. 'Help yourself.'

This was how the time passed. One lunchtime Michael took Bill to a country club attached to a caravan park overlooking the Channel at Caple-le-Ferne, a village situated between Dover and Folkestone. On an earlier visit Michael had made to the bar, it transpired that the owners were friends of his father and had previously owned a carpet business in London. Bill had apparently employed them to lay carpet in The Beehive Club and they had made Michael promise to bring his father in to see them the next time he visited. Unfortunately, the couple were away, so the surprise didn't happen and Michael kept the knowledge up his sleeve for a future outing.

On another day, after a series of early telephone calls which Bill made while Michael was in the shower, Bill asked if it would be possible to have a trip out to Howletts, a safari park a few miles south of Canterbury, less than ten miles from where Michael was living. This suited Michael quite well as he had gaming tables on ferries sailing from Sheerness to Vlissengen in Holland. Normally, he would have visited the vessels at least once a week but he had put it off while his father was staying. Michael was happy to schedule the trip to the safari park either prior to or on the return journey. Bill plumped for calling in on the way home.

Sheerness was a large cash pick-up. The takings on the Olau Line vessels were good. There was a long period at sea with a substantial boredom factor. Also most of the people travelling who were potential punters could afford a cabin, so even on busy trips there was no panic about leaving your seat and finding it taken when you returned. By the time they arrived at the port, the weather had come round. There was a light rain in the air and the wind had picked up. Sheerness docks were desolate – few coaches waiting to embark and stacks of TIR tractors waiting to go aboard. Some would wait days until non-booked spaces became available. The odd person dashed from Portakabin to Portakabin. Everyone who wasn't needed had gone home. It was a well-known fact that customs officers who fell foul of their senior officers in Dover were dispatched for a tour of duty at this outpost. Michael boarded the vessel, leaving Bill waiting in the car. At the purser's office he collected and signed for the takings and then went to find the croupier for a quick chat, a check that the table was in peak condition and to collect the originals of the play reports. The walk back to the car was completely unhindered. No passport check, no customs check. Dover, Michael considered slack. Sheerness just seemed to have been forgotten, not even an uncaring, disinterested glance. In the boot of the car, Michael secured the cash in the well which was designed to hold the spare wheel. During the height of the season, Michael could visit anything up to ten vessels, picking up takings from each vessel one after the other. Security was an obvious concern. Michael hoped that Bill would not let slip, after a few drinks, information to any of the chaps who could make Michael a target in the future.

At Howletts, it was Michael's turn to remain in the car.

'I shouldn't be long,' Bill said, pushing himself up from the low passenger seat.

'No hurry,' Michael replied. He watched his father walk across the car park. Michael was not sure if it was only his imagination, but he felt his father looked taller. The roundness that had crept into his shoulders over the past few months seemed to have gone and Michael was sure Bill was a lot steadier on his feet than when he had been walking from the entrance of Priory station ten days earlier.

In the car, Michael double-checked the accounting on the paying-in sheets he had collected and compared them with the figures that the croupier had telephoned through at the end of each sailing. Fifteen minutes passed. Michael felt sure his earlier impression was right. His father did look as though he had been given a new lease of life. Almost striding, Bill crossed the half-empty car park, a carrier bag all but swinging in his hand as he walked. Bill pushed the bag into the foot well, not passing it to his son who was ready to take it, and climbed in.

'Toys for the kids,' Bill offered by way of explanation and did not elaborate. Michael did not pursue the issue.

Back at the flat, Michael placed the casino takings in the safe. The 'toys' Bill stuffed into his suitcase without further discussion. The remainder of the stay was low-key and while Michael disappeared now and again to oversee his business, his father seemed content to eat, rest and drink only small amounts. Hitler was doing well. At one point Michael became suspicious at the lack of alcohol being consumed and checked out a few possibilities. The seals on the bottles standing on the drinks trolley remained firm, a quick scout around the inside of the flat and outside at the bins gave up no evidence of undeclared bottles and a visit to the local, still devoid of customers, did not shatter the good news. It was not difficult for the barman to remember Bill, he had been in only on three occasions and Michael felt that these visits had been the highlight of the man's day. On the pretext of his father being on strong tablets, when questioned the man confirmed that Bill had drunk no more than two single brandies on each visit and that if he remembered rightly, on one occasion Bill had also drunk a half of bitter.

Michael dropped Bill at the station, they shook hands and Michael promised to pop up in the next couple of weeks. Bill promised not to leave it so long next time before coming down to visit. 'I'll see if I can keep it under 30 years next time.' Michael smiled. Laughing Boy was laughing again.

That evening Bill telephoned Michael to thank him for the stay. Michael knew how bored his father must have been. He thought a couple of weeks had worked well, any longer would have been a strain on the therapy. Hitler was sitting almost finished in the corner. Michael wondered if he should take it up to Brixton the next time he visited, but decided it would be a good intro on Bill's next stay. Over the following few days, Michael mulled over his time with his father. In many respects it had been strange, quite relaxed but without any intimacy. Lives were not discussed. All exchanges dealt with now, current events. At the time Michael had not thought twice about his father's out-of-character visit to Howletts. However, Michael did later wonder whether Bill's previous reference to Canterbury being a jungle referred to the safari park, not the city's prison.

* * *

The next day Bill was back in the pub. Two or three messages were waiting behind the bar. One was from the council, suggesting a meeting, another was from Brixton Police Station. Both messages were from friends using only first names, but Bill did not have to guess twice as to who was trying to contact him. And he did not have to think too hard to know they were both missing their bung.

The meeting with the filth about reopening a spieler was simple and was exactly what Bill had expected, but there were two other subjects that he had not expected on the agenda. The sergeant sitting opposite Bill was a power broker at the station, working deals and payouts both up and down the ladder. He was strong enough to keep any young innocents in line and relied upon to keep all the underhanded action and gossip away from the station hierarchy.

'Silver wedding anniversary, me and the missus thought it was time to buy that bungalow or a little pub with roses round the door.' The sergeant sipped his pint, knowing Bill would not be pleased to lose influence, despite assurances there were other people more than happy to see that the wheels were oiled. Keeping in mind the set-to he had had with the station only weeks earlier, Bill felt wary, particularly with the offer of a blind eye over a new spieler site. The second item was a proposition, which in many respects Bill felt could easily be turned into an insurance policy. The proposition was to re-establish a business they had operated together a number of years earlier, that for one reason or another had ceased. If Bill recalled correctly the lease on the property being used came to an end and the block was redeveloped. Bill agreed to see if he could find somebody suitable to front the operation.

The meeting with the contact at the council was even more straightforward. The suggestion was that Bill be given access to the block of flats directly opposite the pub, through some big iron gates that opened into a courtyard, off which doors led to a labyrinth of empty accommodation.

'Take your choice. Replace one of the locks and it's all yours. As long as there's no trouble, no one's going to bother you,' Bill was assured.

'I was happy in Electric Avenue. That was meant to be no bother.' Bill let his displeasure show in his tone.

'That's all sorted now.'

'It had better be. I don't want to get things running nicely and then find someone from your place has been down the nick every two minutes causing trouble. I'm telling you, you get the bung and you sort out the problems. It's your legs.'

The council official considered himself a friend of the man he was standing next to, but he still felt a shiver run down his spine. If he hadn't needed the money so much he would have backed out, but he did. So he nodded his agreement.

Within a week, the lock had been drilled on the entrance to stairs that led up to a group of second-floor flats and new locks had been installed. Scouse had found a few lads to get the place sorted and Bill obtained some paint from the council yard. Mickey Rice, always wanting to ensure the best for Bill, set to with the brushes and the skill of a good decorator to turn two of the units into habitable areas. Scouse got the job of painting the glass with green paint to deter prying eyes. Heavy curtains and other items were obtained from the back of a lorry clearing fixtures and fittings from a West End hotel refurbishment, and the tables were trucked around, again courtesy of the council. Scouse took time to ensure his coffee bar was well equipped, although to everyone else coming and going it did not seem to look any different from its previous incarnations. In the flat next door, Bill had a bed brought in and turned the accommodation into a place where he could crash on the occasions when games continued late into the night. He let it be known that he was in the market for a comfortable easy-chair and a couple of blagged TVs – one for the spieler and the racing, the other to provide home comforts should he wish to put his feet up on a quiet afternoon. Mickey came up trumps with a sofa and other furnishings that his parents were replacing. Bill was back in Brixton and back in business.

Why Bill had not asked Michael for a set of professional dice while he had been staying with his son, Bill did not know, but he felt a set would add the right touch. Michael again dispatched Luke from Dover with a few sets of the clear, red-tinted plastic dice, each serial-numbered to ensure authenticity. Bill knew his new spieler was neither Winston's nor The Beehive, it was what it was, a squat in an otherwise dingy, deserted tenement. The one thing it was, was Brixton. He felt at home here. He really liked the people, well, the whites, and in truth most of the blacks if he really thought about it. One or two of the blacks he preferred to a good few of the whites. This was not the case with many of the whites, and the feeling was mutual with most of the blacks. It was difficult to keep a foot in both camps, but that had been the story of his life. Nothing changes.

Both the council and the filth were as good as their word. The spieler opened without hassle from either. Business was slow, even though a lot of the lads that had previously frequented Electric Avenue looked in. Some stayed and played, although rarely for high stakes. Most were saving their extra few quid for the family holiday. Occasionally, greed would get the better of one or two and a big game would develop and last until the early hours. However, this was not a nightly or weekly guarantee. A lot of the house money went to bung the filth and the council – these amounts were not proportionate to profit, or even turnover. Then there was Scouse to square, and without fail the handful of notes Bill would consistently push into the pocket of one loser or another, partly to prevent them getting a bashing from their wives if they went home without the day's takings and partly to ensure they returned the following day to lose more.

Trips up West were depressing. Bill would have not bothered crossing the river had he not felt he still should. Since the death of Dimes, Soho was a poor excuse for the past. Now there was nobody on the ground in daily control, nobody controlling the streets or the businesses. This was not his job, it never had been. He had brought order to the competing gangs and had provided insurance to their business interests. If the various gang leaders could have been referred to as managing directors, he had been the chairman, the consultant and the banker. Now there seemed only to be bits of kids who thought crime as a long-term career was simply about a bit of violence and a few quid today. That and drugs. On the street level, most of those involved were in a worse state than their customers. The importers were further afield, and the money men long gone. Soho was no longer the small village where respected faces drank coffee, passed the time of day with shop and restaurant owners from whom they collected protection money and held court with young hardmen who did their bidding.

Bill realised that this might have been a rose-tinted view of the area he had always enjoyed and remembered with nostalgia. If Brixton was his home, then Soho and Mayfair were his playgrounds, the greater area of the West End and south London his corporate entity. Everything had moved on and he realised that in many respects he had become a dinosaur. Most of the chaps from his era were banged up, probably for the remainder of their natural, and the rest were on their toes. Those who weren't brown bread, that was. Only one firm had remained constant, a change of face, a setback here and there, but the filth had succeeded in cutting out the middlemen. In some ways, the more the 'bad' ones had sought to clear out the corruption, the stronger the 'good' 'uns had got. Corrupt officers, Bill believed, were now less widespread through the force, but they wielded more power, controlled greater criminal activities directly and in some cases were not only involved in crime but were actually organising it. The patients had taken over the asylum.

New faces in the force had wanted a clean sweep on both sides of the fence. They had seen that the only way of maintaining control was to ditch those officers who had been tarnished over many years, who would always be susceptible to criminal blackmail, the threat of prosecution from the Countrymen of this world and of lifestyle exposure. On the other side, villains capable of pulling down the house of cards in return for liberty needed to be discredited, fitted up and seriously banged up. Over the next few months, Bill continued to have meetings with faces on both sides of the fence – in the main, small favours being sought by older members of the criminal fraternity for themselves or their offspring's misdemeanours. Small amounts of money changed hands, usually in return for the loss of evidence or the scaling down of previous offences being made known to the court before sentencing.

At the time it was agreed that Bill should reopen a spieler in Brixton, the police had put a second proposal forward. Bill had not had any great success achieving this, mostly due to his own inertia. On two previous occasions he had been instrumental in setting up pawnbroker's shops. The deal was simple. The shop was fronted by someone who, if not totally clean, had been for some time. It was ideal for providing a nice little earner for one of the chap's wives that had been put away, or one of the chaps that had decided to retire from active duty. The shop was used by the police to convert stolen goods they retrieved, particularly jewellery and silverware, into cash. At pre-agreed times they would also carry out raids on the premises and retrieve some of the items that still remained on the stolen list. The owner of the shop, of course, could not remember who brought the item in and the name and address in the book would naturally be false. The police were the benefactors of a win, win situation – substantial amounts of cash to line their pockets, plus they could claim that goods had been recovered and returned to the owner. The cash paid to the filth in the first instance when they brought the goods in was a loss the shopowner had to stand.

Bill met an old adversary in the cafe one morning. Over the years the younger man had grown to respect Bill and they had become, if not friends, friendly. Bill put the pawnshop deal on the table, but the younger man rejected it out of hand. He hated the filth and wanted nothing to do with them. Bill understood his attitude. Dealing with the filth was considerably more difficult to control and whilst he did not believe in honour amongst thieves any more than among the rest of society, even good coppers were filth. On reflection, Bill felt that Brixton no longer merited a pawnshop where quality items could confidently be fenced. Going outside the district posed the problem of retrieving goods on regular raids, although if this was not restrictive, opening a shop outside the Metropolitan area had its attractions. Brighton seemed to be the obvious choice.

Bill had made Brighton a regular race outing over many years, but now, like everything else in his life, things were scaled down. It was more than a year, maybe even two, since his last visit. Going back over the years, he had regularly stayed at The Ship and one or two of the other prestigious hotels scattered along the seafront. On this occasion he telephoned the Iron Duke public house and told the landlord he wanted a room. It was a big old pub, a short walk from the seafront, along a side-turning in the direction of Hove. It was a favourite haunt with a lot of the chaps, and a few of the bookies who wanted to drink and party all night without the night manager of one of the hotels threatening to call the police because the other guests were complaining. During race weeks, the Iron Duke was taken over. It was an ideal time to be in town without too many people paying much attention, and it was certain the chaps he thought might be interested in fencing the stolen goods would be around. It was almost a rehash of the situation that had been operating prior to the Brighton Conspiracy trial.

When Bill arrived at the pub, everyone was at the course and the bar staff were still clearing up from the night before. Bill visited a few pubs and called in to speak to the owners of a couple of jewellery shops, antique dealers and a bullion dealer who specialised in scrap gold. Most of the bits that came in were either sold on within the hour to someone he knew was looking for a special piece, or they were broken down, cut up and sold on to a bullion dealer in Hatton Garden. Bill did not put the deal to any of the people there and then. He was really checking the lay of the land. Plus, he felt that it was only polite to run it past the local governor before setting something up.

By ten, the Iron Duke was heaving.

'Mr Howard.'

Bill did not recognise the heavily built young man who was pushing an open bottle of Moët into his hand, retaining a second bottle for himself.

'I saw you when I was at the bar and thought you could do with a drink,' the man said, giving Bill a friendly punch on the shoulder.

Bill was still trying to place him, gold chains, gold sovereign rings and gold-rimmed bins. Before Bill could gather his thoughts or even thank the man, he was heading off.

'If you fancy a few lines of coke, come over to the table,' he invited Bill, pointing towards a table in the far corner occupied by three skinny girls with extremely white complexions and bleached hair. Bill guessed they were on the game.

The next time Bill saw the man was at 3 a.m., lying unconscious on the stairs, champagne dribbling from a tightly held bottle. As Bill picked his way around the body, trying to retain a hand on the bannister to ensure his balance, more bodies came into sight on the landing. Sitting on the top step was one of the brasses, a short turquoise dress hitched up round her waist, her head between her sore, spotted knees and thighs. A vomit trail cascaded down four or five stairs below her. As Bill weaved past, she looked up, her lips and chin still wet, her eyes glazed. Without recognition of human life, she dropped her head back down and immediately heaved.

The following day Bill declined breakfast. The smell of booze and vomit and the snoring of outstretched bodies, still sleeping it off on the banquette seating, made it an easy decision as he walked light-footed across the sodden carpet in the direction of the street and fresh air.

The air was clean, the sun reflected off shop windows, but it was deceptive. The cold salt air cut deep into his lungs, snatching his breath away. He had been left a ticket to the enclosure by one of the chaps in the bar, so the landlord told him, and he had intended using it. But now he was having second thoughts. Halfway along the seafront he had to sit. He found a spot out of the wind that benefited from the sun. It was 20 years, maybe nearer 25, since the magistrate had issued the order to find Billy Howard. He smiled, took his folded handkerchief from his pocket and wiped his mouth.

Service of breakfast had finished by the time Bill arrived in the dining-room of The Ship. A table of bookmakers, most of whom had used Bill's services in the past, invited him over and managed to persuade the waiter to bring an extra cup, fresh coffee and two slices of toast. With the offer of a seat in one of two Range Rovers, Bill accepted their hospitality. Some realised that what he had done for them had taken its toll; a younger couple, Bill knew, only saw him as someone out of the past. During the drive, one spoke clearly out of order, making a snide remark about Jan, Bill's ex, and then laughed. Bill quietly leaned forward, cupped his hand round the base of the man's neck and twisted his head very slightly. 'I don't think that was a very nice thing to say,' Bill said in a quiet voice, giving the man a thin-lipped smile and a sideways glance.

For a moment, the noise of the engine was the only sound in the car.

'Apologies, Mr Howard. No offence meant.'

Bill loosened his grip, the muscles in his arm already beginning to hurt. He tried not to show the wince in his face. 'None taken.'

The chat in the car resumed.

At the course, Bill found a sheltered spot close to the bar where he could sit and watch the racing. Life was becoming one continual search for sheltered spots, he reflected. Throughout the day he would be recognised and large brandies sent over with best wishes. In his mind he knew that this would be the last race meeting he would attend. Not that he thought his life was coming to a close, but it was something for which he felt he no longer had the energy or inclination.

He did not place any bets and after the first two races he didn't even bother to try to pick winners. He sat, sipped from the ever increasing quantity of brandy in his glass and allowed his thoughts to wander through the history of what had brought him into racing in the first place. It was the backbone of the British underworld. It was the backbone of his world. Racing had always been corrupt, corruption created large quantities of black money and that needed to be protected. Protection needed vicious men and they could enter that world without capital investment. Clubs and things cost money, and blagging, as Billy Hill had found out, required a certain type of person that was prepared to do regular stretches of bird. Both Bill and Dimes had managed to avoid those unhappy holidays. Only mugs go down for long stretches.

* * *

At the end of the First World War, a year after Bill's birth, the Birmingham gang known as the Brummagen Boys, led by Billy Kimber, ruled the racecourse. Their foothold had been established in those courses close to Birmingham but as their gang grew in numbers with hardmen from the Elephant and Castle joining the ranks, their power became stronger and they expanded their influence further afield. They were not bookmakers, their business was straightforward protection. Demanding money with menaces. They spread their demands both to the north and the south. Their MO was simple: the better the pitch occupied by a bookmaker, the higher the levy demanded. Any slowness in paying up would result in the stand being smashed. Any refusal to pay would result in the bookmaker and his assistant being severely beaten.

Like most gangs or conquering armies, success and time provided a soft underbelly. By the early 1920s, the Brummagen Boys found their authority being challenged by an up-and-coming Italian gang led by Darby Sabini and his brothers. Within a short period of time the Italians were appearing on racecourses previously dominated by the Birmingham gang, who found their main source of revenue being curtailed. It soon became clear to everyone that before long a battle must ensue so that the Brummagens could re-establish their control or be deposed by the Sabinis.

The venue, a large pub a short distance from Epsom racecourse, was where they finally came face to face. Within minutes, a vicious battle with razors and iron bars was in full flare, the pub was wrecked and screams, shouting and verbal threats of killing and maiming reverberated throughout the building. On that day, blood flowed faster than beer. It was not the first attack, though. Earlier the Brummagens had ambushed a coach-load of men heading for the Derby. The passengers were dragged from their seats into the road and thrashed without mercy. Within minutes bodies lay unconscious, badly bruised and oozing blood. Victorious, the Birmingham gang retreated, only to find out that they had in fact not inflicted severe punishment on their arch-enemies, the Sabini boys, but had attacked a party of Leeds bookmakers who generally looked towards Billy Kimber for protection.

It soon became apparent to Kimber, who was considered an astute gangland boss, that maintaining control of the racecourses in the south from his base in the Midlands was an impossible task. At a meeting between the two men, Billy

Kimber and Darby Sabini, an arrangement was made. Sabini was to pay Kimber an agreed amount and the racecourses would be carved up. Sabini was to take control of those in the south and Kimber would concentrate on the Midlands and the north of England. But before the meeting ended, members of the Sabini gang burst in and the sound of shots filled the room. In the belief that Kimber was dead, they left him bleeding badly on the floor.

Kimber pulled through and an agreement was finally made after a decisive battle that involved running fights across Bath racecourse which lasted for hours. Bookmakers protected by one gang were beaten, slashed and bludgeoned by opposing gangs. Their pitches were overturned and their books were torn up or set alight. Punters were threatened and chased off, and the troops from both gangs were hunted, ambushed and set upon without fear or mercy. After this, a settlement was agreed but the cost to the Sabinis also now took into account an amount that prevented retaliation for the shooting of Kimber.

Kimber missed operating in the capital and within a few years returned to become a major player in the greyhound scene, exploiting the connections he had established within the Met and the Racecourse Police, set up by the Jockey Club to crack down on the battles that had become a running sore at many of the race meetings. He was even approached by Darby Sabini's brothers to arrange assistance from the police concerning some trouble they were experiencing. This is not to say that the Sabinis did not have their own connections, but as time lapsed and Kimber's gang faded his own individual influence increased.

Bookmaking was a favourite occupation of some members of the Jewish community and to bring them under the protection of his gang, Darby Sabini recruited Jewish hardmen from Whitechapel to fight alongside his Clerkenwell Italian boys, and for a while this proved successful. But, many of the Italian hardmen were supporters of the fascists and followers of Mussolini in their own country. Along with this came the inevitable anti-Semitism. This naturally caused the loss of support from the Jewish community and opened the way for a challenge to Darby Sabini. Harry White and the King's Cross Boys made a move. The Italian gang faced their bloodiest fight yet. The two gangs clashed at Lewes races, a confrontation that proved to be the most vicious of battles in the history of British races. Unlike that at Bath, where much of the violence was intent on destroying pitches, on this occasion it was a straight fight between gangs and saw the introduction of the new weapon – the springer knife, later to become better known as the flick knife. But these small, sharp blades, which were ideal for concealment and street altercations, were no match for the cutlasses and hatchets wielded by White's boys.

It all started when White's boys attacked the bookmaker Soloman and his helpers, which drew out Sabini's men. It became a day when most of the bully-boys, on both sides, would receive the battle scars they would carry for the rest of their lives. As day turned to night, London found itself with a new face at the head of its underworld. A bookmaker himself, Harry White prepared himself for a Sabini counter-bid, but with the onset of the Second World War many of the Italians faced internment and many of the British gang members donned uniforms to be shipped off to fight in a larger arena.

Earlier, sitting in the warmth of the sun's rays on the south coast seafront, Bill had glanced along the promenade, his eyes focusing on the large Hove houses. It was in a flat in one of those mausoleums that Darby Sabini had breathed his last breath, in 1950 — an old, sad man whose unattended funeral reflected his loss of status. At one point he had declared himself bankrupt, despite the fact he had been raking in sums of more than £2,000 per week.

Bill reflected on the wealth that had passed through his own hands over the years and wondered how fortunes could be eroded so quickly.

* * *

Over dinner at a quiet table in Bianchi's Frith Street restaurant, Bill had put forward his proposal for effectively franchising out the criminal activities in Soho. If rival gangs wanted a piece of the action, a price would be levied and an agreement reached, so that it did not interfere with other existing operations. A deal would be struck. Bill knew that if he could get Dimes 'signed up' to this arrangement, he would be well on the way to making Soho a business entity. In return, Bill would provide additional muscle if people stepped out of line and, most importantly, he would negotiate agreements with the police and the local council to allow criminal businesses to thrive without the constant problems associated with the law. Dimes had proved to Bill that he was not only hard, and business-like, but was capable of staying out of prison, a trick that many of the other hardmen lurking on the edges of gang leadership were not capable of, some even waving their record like it was Tin Pan Alley's top tune.

Bill had liked Albert Dimes and the feeling was mutual, but Dimes was his own man. In many respects this was the way forward; each gang leader with his own interests, working as a network, not as a competitor. Competition brought trouble and trouble only brought profit to the press. If Dimes was going to side with either Hill or Spot though, it would inevitably be Hill, as there was definite animosity between members of the Italian community and the Jews. When the Hill–Spot break-up finally came, Spot was left on the outside. The Old Compton Street fight between Dimes and Spot hit the front pages and landed both men in court. But it did not end there. Further attacks on Spot took place and there was an attempt to put Spot away when Tommy Falco, Dimes' driver, was attacked, supposedly by Spot, and slashed down the face as he was leaving Bertie Green's Mayfair club, The Astor. Spot was charged but found not guilty. However, his career as a top London gangster was finished.

The Crazy Gang, as the Italians called the Kray firm, was not a gang that Dimes feared. It was clear to Bill that Dimes was a man in control. Some people, as in legitimate business, like to surround themselves with people weaker than themselves. Bill saw the advantage in dealing with people who could maintain order within their own province. Decisions taken and arrangements made could then be relied upon.

Bill and Dimes were both players and there were few people who were aware how often they talked. Sometimes it was politic for them individually to bad mouth the other to the chaps, but most of the chaps, both knew, could not see beyond where the next few quid was coming from, or who was taking liberties today. Dimes had died of cancer before the death of his little boy, and while Bill was sorry to see him go, he was pleased he did not have to face up to the death of the younger man he had nurtured since a lad. Equally it did not mean Bill considered that Zomparelli hadn't got what he deserved. Then thoughts of the Twins touched the edge of his memories.

'Mr Howard. Mr Howard.' Bill slowly lifted his head.

The smell of brandy, which had seeped from his overfilled glass on to his coat, filled his nostrils. The sound of the Tannoy and cheer of the crowd filled his ears. For a moment he did not know where he was, then slowly the reality of his position fell into place.

CHAPTER TEN

It's a Bloody Liberty

Over the coming months, the spieler in Clifton Mansions, opposite the Prince Albert public house, operated in much the same way as its Electric Avenue predecessor. Big games of faro, craps and poker provided excitement outside the norm of the daily low-level routine. The police were looked after, as were the council. The usual winners tended to continue winning, generally because their playing skills were more finely honed than those who played and continued to lose. The losers remained convinced that their luck would change, and when it did, usually their skill level was not sufficient to take advantage of the situation. It remained Bill's policy to stuff large proportions of the table money into the losers' pockets, so they did not go home skint, regardless of the fact it meant, after ex's, he regularly was left without the price of a decent meal. As with the ups and downs of the gambling, but not necessarily in unison, Bill's health continued to fluctuate. More than a decade had been swallowed up since Bill had approached Michael in the foyer of the West End hotel. Since then life had taken its toll – the loss of his home, the break-up of his family and a new era that had brought change. But more than anything the effects of prolonged heavy drinking over too many years had sucked Bill down.

During this time Mickey Rice constantly kept an eye out for Bill, having admired the power of his punch, having benefited from advice he had offered on such occasions as the upset at The Craywood Club and having prized the ten-shilling note Bill had given him when he was little more than knee-height. It was not a one-way street: Mickey was looking for a new occupation and turned to Bill, who was able to show him the ropes of running a wet fish stall from his experiences of the family business in East Lane. Having enlightened him in the tricks of the trade, Bill then spoke to a south London landlord with a large forecourt and set Mickey up with a Sunday stall on the premises. Over the years Bill had found a pleasure in cooking, so it was not unusual for Mickey to bring over a large rib of beef on his way to set up his stall. With the spieler now regularly closed on a Sunday, Bill would undertake the cooking of a late lunch with all the roast trimmings. But Sunday morning was the pub.

'See the way they have been ripping off our boys, the buggers?' The short, weaselly man in the soft peak cap and none-too-clean stone-coloured raincoat said, drawing Bill's attention to the front page of the Sunday tabloid. A large front-page picture depicted a croupier behind a dice table, around which a crowd of young men, with obvious eagerness, were betting on the result of the next roll. 'They're fleecing our young squaddies on the way back from Germany to see their families. It's a bloody liberty,' the old man added.

Shortly before the man had drawn this exposé to Bill's notice, Michael, Bill's son, had joined him at the bar. Bill looked at Michael, who smiled.

'Those dice tables belong to my son,' Bill told the man quietly.

'I'm sorry, Mr Howard. I didn't know. Truly, I didn't mean to speak out of turn. I didn't mean any offence.' The man was clearly horrified at having unwittingly criticised any friend of Bill's, let alone his son.

'It's OK. It's not what it seems. I sacked a croupier for stealing and next thing another croupier, one of his friends, has gone and sold a story to the newspapers. The maximum bet is 50p and the odds are clearly marked on the table, so it's not a secret,' Michael said, trying to make the man not feel so guilty at having spoken out.

'Sir, I was out of turn, I should have kept me mouth shut,' the man repeated. 'I 'ope everything goes all right for ya,' he added and skulked off to a corner at the other end of the pub.

'I hadn't expected to see you so early,' Bill said, ordering another round of drinks to include his son.

'I stayed in a suite at the Royal Garden last night. I didn't get to bed till almost four, and then shortly before eight I got a call telling me we were all over the front page. After sending out for all the papers, I couldn't get back to sleep,' Michael explained.

'What will happen now?' Bill asked.

'Who knows? The odds are not as good as a shoreside casino but they are a lot better than many licensed betting shops offer on large bets and on evening racing. About the same as a fruit machine, for what it's worth. I'll write a report to the shipping companies, but it's all offshore so there are no legal ramifications,' Michael explained.

On this Sunday morning Bill seemed to be in reasonable health, but before closing time the intake of spirits had reached silly proportions. Drinking brandy like his father, Michael noticed that double brandies were arriving in his glass simultaneously from either end of the long line of drinkers spread the length of the bar. At one point, what Michael thought was a half-pint of beer being placed before him was his own tall glass almost overflowing with neat brandy. Michael wondered how long it would take for Bill to have a major relapse if drinking sessions of this magnitude were again becoming a way of life.

* * *

The day was like most others in Brixton. Bill was shaky and slightly short of breath, Coldharbour Lane was its usual busy self. The weather was overcast and traffic fumes hugged the ground. Bill headed directly across the road, the lights having changed at one end holding up the constant flow, and the traffic from the other running at barely a trickle. Bill had not paid much attention to what was happening on the other pavement and on arrival still did not think much of the black man hanging around outside the door of the pub. Bill's right hand came from his coat pocket, grabbed the door handle and made to pull it open. The door did not budge. At first he thought it was jammed but as he shook it, it became clear from the rattle that it was bolted.

'Tarase clart, marn. Fucking white honky bumba arse, lock door, marn.'

It was only now that Bill paid attention to the jittery black man who pushed him to one side and began pummelling the door. Bill was about to walk off, having seen a figure inside the pub signal to him that he should come back when the person causing the nuisance had got fed up and moved off. But before Bill could leave the scene he felt a sharp pain in his lower arm and side. As he looked down he saw the man's outstretched arm draw back and the blades from a pair of scissors glisten in the light, wet with blood. Bill heard words of abuse or excuse being shouted over the shoulder of the retreating figure and was thankful that although damage had been inflicted, for what reason Bill was unclear, his assailant was not hanging around to finish the job.

The assault, it transpired, was nothing whatsoever to do with Bill, it was purely random. The man with the scissors had been in the pub earlier and, after causing trouble, had been pushed out. When he was seen returning, the landlord had locked the door to prevent him re-entering. Bill had simply been unlucky to arrive at the front of the pub at the same time. The man had only recently been released from a psychiatric institution after a previous unprovoked stabbing. Mickey Rice searched the streets in an effort to locate the culprit and exact retribution, but without success – an outcome that was probably to both their benefits. Bill was not held in hospital for long as the wounds were not life-threatening, but the damage caused to his hand was irreparable. Control of his hand at the wrist was completely lost, the nerve having been severely damaged.

Visits from social services to ensure his wellbeing on release and assist with paperwork associated with a claim to the Criminal Injuries Compensation Board indicated to the health visitor that as far as the State was concerned, William Howard did not seem to exist. This was a status Bill was content to maintain.

'I'll forget about you if you'll forget about me,' Bill told the authorities, but this was not a line they were prepared to accept.

Bill was found a council flat on the main road coming out of Brixton in the direction of the Oval. Neighbours in the block liked Bill as much as he was drawn to them. Loud Jamaican music throbbed the walls night after night. Bill travelled the mile or so to the spieler and the Prince Albert less and less, taking to frequenting the pub nearer his new home. During this period Michael had lost the gaming contract operating out of Dover and had travelled on an extended business trip to Zimbabwe. Bill was again hitting a low point.

Mickey Rice was a regular visitor, along with Bill's youngest son Billy and Jan his ex-wife. With the spieler only operating at a low level and Bill often sleeping throughout the day, he lost touch with many of the chaps requiring his influence. Even the modest funds on which he had been living began to dry up. Not every day was a bad day, but the bad days began to outweigh the good. On each occasion Billy visited his father, Jan would ensure that Bill had everything he needed in the flat and would provide funding for the next few weeks.

Shortly after Michael's return to the UK, he visited his father, who had now started sleeping nightly in the 'day room' of the spieler. For whatever reason, Bill did not mention the attack and concealed the damage to his hand. Despite this, it was clear to Michael that Bill's living conditions and the volume of business generated in the spieler had, over the last few months, taken a considerable downturn. At about the same time, Michael was offered a lease on a Margate basement premises, which had previously been used as a seedy coffee bar. The smallness of the property precluded it from any interest as a potential business, but it occurred to Michael that if a licence could be obtained, it could make an ideal little drinking club which would provide a suitable retirement business for Bill in a reasonably relaxed location.

Michael decided that it would be better to have some positive progress on the project before approaching his father. Within a week he had secured the property and rented a flat overlooking the sea on the beachfront.

'What happened to the casino tables on the ships?' Bill asked when he next saw Michael.

'The report I produced exonerated my position, but the directors of the shipping company felt that the casino operation no longer represented an image they wished to portray. So regardless of the rights and wrongs of the allegations the contract was terminated,' Michael explained.

'What, on all the shipping companies?'

'Well, they did not pull the contracts on the ships out of Portsmouth, basically because they are longer journeys.'

'What difference that make?'

'I think they just thought it was more appropriate.'

'So you've still got those?' It was a question rather than a statement.

'No.'

'Why?'

'It's complicated. Only some of the ships were included in the company I owned. The others were owned purely by the other director.'

'That doesn't sound right. It sounds to me as if you're getting ripped off.' Bill looked at Michael while he was speaking, watching to see his reaction.

'I can't say I was particularly happy with the way it was done. I think I ended up holding the baby. One phone call to say it's over and then no further contact,' Michael said, shrugging it off.

'Look, if he's turned you over, I'll go down to Portsmouth and kill him. My life's over. I've got nothing to lose.'

Michael could have thought that his father was joking, but he knew that he wasn't. All he had to do was give the word and he was certain that his ex-partner would be dead.

'Bill, if you only had an hour left on this earth, I'd value you more than him. He wasn't worth it then and he isn't worth it now. But thanks for the offer.'

Bill looked at his son to see if it really was a subject on which he could wipe his mouth. Michael slapped his father on the arm and told him to forget it. Bill winced.

'What's up with your arm?' Michael asked.

'Some crazy black geezer stabbed me a few weeks ago,' Bill said, the pain obviously still causing him trouble.

'Why didn't you say?'

Bill did not answer, he just shrugged his shoulders as much to say 'what's done is done'.

At this point Michael considered it opportune to put forward the suggestion of the drinker down in Margate.

As Michael had anticipated, Bill was going to need some persuading.

Over drinks and a lunch in the cafe, Michael did his best to make the proposition sound appealing. The fact that it was out of London, away from the hustle and bustle of city life, away from all the aggravation. The fact that Margate was a favourite seaside town with lots of the East End and south London chaps who, once they knew Bill had a drinker down there, would flock down for the weekend, even for a Monday session. Michael felt that this had overcome the 'I don't know anyone' argument, but there were a string of other hurdles.

Michael assured his father that he would be around a lot of the time and that he would sort out a lad to do all the running around and keep an eye on the place on the occasions Bill had to come back to London on 'business'.

'Bill, there's a decent flat down there, you aren't going to choke on traffic fumes and you can pop up to London whenever you feel the need. Why don't you give it a try? If you don't like it, give it a miss. But at least give it a try.'

'I need to visit that animal place again next week. I'll come down then and we'll see how it goes,' Bill conceded.

Michael was beginning to become intrigued about these ad hoc visits to Howletts. He wondered what the rhythm was. He then wondered if Bill had been visiting the safari park on other occasions and only used him as a method of transport when his trip to Margate coincided.

Rather than have the Margate basement shut and not providing cash flow towards the rent while the red tape was being sorted out, Michael decided to open the place as the cafe it was previously. He installed Luke and gave him a bedroom in the flat to ensure that Bill did not feel isolated. He also tried to spend as much time down there himself as possible.

The weather in Margate that summer was unusually good. Most days the sun shone and the seafront seemed to ooze an atmosphere of 1950s British holidays. Luke pottered about in the cafe, which attracted sufficient business to pay the ex's, and every few days went back to Dover to keep in touch with friends and family. Bill had taken on a dandy style of dress over the past few years and did not look out of place in his white shirts, grey slacks, red and black striped blazer and yellow cravat. His days seemed relaxed. A late breakfast, which he cooked for himself in the flat, a brandy and a couple of halves of beer in The Cottage public house, and then most of the afternoon stretched out in a deckchair in the middle of the large sandy beach, reading the newspaper or dozing under a handkerchief neatly protecting his head from the warm sun. Visits to the cafe were generally confined to a quick look round the door as he passed in one direction or another, or when his appetite called for a couple of cheese rolls. As the weeks went by, applications for licences and change of use and all the other red tape were kicked into motion.

Again, during a visit to Howletts, Michael stayed in the car and again a plastic bag was collected by his father. On this occasion, however, Bill asked his son if it would be possible to place the rolled-up bag in his safe until Bill was due to return to London for a few days the following week. Michael agreed, but felt that this request at least allowed him to plant a question. It would have been a lie to have said that he did not feel a little curious. Michael was fully aware that the owner of Howletts, John Aspinall, had a lengthy background in London's illegal gambling. He was, in fact, the first person to have a charge brought against him under the Gaming Act which was subsequently changed in the early '60s. Further changes took place in the late '60s that made many of the small clubs illegal and imposed stringent restrictions on the larger, more professionally operated units.

To obtain evidence against illegal casinos, it was essential for the police to witness the gaming in progress and to see money actually changing hands. John Aspinall and his mother were noted for their high-society gaming parties – however, entrée was tightly restricted to well-acquainted personal friends. It was therefore difficult, almost impossible, for the filth to gain entry and make the necessary observation. Raiding the establishment, a private flat, required sufficient evidence for a search warrant to be obtained. The likelihood of the cash side of the operation being cleared from the table during the time it would take for doors to be smashed down and entry gained made this course of action unattractive. In final desperation, an inspector was ordered to place a ladder outside the Aspinalls' Marble Arch property and balance on the top in an attempt to gain evidence by peeping through a narrow slit in the curtains. A conviction was finally obtained and Aspinall's illegal gaming career was brought to an end.

Years later, John Aspinall, who had two passions, gaming and wildlife conservation, opened a swish Mayfair casino – legal this time – and two safari parks a short distance from the Kent coast. But his earlier prosecution was not to be his last brush with the law.

'So what's with all the toys?' Michael enquired of his father as he took the package for safekeeping.

'Playing games is an expensive hobby.'

Michael remained silent, in the hope the space would persuade his father to elaborate. It didn't.

The money was not hidden or well wrapped. Certainly it was not sealed – bundles of £10 and £20 notes, held together with wide elastic bands and pushed into a brown paper bag, which in turn had been placed in a rolled-up plastic carrier bag. Before stashing it away, Michael shook open the bag and, using a ruler from his desk, poked open the brown paper bag to establish the contents. Father or no father, Michael wanted to ascertain what it was he was being asked to hold. Giving money to someone did not seem to be criminal in itself. Michael felt that it was not cash that had been stolen, as these transactions were not isolated and there had certainly been no outcry today or previously. Whatever it concerned, it seemed to be personal and had the tacit approval of the owner, John Aspinall. Equally, Michael felt convinced that his father was purely a conduit in the transaction. There was no indication that the sum, which he had not counted but estimated to be in excess of £5,000, was destined for his father's pocket, although he felt sure his father would receive a cut, a commission. Michael took one further piece of action to help satisfy his curiosity. He telephoned Howletts.

'Can I speak to John, Mr Aspinall?'

'Who shall I say is calling?' The voice on the other end enquired.

Michael did not answer. He simply replaced the receiver but was convinced that John Aspinall was on site.

A few days later, Bill returned to London and took the package with him. No further visits, to his son's knowledge, were made to Howletts. So from that he deduced that although the payments were regular, they were made over long periods. Two or three times a year, even annually.

★ ★ ★

Shortly after Michael had reopened the cafe, a group of menacing-looking skinheads bowled down the stairs, rowdily pushing and shoving. Michael's attitude was clear – the place might still be a bit of a tip, but he did not want trouble, particularly with an application for a liquor licence pending.

'Yes?' Michael demanded

'Is it open again?'

'Sort of.'

'I suppose you're not gonna want us down 'ere now!' It was a statement rather than a question, the tone clearly indicating that they thought Michael would be confrontational and they might just decide to smash the place up before they left.

'I asked you what you wanted. If I had wanted you to leave, I'd already have told you.'

'You mean you don't mind if we stay?' There was an obvious note of surprise in the voice.

'Subject to,' Michael said.

'Wot?'

'Subject to the same ground rules as everyone else.'

'What's that then?' There was a sneer to the question, as much as to say 'I thought so' or 'Here we go'.

'The house rules for everyone are the same. One, you've got enough money to buy what I'm selling. Two, no bad language or bad behaviour and three, you wear suitable clothing. That's about it,' Michael explained.

'What sort of clothes?' one of them asked, butting in on the tallest of the group, who until now had dominated the conversation.

'Not T-shirts like he's wearing,' Michael replied, pointing at a short, thick-set lad in his early 20s.

'It's not up to you what he wears,' the same lad said, sticking up for his mate and trying to turn the situation from one of reconciliation.

'In here it is,' Michael held his position.

'Wot's wrong with it?'

'I don't like it.' Michael could see that it was the intention of the mouthy one to draw him into an argument on the rights and wrongs of a T-shirt boldly bearing the slogan, 'Kill Jews and Pakies', stencilled across a bright-red cross with a swastika in the centre.

'Look, life is reasonably simple. You want to come in here, you play by the rules, if you don't, you don't,' Michael added.

Seeing they weren't getting anywhere on that tack, it was the turn of the flag-wearing lad to speak up.

'How about our weapons? We used to keep our weapons down here.'

'What weapons? What for?' Michael asked, now sounding more than a little bored.

'Tools, mate. Blades, bars, axes. Whatever we can lay our hands on. If any of them come inta town we 'ave ta sort it. We gotta protect ourselves.'

'Look . . .' Michael was about to explain when Flagman butted in.

'No, you fucking look.'

Five to one didn't look good and it was beginning to seem as though things might at any moment take a turn for the worse. Michael knew he had a pot of hot fat on the stove, and he had made up his mind they were getting it before he was going to get his head kicked in.

The tall one spoke. 'So if he doesn't wear any of his shirts and we don't bring our tools in, we can come down here?'

'As long as you buy something. It's not the Salvation Army. You buy something and behave yourself down here, you're welcome.'

'We're barred from everywhere else. Why you letting us in?'

'I've got nothing against bald people.'

'Do you do burgers?'

'Yeah.'

'And chips?'

'Yeah.'

'Can we 'ave five burger an' chips, three teas, a weak cup of coffee and a Coke? Oh, and can you do an egg on one of the burgers?'

'If you want to sit down, I'll give you a shout when it's ready.'

The skinheads became friendly faces almost every morning and caused a lot less trouble than most two-year-olds in a crèche.

Luke and Bill got on well. Bill seemed to enjoy cooking a meal each evening but showed signs of irritation when Luke bowled up late. At one point, Michael thought he was going to hear his father tell Luke that it was in the oven and it was probably dried up by now. But he refrained, although he did speak to Michael about the washing-up.

'I'm happy to cook Luke a meal, he's a good lad, but I'm not doing his washing-up as well.'

Michael passed on the complaint and after that Luke did his best with the domestic duties, although it was obviously an alien concept.

The situation with the skinheads took a turn for the worse weeks later, shortly before the Bank Holiday weekend. Luke went to check the toilets before opening and found some ceiling tiles had been displaced. On further investigation, a stash of iron bars, machetes and kitchen knives had been lodged in the roof area. They had not been there long. The fingermarks around the ceiling were recent and they would have been noticed a lot sooner. Besides, the whole place had been thoroughly cleaned and given a coat of paint before reopening. Michael instructed Luke to drop the lot in the messiest swill bin at the rear of the premises, while he stood on the door. It was not long before the faded blue denim group appeared on the opposite corner and crossed in the direction of the front door.

'Sorry, lads,' Michael said, standing in the doorway, as they approached.

'You not opening today?'

'Yes, we're open, but I'm afraid you're not allowed in,' Michael informed them.

'Why, we ain't done nothing,' they protested.

'I found all the weapons you left down here. And that was part of the deal. No weapons. So I'm sorry, but you're barred.'

'We didn't use them in your place.'

'I said no weapons. I kept my side of the agreement, you didn't keep yours.'

'So we can't come in any more. Is that what you're saying?'

'That's right.'

'How long for?'

'Forever. You're barred, you're barred.'

'We weren't going to use them down there, we just stored them there. There's going to be lots of trouble over the weekend and we need to have them handy to protect ourselves.'

'That's not my problem. We had an agreement. You broke it. Not me,' Michael said.

'Well, can we at least go down and get our things?' one of them asked.

'I threw them out.'

The whole group bristled.

'If you're so scared of wandering round town without them, they are round the back in the garbage. Be my guest,' Michael pointed round the corner. 'The back gate's not locked.'

'Fair enough, mate. You were straight with us. But I'm warning you, there's going to be a lot of trouble this weekend. I'd close up if I was you,' the tall one who had been reasonable from the beginning said. To Michael's surprise he had been quite chatty about mainstream issues, movies and books throughout the period they had been welcome. He certainly had not seemed the archetypal racist skinhead thicko. Later, after they had gone, Michael was not sure if they had sorted through the bins, but Luke had assured him that, if they had, the weapons were buried so deep they probably would not have to use them in any battle, the smell would have been enough. The smallest of the group, who had been wearing the offensive T-shirt on the first visit, came back and from the top of the stairs, shouted down, 'You're all fucking dead,' before scarpering.

'What was all that about?' Bill asked, having recently surfaced.

Michael explained.

'I'll stand on the door for the next few days,' Bill offered.

'OK, but keep Luke up there with you and give me a shout if it looks like there is going to be any trouble,' Michael insisted.

Michael was putting more time into this project than he had ever intended but he hoped that once it was finally up and running, it would need little further attention and would mean that he could pop over to Margate regularly to see his father, without the drag of traffic that was routine when he visited him in London.

Friday, Saturday and Sunday were beautiful. The beach was packed and the arcades were busy with day trippers. No sign of the predicted war. Bank Holiday Monday was the day this event traditionally happened, dating back to the mods and rockers in the early 1960s. Monday morning, Bill was on parade early. As soon as the pub opened a brandy was called for and guard duty was taken up, neatly pressed shirt and slacks, polished pointed shoes, Paisley cravat lightly tied and glass in hand. Walking down the stairs, Bill seemed to have taken on the air of the camp prison baron played by Noel Coward in *The Italian Job*, but this was a thought Michael refrained from voicing.

Luke alternated between the entrance and the kitchen. Crowds started to build and the possibility of the resort enjoying a bumper weekend looked assured. By the early afternoon, Bill reported that he had seen the group of skinheads pass on the other side of the road on at least two or three occasions. It was also noticeable that other groups were gathering and there seemed to be considerably more police vans floating around than there had been on the previous days.

The cafe was busy and Michael realised Bill had not been down for a break for over two hours. Walking up the stairs, Michael saw a group of high-laced feet crowded around the door. There was little doubt that, even if they did not belong to the skinheads who were barred, they were owned by a similar ilk. Not wishing to inflame a situation, Michael stood out of sight ready to pounce if it went off. Minutes passed, there seemed to be some talking going on but voices were not raised. Then Michael saw the boots turn and move off.

'Problem?' Michael asked his father, as he stepped alongside him into the sunlight.

'No. The Wimpy is full and they wanted to know if there was anywhere off the front where they could get something to eat,' Bill explained. 'Everywhere they're queuing out the doors.'

'Where did you send them?'

'I told them to try The Cottage. The food in there is pretty decent.'

'Where's Luke? I thought he was up here with you?' Michael asked.

'Good doorman he is. He disappeared about an hour ago when he saw another lot heading this way,' Bill said, laughing.

'You should have called me.'

'It wasn't a problem.'

Luke finally reappeared another hour later.

'Where have you been?' Michael asked, as no explanation seemed to be immediately forthcoming.

'I was hungry, so I went back to the flat to get something to eat. You know what I mean?' Luke replied.

'What do you mean, you went to the flat? This is a cafe. If you wanted something to eat, there's plenty of food here,' Michael said in disbelief.

'Yeah. But I thought . . .'

'You mean at the first sign of trouble, you left a 65-year-old man to deal with it on his own. I think you'd better get up there so Bill can get a break. He'll probably give you a clip round the ear when he sees you.'

'I was just going to get a burger,' Luke said, with a touch of disappointment in his voice.

Michael shook his head and sent him off in the direction of the door.

Later, when they all returned to the flat, the food that Bill had got in had been eaten and Luke was again in the doghouse.

Over fish and chips that Bill insisted Luke queue and pay for, they discussed the damp squib that the skinhead threat had turned out to be. This chat seemed to open Bill up to conversation.

Luke spent fewer evenings in Margate, feeling after his fall from grace he needed to be on his best behaviour around Bill. So Michael and Bill spent long evenings, well into the early hours, talking. For no apparent reason, Bill seemed suddenly prepared to talk of his life, right back to the early years. Michael was happy to just listen, not asking questions but occasionally butting in to clarify details on which his father had not made a point clear. For fear of his father clamming up, there were specific questions, one being the cash pick-up from Aspinall, that Michael was dying to ask, but for the time being he was prepared to soak up the history. The biggest confusions were over people's names. Almost always, only first names were used, and the amount of Billys, Jimmys, Ronnies, Frankies and the like sometimes made things more than a little complicated. The cardinal rule of not asking what people do, as Michael was introduced to various chaps, was also confusing.

'Have you met Jean? She was a top shoplifter.'

'Well, I met a Jean, but no one mentioned if she was a shoplifter or not.'

Over the coming weeks, listening to his father's tales of Soho, London's West End and the escapades in south London became Michael's passion. At every free moment, the opportunity to glean further information was exploited – lunch in a corner of The Cottage, a couple of deckchairs on the sands or the insistence of driving Bill up to London, where on previous occasions his father's assurances that the train was fine would have been accepted.

* * *

Bill was due back in Margate for the Thursday Brewster Sessions. The licence was to be in Michael's name, but it was an important day for the future of the drinking club and equally important if Bill was to have any future in Margate. As it transpired, the justices required further information concerning the proposed layout of the premises, so no decision was made. But what slightly concerned Michael was that Bill had not shown, and by the evening he had not even made contact. Michael was concerned, almost disappointed, that his father had not at least phoned to find out how things had gone. With no word, Michael expected Bill to turn up sometime over the weekend.

Nothing. It was Tuesday before Bill phoned and he made no mention of the messages Michael had left in various pubs he knew Bill would be likely to frequent. All in all, the excuse provided seemed to Michael pretty thin.

'I thought it would be better if I stayed out of the way. If anyone clocked me in the back of the court, it might have gone against you,' Bill had explained.

Bill had not asked his son the outcome. He had given no reason why he had not come down and just stayed away from the court. Also, there was the reference to 'you'. Michael had never considered this deal to be anything other than his father's. Michael had the feeling something had happened and that something was going on. He didn't know what had changed, and he certainly knew better than to ask his father. The change was noticeable even to Luke who, despite his lack of domesticity, really did get on well with Bill. They seemed to be comfortable in each other's company. Bill had become very elusive and the odd couple of days back in London had been stretched. Now Margate was getting the short end of the straw.

The weeks passed and the summer was succeeded by the damper, more blustery days of autumn. The holidaymakers were gone and the holiday seemed to be over. Business in the Brixton spieler was, according to Bill's conversations with his son, picking up. Christmas was still far enough away for those wishing to gamble their money, as long as their losses were not too great. Plus, the anticipated boom in Christmas takings always put a stoke of optimism in the thought that sufficient funds would materialise, which was not always the case prior to the summer break.

Bill was due back in Margate early on the Tuesday morning. He did not arrive and he did not phone, which was the same situation as on the day of the Brewster Sessions. Michael was beginning to have second thoughts about Bill's commitment to Margate as a retirement plan, and to the idea of the drinker as a pension. This called Michael's own commitment into question. The last thing he wanted was to get stuck in Margate. He was not looking to retire. If the project did go ahead, Michael did not envisage Luke being prepared to sit in there once the initial enthusiasm had worn off. Luke needed to be around people and soon lost interest in anything if he was left to his own devices.

Bill finally telephoned Michael late on the Thursday morning.

The call came from inside Paddington Green Police Station, a high-security unit, which was generally known as the police station used for interviewing terrorists. Numerous suspected IRA members operating on the mainland were among the previous occupants and dangerous criminals, particularly those who it was felt might have had the connections to mount an escape, were held here. As far as Michael was aware, Bill hardly remained in this category.

'Hello, Michael, I'm being held at Paddington Green,' Bill had told his son.

'I got brought in on Monday. That's why I couldn't get down to see you.'

'Are you all right?'

'Yes.'

'Do you need a solicitor?' Michael asked.

'No. I've got one who looks after a lot of the chaps in here. He's even better than Blok. They can't keep me much longer. I'll stay up here for the rest of the week and then come down Tuesday next week,' Bill said. His voice did not seem to hold traces of concern over his position.

'If there's anything you need, get the solicitor to give me a ring,' Michael said, and a moment later the line went dead.

* * *

Two extremely bold armed robberies had taken place in 1983. The Security Express robbery in London's Curtain Road, Shoreditch, netted the robbers a little short of six million pounds. The high-security building was known by the workforce as Fort Knox because of the impenetrability of the unit. On 2 April, the security was breached by a gang whom the press dubbed 'The League of Gentlemen', after the British film starring Jack Hawkins. To obtain the co-operation of the staff, who were quickly bound by the raiders, petrol was poured over them. The haul weighed more than five tons and the security firm offered a £500,000 reward. In January 1984, Johnny and Jimmy Knight – brothers of Ronnie – were arrested. Both were found guilty in 1985. Johnny received the heavier sentence of 22 years.

Seven months or so after the Security Express job, an armed robbery was carried out at the Brinks-Mat depot, Heathrow. The raid took place on 26 November, and netted the gang gold bullion worth £26 million, a total of more than 6,000 bars. On this occasion, the person on the inside did not need to be encouraged with a petrol shower. Tony Black worked at the depot and was the brother-in-law of the south London villain Brian Robinson. In February 1984, Black was given a six-year sentence, lightened possibly after naming Robinson, Mickey McAvoy and Tony White, who were also brought before the courts. Robinson and McAvoy were both given 25 years at the Old Bailey. White walked free.

The police had achieved a limited level of success, but none of the bullion had been retrieved. In an effort to trace the proceeds of the robbery, Kenneth Noye and Brian Reader came under scrutiny. The consequences of this and an SAS-style of surveillance resulted in the stabbing of the police officer John Fordham on the front lawn of Noye's Kent mansion. Later, when both Noye and Reader came to trial for the killing, they were acquitted.

Whilst there was no suggestion that Bill was connected to either of the robberies, he had been arrested and questioned for threatening potential witnesses and an overriding concern that he would become involved in jury nobbling when a case was brought to court. The team of detectives who had arrested Bill, detaining him in Paddington Green, wanted to talk to Jan, Bill's ex-wife. Jan had already sold The Ellerslie Hotel, and moved to The Winter's Tale, a pub in the beautiful Oxfordshire countryside on the Burford crossroads, an area popular with the racing crowd. They travelled to the pub to interview Jan, who they believed had been using the name Reader and might have been connected to the man they were keen to charge with handling the stolen bullion.

The person called Reader, whom the police were interested in, was a person Jan has said that to the best of her knowledge she has never met and had not had any previously knowledge of his existence. Her previous marriage to Bill, her association with Freddie Foreman, who was later brought back from Spain to face charges in connection with the robbery, plus her connection with the name Reader had brought her into the net cast in these investigations.

Despite days of interrogation, the police were unable to bring a charge of attempting to pervert the course of justice against Bill. At the time he was arrested, he was an old man whose drinking and high life had caught up with him. If he were to be described as feeble, it might have been a little too strong, but the police did not arrest him purely on his MO. They were well aware of the state of his health, yet they remained more than convinced that he still held sufficient power, both with the hardmen of the underworld and within the corruptible element of the judicial system, to threaten the sanctity of the British legal system – a capability to set powerful criminals free.

* * *

Two weeks later, Bill decided it was time to talk to his son Michael and to be truthful. Returning to Margate, Bill was reluctant to say what he had on his mind. He sat with Michael in the flat talking, sharing bottles of wine and cooking food, while the wind and rain lashed the windows and drove the few remaining tourists into the pubs, fast food restaurants, bingo and machine arcades. Margate had returned to the typical English resort in winter.

Most of the conversations were confessional, Bill talking again about his past life, often repeating stories he had told Michael on various other occasions. At no time did Michael refuse to hear the details repeated or show any sign of boredom. His attention was total, there was no thought in the back of his mind of 'here we go again'.

Before long, Michael brought the possibility of a book into the arena. He did it tentatively, allowing it to be laughed off if the idea gave offence. To his surprise, Bill was compliant.

'If you want to do it and can find someone interested, go ahead. *The People* asked to do my life story years ago, but I wasn't interested,' Bill explained.

Maybe this was a sweetener. He knew Michael had put a lot of time into attempting to set up the Margate drinker and until now Bill had not found the right moment to tell the truth.

'Michael, while we are talking about the future, I don't think I'm going to be able to spend the time in Margate that this drinker is going to take. If you want to go ahead with it, I'm happy to come down regularly, but being down here all the time is difficult. And Luke is a good kid but he's not reliable. He's young and wants to be out and about. I don't think it is worth keeping the flat on.'

'Look, Bill, it was for you. There's no point in doing something you're not going to be happy with. There's no sense in it,' Michael said, without disappointment.

'I've still got to be in London and I don't want to let you down.'

'It's OK, really,' Michael assured his father.

Dinner, a few days later, signalled the end of a short era. The restaurant at the casino offered reasonable fare and good value, although Michael did wonder if they would both be given the opportunity to finish their meal before being ejected – Michael, for having worked in the industry, and Bill for his multitude of gaming convictions. As it transpired, their presence in the dining-room did not bring them into the realm of the pit boss, the man usually charged with ensuring the punters are of good character and limited knowledge. It was a time that could have been missed without either of them ever having noticed. But the fact that it hadn't seemed, without verbal verification, important to both men. A shared time.

In the flat, Bill opened a bottle of red wine and Michael put on a kettle of water for coffee. As he returned to the sitting-room, he saw his father relax back into the sofa, his chin fall on to his chest and his hand, in the process of lifting the bottle to pour the content into the glasses, drop. The bottle spun out of control on to the carpet, the red liquid gulping from the neck.

'Bill!' Michael's voice was loud and clear from the doorway, but the sound did not stimulate a reaction.

However, within seconds, almost as if nothing had happened, Michael watched his father jerk back and pick up the bottle as if he did not realise what had happened.

'Are you all right?' Michael asked. Stupid question, he thought.

'Just slipped out of my hand,' Bill replied, clearly unaware that he had not only dropped the bottle, but for the shortest of moments had also been unconscious.

Michael sponged up the wine from the floor and Bill, using his neatly folded handkerchief, dabbed spittle from the side of his mouth. There was a persistent dribble down his chin. Michael skipped the coffee and after a single glass of wine each, he suggested that they call it a day.

The following morning Michael had it in the back of his mind to take Bill to the doctor, or at least ask his own doctor to come out. But before the subject could be broached, Bill had checked out the times of the trains and booked a cab to the station. Michael made an appointment for himself on some pretext and mentioned his father's problem at the end of the consultation.

'Well, it sounds as through he might have suffered a very slight stroke,' the doctor said. 'It's difficult to be sure without tests being carried out. But that might cause him more anguish than it's worth. There is very little that can be done. If you can persuade him to stop smoking and cut his drinking right down that's the best thing.'

Michael had mentioned that his father was still attending the hospital following the stabbing incident so the doctor felt confident that any problem with his blood pressure would be monitored by the doctors there. It occurred to Michael that the blackouts Jan said Bill experienced during the months shortly after Bill had moved out of The Ellerslie Hotel may not have been totally due to his body craving alcohol, but were possibly the result of a series of minor strokes.

Within a few days, Michael had jettisoned the Margate opportunity. It was clearly not what Bill wanted and had the potential of becoming a millstone. That done, Michael went back to visiting his father in Brixton. If he had wanted out of south London, Michael realised, his father would have bought a villa in Spain years ago and sat on the beach there. Brixton was not a place where Bill had found himself washed up and near destitute, but a place where he felt at home, a place where he had elected to spend the last days of his life. Be that sooner or later. And if Brixton tore itself apart around him, then so be it, they would go down together.

Scouse, Mickey Rice and Bill's younger son Billy, who was now growing into a young man, all regularly kept an eye on Bill while he slipped back into his daily routine. Breakfast in the cafe, a liquid lunch in the Prince Albert, the afternoon and evening socialising, and doing any necessary business in the spieler. More often than not Bill slept in the spieler, in preference to the flat.

Michael's visits were once again punctuated with trips overseas and short liquid lunches with his father as he went to, or from, Heathrow.

* * *

Michael did not know if his hand gripping the counter had been noticeable. He could not be sure of what the barman had actually said. Michael had arrived unannounced and Bill was not in his usual spot. The enquiry of the barman seemed positively direct, but Michael faltered over the words. He thought the barman had said that they had found him hanged this morning and everyone was over at the club. Michael did not like to say, 'Did you say Billy Howard hanged himself?' Instead he refused a drink and walked across the street. Pushing through the iron gates and brushing the street dirt from his hand, he walked through the open door and up the half-lit stairs. Michael could hear feet

walking around, but there was no sound of talking behind the closed door
leading into the card room. He glanced sideways at the door leading into the
room where his father slept. The door was ajar but there were no lights on.
Taking a deep breath, Michael turned the handle in front of him and walked
in. The person in the room must have been bending or kneeling behind the
coffee bar – apart from that the room was empty.

'Scouse,' Michael called.

The person behind the bar lifted his head.

'What are you doing here?' Bill asked, putting his hand on the top of the
counter and using it to help lever himself from the floor.

'I was passing and I had a bit of extra time so I thought I'd pop in for a few
minutes. I looked in at the pub, they said someone was dead or something.'

'Scouse topped himself,' Bill told him.

'What!'

'Completely out of the blue. I mean, it must have been something he
planned but he didn't mention to anyone he was thinking of doing it. He just
told all his friends to meet him down the pub last night. He bought everyone
a drink and then went home and hanged himself,' Bill explained.

'Does anyone know why?'

'He was due in court today and he said he couldn't stand the thought of
going back inside.'

'What for?'

'Nothing much, shoplifting, non-payment of a fine. He probably wouldn't
even have gone down.'

'Bit extreme.'

'Yeah, well, I think there was something to do with a woman he was in love
with as well. I think he thought she might have left him if he went down.'

* * *

Michael spent much of the coming year as opening manager for a large hotel
group in Scotland. He spoke on the telephone to his father from time to time and
called in once or twice when he returned south for the odd couple of days. During
this period, Bill seemed to fluctuate both in health and in mental attitude. On
one occasion, calling into the spieler unannounced, Michael found Bill sleeping
on a bare mattress, his body covered only with a couple of old coats. Bill said that
the woman that did his laundry had stripped everything and taken it to the
launderette, but Michael was not convinced that this was the truth.

Bill's youngest son, Billy, was making regular visits, according to the
landlord at the Prince Albert, and Jan continued to ensure that Bill always had
money sufficient to stock the cupboards with food. On one visit, she pawned
jewellery so that Billy could try to re-establish his father's accommodation
above the level of squalor in which they had found him. All efforts were short-

lived. There seemed to be a general malaise enveloping his whole situation. Washing and shaving were now becoming spasmodic. Sleeping in his clothes, clothes in which Bill had always shown pride, was a regular event.

In an effort to break the monotony of the routine, Bill's brother and his wife took Bill for a drive to Brighton in the hope that a change of scenery would kick-start some sort of hope, some sort of will to live, into the man they loved and had laughed with over many years. The drive to the coast was in total silence. Bill sat hunched in the back seat, making no sound and taking no notice of his surroundings. Finally, Bill's brother could stand it no longer. Pulling the car over, he popped into an off-licence and purchased a half-bottle of brandy. Bill drank straight from the bottle, and it was only after the alcohol took effect that there was any noticeable change in his demeanour.

Several visits from a social worker, follow-up action on the Criminal Injuries Compensation Board award that could not be paid out until the injury had been fully treated, thereby allowing an assessment of the long-term damage, made little difference. Bill, now unable to erupt violently, simply refused to cooperate. An interim payment of £1,000 was made, but where the money went remains unclear. It brought no physical change to Bill or his surroundings.

With Scouse no longer at Bill's side, Mickey Rice was probably as close as anyone to the man he had admired since his childhood. But it was apparent that all the help in the world had little chance of success without Bill being prepared to help himself.

Michael made calls from Scotland, leaving messages. The calls were rarely returned. One call Michael made to the pub caught Bill at the bar. They talked for more than half an hour, but at no time did Bill give any indication of his current poor state.

'How are things going up there? It looks a really nice place,' Bill chatted, having seen the brochures of the Irvine Skean Dhu hotel Michael had posted down a few weeks earlier.

'It's going really well, but they have got a few problems with their other hotel that has just opened in Glasgow. Three hundred and thirty-six rooms, in the centre. It looks as though I will be going up there after the New Year to sort things out.'

'What's the problem?'

'Lots of things. Major staff problems, problems with one or two of the contractors over snagging, and a top man at head office has said it's likely I'll be getting demands for protection money.'

'What's the threat?' Bill asked.

Michael could hear his father's attention heighten.

'The suggestion is that some of the building workers will be persuaded to come out on strike if payments aren't made.'

'You worried?'

'Not especially. It's just one more thing to deal with. Head office said to let them know and they would have a word in someone's ear if anyone tries it on.'

'Phone me tomorrow,' Bill said.

'What time?'

'About the same time.'

The following day Michael telephoned his father, and for once Bill was true to his word. The barman said just a minute and was obviously passing the phone across. Michael thought his father's voice was shakier than on the previous day. He seemed really short of breath. Probably he would not have come out had he not arranged to be there. The call was not lengthy. Bill gave his son a number and a name and told him that the man was expecting his call.

The following day Michael rang the number he had been given. The person who answered was not the person he wanted to talk to. He telephoned again the day after and again the day after that. Finally, they spoke. He arranged to meet with his contact in the hotel bar. Sitting opposite him was the man his father had said was the Governor in that part of the world.

'You won't get many of the locals coming in here, Michael. It might be fashionable down south to have bare wood floors, but up here the smart places have now just put in fitted carpet.'

The comment was right. The bar was fitted out with the theme of a clipper sailing vessel, with lots of polished wood, and encouraging customers to frequent the place proved extremely difficult.

'Your father and I always got on well the few times we met. I don't know what he was quicker with, a blade or a card from the bottom of the pack.'

'Did he come to Glasgow a lot?'

'I think other than Gold Cup week, Ayr races were his favourite. Long time on the train. Plenty of time to fleece a school.'

As they were finishing their drink, Michael offered a refill. Arthur Thompson declined.

'Mr Howard,' he said with a smile, his thick dark eyebrows furrowed across his face, 'said you were expecting some problems?'

'Just a whisper,' Michael said and explained what he had been told.

'Well, it's none of my making,' Arthur Thompson replied, rising ready to leave. He stretched out his hand, took Michael's and shook it firmly. 'I've promised your dad I'll keep an eye out for you, so if you have any trouble just refer them to me.'

Michael invited him and his wife back for dinner and later sent him an invitation to a boxing dinner, but neither was taken up. There was a great deal of trouble at the hotel not long after Michael's meeting with Thompson, but not extortion and not of the type that required support from Glasgow's Governor.

* * *

The deputy general manager found Michael wandering the upper floors of the hotel. Forty-two pages of snagging to date, the inspection of the newly built city block seemed to be never ending. There was constant discussion with staff about the problems they were experiencing in their departments. Bringing the property, staff and service up to a five-star standard was proving mammoth. Michael took the call in his private office at the top of the building.

'I'm sorry to have to tell you, Michael, Bill died in hospital three days ago.' It was Henry, Bill's brother. 'I'm sorry I didn't phone sooner, but I had difficulty finding a telephone number for you. Finally, I spoke to the hotel you were at previously and they gave me this number.'

Michael did not really know what to say. 'Thank you for letting me know' somehow seemed inappropriate.

'When is the funeral?' Michael asked.

'The day after tomorrow. There's no need for you to come down.'

'It's not a problem. I can come down tonight on the sleeper or hop on a plane.'

'There's no need, Michael.'

'How long had he been in hospital?' It was a question that just seemed relevant at the time.

'Three days. He was in a pretty bad way. It was pitiful to see. His going was for the best really, Michael. Young Billy phoned me, he went to see him and found him in a bad way. So we got him straight into hospital. Nobody thought he was going to die,' Henry explained.

'Henry, look, it's not a problem, I can jump on a plane,' Michael again offered.

'It's not worth it, Michael. Billy's here and there will be a few other people, it'll only be a few of us.'

'OK, well, if I can do anything let me know, you've got my number now and thanks for letting me know.'

Michael replaced the receiver and contemplated whether or not he should phone his mother. There had been two deaths in the family within weeks and he wasn't sure if telling her at this time was the right thing to do. Finally he picked up the phone.

'I've just had a call from Henry. Sad news I'm afraid. Bill's died.'

'I'm sorry. Are you all right?'

'Yes.'

'Will you send some flowers from both of us?'

That was about the extent of the call. Michael arranged for a huge number of flowers to be delivered to the undertakers in time for the funeral. He had not attended his stepfather's and his uncle's funerals, both of whom had died only weeks earlier. 'Funerals were for dead people.' It was a line written by Ian Fleming, and Michael guessed it was about right.

EPILOGUE

Face to Face

In 1954, Vera married. Her new husband moved from Ireland with his son, who was the same age as Michael, and they set up home in the Kennington Lane flat. Within a year, an opportunity to move to the Cotswolds presented itself and preparations to move the family were put into motion. Vera approached Bill and requested that he sign adoption forms. It was a decision he took reluctantly, but he believed it would be in the best interest of his son. This was the last time he was to meet with Michael until the day at The Regent Palace Hotel, a fact that he insisted to members of his family and later to Jan, that he had not realised would be the result of his agreement.

Michael Howard was seven when he was taken with his mother and stepfather to the room in the court where the formalities were to be finalised.

'Do you understand what is happening here today?' the judge asked Michael.

'Yes,' Michael replied.

He knew he was there to have his name changed. But as for fathers, he did not really understand the concept. He did not think, looking back years later, Bill had ever been a father in the recognised sense of the word. The papers were signed and minutes later, holding his mother's hand, Michael Connor walked from the court.

A few Sundays later, at Saint Anselm's Church in the Kennington Road, I was christened Michael William Connor. Doused with God's blessing for a second time! My godfather, Mr Mackeand, was a London policeman, whom I am told was of impeccable integrity. My godmother was my mother's childhood friend, Rita, wife of Alby Day a noted boxer and bookmaker, who in years to come would use Bill's services. Friends told my mother that, during the service, they had seen Bill loitering around outside, but he had not come in and was gone when we emerged.

I do have memories of Bill from when I was very young, but only snatches. That is probably because he was only ever around for what would today be termed soundbites. I remember meeting him when walking with my mother in the Kennington Park Road. A street vendor on a cycle was peddling by and he stopped him and bought me a stool and two pearl-handled pen-knives. I was probably four or five at the time. The stool I still sat on to do my homework ten years later. The knives, well, one I lost within months while on holiday on the Isle of Wight with my grandmother. I was throwing it into the hotel lawn and it bounced into the flowerbed, never to be seen again. It did occupy a great deal of the holiday searching for it. I considered it an important possession. The second sat on my desk at home for many years and slowly I took less interest in it. Then one day it was gone. But it was one of those days you can't put your finger on. By then I was in the Scouts and probably owned a Bowie knife or the like.

My mother kept in touch with Bill's brother by phone and went to London to see friends at every opportunity. Toys intended to be Christmas presents from Bill, via third parties, were apparently returned. Clean break etc. But it always puzzled me why in my early teenage years, when my stepbrother and I were taken to London on an outing, we were always paraded through the seedy streets of Soho, as they were at that time. The odds of bumping into Bill, although it never happened, must have been phenomenal. A bet that even Bill would have put money on!

Applying for my first job, I had every intention of working in London, but I was dissuaded from this and took a job in the Midlands, well out of harm's way. Or so you would have thought. My eye fell on a young lady and I was soon receiving her boyfriend's thoughts on why I should forget it. It transpired that he worked as a bouncer at Bertie Green's Astor Club in London's Mayfair. Ignoring the advice, it was not long before I was treated to a visit from a couple of heavies who were frequent guests at this notorious gangland watering-hole. I recently wondered if they appeared in these pages without my knowledge. I knew Bill was involved with this crowd and I could easily have dropped his name, but I didn't. Another chance missed, and I don't think either of us ended up with the girl.

My mother did see Bill again a couple of years before he died. She telephoned Bill's brother and an arrangement was made to meet one Sunday morning in East Lane. I think it was at a time when I was working overseas. Bill had been helping on the stall and they went across the road for a drink. I think they just talked about old times. Bill said that he was impressed by the way she had brought me up, which pleased her greatly. As far as I'm aware that was the last time they met. She did tell me that she found it hard to realise that he had become an old man, even if he did still have a sparkle in his eye. They would both have been in their early '60s then, and I guess my mother, some 20 years later, is probably more sprightly now than Bill was then. Life's excesses have a way of not only catching up, but taking over.

Jan was extremely upset by Bill's death, regardless of the fact they had split up almost a decade earlier. She told me she had been visiting Bill with Billy a few days before Bill died and was shocked by the state that he was in. By then she had sold The Ellerslie Hotel and moved to Oxfordshire. She had insisted Bill return with her and Billy so that he could be looked after and have a nice place to live. But he refused, promising to make the journey in a week or so, after he had kept an appointment with the doctor. All the animosity Bill had felt, at their divorce, time had put into perspective. Jan took Bill's dog and left Billy to keep an eye on his father and make arrangements for the move. The following day, Bill could hardly breathe and Billy got him into hospital.

Mickey Rice visited Bill every day. The only other person Mickey saw at the hospital was a very smart woman, whom he said he did not recognise. She could have been Bill's long-term girlfriend, an American woman Jan knew Bill had received letters from over many years, or the wife of a High Court judge that Bill had met in a Soho restaurant. On her insistence, Bill had escorted her around the more seedy spielers and drinking clubs, with which she was fascinated. Mickey was the last person to see Bill alive. Bill looked well, not drinking – nothing smuggled in – eating and sitting up in bed. Nobody thought he was going to die, but a few hours later and without warning, he was dead.

Billy was devastated. Jan made all the funeral arrangements and picked up all the bills. He was buried in a south London cemetery, with a few close friends and family at the graveside. One of his two daughters, with whom he had kept in touch over the years, attended. The other had been adopted as a baby and I assume was unaware Bill was her real father.

I did not find anyone who had a bad word for Bill. Strangely, even his enemies seemed to like him. Jimmy Evans, author of *The Survivor*, the man who had come close to shooting Bill in the toilets of Winston's Club, had later become a friend. 'He became a bit of a dandy in his old age, despite his bad health and drinking. Bill was a father you can be proud of,' he told me.

Ronnie Knight, the man my father considered his protégé, failed to take up the mantle. For a while he probably stepped into Bill's shoes, but before long had chosen Spain in preference to Soho – or prison, which finally caught up with him, as it did with many contenders. He had escaped a long incarceration in 1980 when Queen's evidence was given by Maxi Bradshaw incriminating Ronnie and Nicky Gerard. Both Gerard and Knight faced a jury on charges related to the Zomparelli killing and for a while Ronnie was allowed bail on a surety of £250,000. Both were eventually found not guilty, and while Bill no longer commanded a great deal of muscle, he would certainly still possess the ability to demand favours of the judiciary and nobble juries. Whether this was the case here, it is impossible to say, but Knight was free. Nicky Gerard was serving an unrelated sentence, but after his release he was shot and killed. An agreement had been reached with the Italians that Knight would not face an ongoing vendetta, however, the same had not been negotiated for other people involved in the Zomparelli killing. Knight was guilty and was prepared later to boast of the fact. Gerard was shot, not by an Italian, but by one of his own countrymen. And it is likely the reason behind his murder is not all that it would first appear.

In the mid-'70s I interviewed a close friend of Alfredo Zomparelli, himself responsible for a killing in a Soho club, and much of the background on the Knight/Italian Tony killings came from him. It was interesting to obtain the Italian angle on the events that took place early in the decade. Years later, after Bill was long gone, I bumped into my contact again, still mooching around Frith Street.

'So who runs Soho now?' I asked.

'Now? Nobody. The place is finished,' he replied, an air of disappointment in his voice.

'This is me you're talking to. There must be someone,' I said. Over the years I had always kept my British and Italian connections separate. He did not know and I have no reason to believe that it is still not the case, that I am Bill's son.

'The only people you pay now is the filth.' And with that he ducked into a betting shop that had once been an Albert Dimes business.

There are still a few unanswered questions which I had intended gently teasing out of my father when the moment was right. But time and death . . .

The Aspinall cash collections remain a mystery. I can't imagine it was connected with the zoo operations. To my knowledge, John Aspinall was only involved in two other areas – the ownership of a West End casino and hosting the last supper for Lord Lucan. The police did search Howletts zoo as part of their investigation into the disappearance of the peer and possible links with the murder of his children's nanny, but no evidence was reported to have been found. Some arrangement with a third party concerning the casino is an obvious possibility.

The other question must be what happened to the millions of pounds that passed through Bill's hands over the years. Not paying for anything, Jan picking up the bills for many of the day-to-day costs, should have allowed a substantial accumulation of money. Certainly the police were dipping their hands deep into the pot and certainly Bill was over-generous with even the most unlikely characters, but this hardly explains the fortunes lost. The situation, though, was not unusual. Darby Sabini was said to have been collecting £20,000 a week at the peak of his power, but he died in reduced circumstances. Spot, it has been said, ended his days working as a kitchen porter in a large hotel and was finally sacked for stealing a little meat. Similar stories surround the death of George Raft. They indicate that he died in the back room of a cheap Florida motel where he was working as a night porter. Others spent long years in prison and found when they were released, if they were released, everything had slipped away. Then there were those who died during the rigours of their chosen profession, and they were many.

The one answer Bill was able to provide was the real name of the man Ronnie Kray referred to as 'The Old Fox'. Reggie Kray divulged this gimlet of information quietly to Bill, not at the time of their trouble with the rent boy, but while being held in Brixton Prison. Strangely enough, he did so without being prompted. From what I understand, Ronnie apparently considered the nickname for Lord Louis Mountbatten to be common knowledge.

Shortly after Bill's death, my career branched out into consultancy for the hospitality industry and journalism, developed through food and travel writing. For many years, the prospect of writing my father's biography hovered on the horizon, and over those years, mountains of information accumulated. There are many little stories I have not included, purely because at some point you simply have to draw the line. But one still brings a smile to my face.

Looking back at my teenage years, it was one of the strangest moments, and probably as true today as it was then. I was eating a salt beef sandwich in the Nosh Bar opposite the Windmill Theatre, in Soho.

'You look like Bill.'

I looked over at the skinny newspaper seller, sitting a few feet away from me. His comment had nearly caused me to fall off my stool. Did he really know I was having a sly wander on the off chance I might casually bump into the man I had not seen since my childhood, and if an old newsvendor could make the connection, then maybe my father might notice the resemblance if I passed him on the street.

'Bill who?' I asked, needing to be sure about this.

'If you don't know who the Bill is, mate, you don't have any right being in Soho,' he answered with a look of disgust.

NAMES GLOSSARY

JOHN ASPINALL: Aristocrat, notable gambler and founder in 1957 of Howlett's Safari Park. Charged under the Gaming Act, but later opened a West End casino.

BURT BACHARACH: American composer and songwriter, famous for songs including 'Raindrops Keep Falling on My Head' and 'What the World Needs Now'.

FULGENCIO BATISTA: President of Cuba, although more a dictator, until overthrown by Fidel Castro in 1959. Close links with American mafia, particularly Meyer Lansky.

SAMUEL BELLSON: Brighton bookmaker and club owner. Charged with bribery of police officers.

ALAN BENNETT: Operated the Astor Club, aka the Bucket of Blood, in Brighton. A known thief and main prosecution witness in the 1957 Brighton Conspiracy Case.

JUDAH BINSTOCK: Solicitor and financier with close ties to the American mafia, offshore banking and British casino operations.

EDWARD BLAND: Police Detective Chief Superintendent of South London. Close friend of Billy Howard.

JOHN BLAND: Police Detective Sergeant handling The Craywood Club investigation in Streatham in 1967.

ANTHONY BLOK: Solicitor favoured by many career criminals. Offices in London's West End and Camberwell.

LORD BOOTHBY: Conservative politician, homosexual lover of Ronnie Kray.

BRUCE BRACE: Operated top London West End nightclub, Winston's, with Billy Howard.

BOB BRUCE: Manager of the Craywood Club in Streatham, South London.

BRUMMAGEM BOYS: Early 1920s gang, from Birmingham, led by Billy

Kimber. Fought with Darby Sabini and his Clerkenwell Boys over control of the south of England racecourses.

ANGELO BRUNO: Philadelphia (US) mafia boss in late 1970s. Publicly murdered by a hit man in 1980.

MICHAEL CAINE: British actor, gained fame in 1960s films *Alfie*, *Zulu*, *The Italian Job* and *The Ipcress File*.

HARRY CAPOCCI: see Joe Collette.

CAPONE BROTHERS: Al was the most famous of these American mafia brothers and, along with Ralph, gained infamy during the Prohibition battles of 1920s Chicago.

CARTER FAMILY: A Peckham family, whose brothers were affiliated to the Elephant and Castle boys, and who had close links with Jack 'Spot' Comer.

FIDEL CASTRO: Cuban revolutionary who overthrew Batista in 1959. Subsequently became dictatorial leader and ousted mafia.

CELLINI BROTHERS: Close associates of Meyer Lansky. Strong involvement in mafia control of The Colony Club, Berkeley Square, London. Eventually deported from the UK.

CLERKENWELL BOYS: Gang headed by Darby Sabini, from area of London with strong Italian connections.

JOE COLLETTE: In 1941, arrested for the affray that led to the murder of Little Hubby Distelman, in Soho. Convicted, along with Albert Dimes and Harry Capocci, of unlawful wounding of Eddie Fleicher.

JACK COMER: See Jack Spot.

RUSS CONWAY: British pianist 'with a golden smile'. Chart toppers included 'Sidesaddle' and 'Roulette', both in 1959. Friend of Dorothy Squires and Michael Holliday.

PETER COOK: British comedian, co-owned The Establishment club in Soho with Dudley Moore. Comedy writer for the political satire magazine *Private Eye*.

HARRY H. CORBETT: British actor who played the part of Steptoe's son in the major TV comedy series. Close friend of Billy Howard.

RONNIE CORBETT: Entertainer at Winston's club, who went on to gain fame through *The Two Ronnies* comedy act with Ronnie Barker, and other top television shows.

GEORGE CORNELL: A member of the Richardson gang, noted for calling Ronnie Kray 'a fat poof'. Shot dead by Ronnie Kray, March 1966, at the Blind Beggar public house, Whitechapel.

CRAZY GANG: Italians' name for the Krays' gang.

BILLY DANIELS: Singer, popular in Las Vegas (US). Starred in West End production of 'Bubbling Brown Sugar'. Friend of Billy Howard.

GEORGE DAWSON: East End scrap dealer and millionaire, associated with Chris Glinski, who moved in business circles with Judah Binstock.

ALBERT DIMES: Scottish Italian, head of the Italian firm in Soho. Friend of

Billy Howard. Involved in 'the fight that never was' with Jack Spot.

BIG HUBBY DISTELMAN: Brother of Little Hubby Distelman. Police informer.

LITTLE HUBBY DISTELMAN: Soho club doorman, murdered by Antonio Mancini.

ELEPHANT GANG: Known as the Elephant Boys, notorious gang of south London hardmen from the Elephant and Castle region of the city. Prepared to hire out their muscle to other gang leaders.

JIMMY EVANS: Author of *The Survivor*, published by Mainstream Publishing. Gunman for Joe Wilkins. In later life, became a friend of Billy Howard.

PETER FINCH: British actor who received an Oscar for his role in film *Network*. Also known for numerous other film roles including *Sunday Bloody Sunday* and *The Nun's Story*.

IAN FLEMING: Author of James Bond 007 books.

FREDERICK FOREMAN: South London villain, associated with the Krays. Charged with murder of Frank Mitchell. Skipped to Spain after Security Express robbery 1983.

CHRIS GLINSKI: Professional witness, associate of George Dawson.

BERTIE GREEN: Owner of The Astor Club in London's Mayfair district.

CHE GUEVARA: Noted face on poster of guerrilla fighter. Fought in the Cuban revolution with Fidel Castro. Later killed in South American conflict.

JOHN HAMMERSLEY: Police Detective Inspector, second in command Brighton CID. Charged with others that over a ten-year period he accepted bribes. Defendant in the 1957 Brighton Conspiracy Hearing.

TREVOR HEATH: Police Detective Sergeant Brighton police. Charged with others that over a ten-year period he accepted bribes. Defendant in the 1957 Brighton Conspiracy Hearing.

BILLY HILL: West End gang leader, sometimes allied with Jack Spot. Main influence in London's gangland during 1930s, 1940s and 1950s, operating regularly as a thief.

MICHAEL HOLLIDAY: 1950s and '60s crooner, friend of boxer and club owner, Freddie Mills.

BILLY HOWARD: The Soho Don. As a boy and by those who also used his surname, he was known as Billy. But close friends usually referred to him as Bill.

BILLY HOWARD (jnr): Youngest son of The Soho Don.

JAN HOWARD: See Jan Macauley.

MICHAEL HOWARD: Eldest son of The Soho Don.

GERALD HOWARD QC: A leading member of the prosecution team in the 1957 Brighton Conspiracy Hearing.

HOWLETT'S: Safari Park in Kent (UK), opened by John Aspinall.

SIR HARRY HYLTON-FOSTER: Solicitor General. Head of the prosecution team in the 1957 Brighton Conspiracy Hearing.

JOHN KILBY-GROVES: Police Detective Chief Superintendent found guilty of passing restricted information to Sir Eric Miller, which benefited Judah Binstock.

BILLY KIMBER: Gangland leader, thought by some to be The Soho Don, prior to Billy Howard.

RONNIE KNIGHT: Head of the Knight firm. Considered by Billy Howard to be his protégé as Soho Don. Married to actress Barbara Windsor. Found not guilty of conspiring to kill Zomparelli. Fled to Spain following Security Express robbery.

THE KRAYS: Reggie, Ronnie and Charlie. Notorious East End villains. Took over and expanded Jack Spot's manor.

MEYER LANSKY: Financial brain behind American mafia, responsible for setting up casinos in Las Vegas (US) with Bugsy Siegel in the 1930s and 1940s.

JOAN LITTLEWOOD: British theatre director, famous for numerous productions including *Oh! What a Lovely War*. Directed one film, *Sparrows Can't Sing*, starring Barbara Windsor.

LORD LUCAN: Aristocrat, gambling friend of John Aspinall set. Disappeared after his children's nanny was brutally murdered and he became the chief suspect. To date no trace of Lord Lucan has been found.

LUCKY LUCIANO: American mafia 'boss of bosses' — don of dons. He worked closely with Meyer Lansky.

ANTHONY LYONS: Licensee of Sherry's Bar in Brighton. Charged with others that he bribed police officers. Defendant in 1957 Brighton Conspiracy Hearing.

ARCHIE MACAULEY: Father of Jan Macauley. Ex-Arsenal football player and manager of Norwich City Football Club.

JAN MACAULEY: Wife of The Soho Don, Billy Howard. Mother of Billy Howard Jnr.

TONY MANCINI: Part of the Italian gang in London. Found guilty and hanged, in October 1941, for the murder of Little Hubby Distelman.

BERT MARSH: Also known as Pasqualino Papa. Friend of Albert Dimes and George Dawson. Often represented Italian-American mafia interests in the UK.

PATRICK McGOOHAN: British actor. Starred in *Dangerman* and *The Prisoner* TV series.

JACK McVITIE: Known as 'The Hat'. Was stabbed to death by Reggie Kray.

THE MESSINAS: Five Maltese brothers who controlled vice in the West End during 1940s and 1950s.

SIR ERIC MILLER: Head of the Peachy Corporation and friend of numerous Labour politicians. Business transactions with Judah Binstock.

FREDDIE MILLS: A former world light heavyweight boxing champion and Soho nightclub owner.

FRANK MITCHELL: Known as 'The Mad Axeman'. Considered highly dangerous and unstable. Frederick Foreman admitted carrying out his murder.

DUDLEY MOORE: British comedian, actor and musician. Starred in US film *Arthur* with Liza Minelli and co-owned The Establishment club in Soho with Peter Cook.

ROGER MOORE: British actor. At one time married to singer Dorothy Squires. Made his name playing 'The Saint' in the TV series of the same name, and in the James Bond films.

ERIC MORLEY: Noted for promotion of Miss World competition and directorships in casino and leisure operations. His name has been linked with Judah Binstock.

SIR OSWALD MOSLEY: English aristocrat, supporter of Hitler's Nazi party. Founder of British 'Blackshirts' nationalist organisation.

LORD LOUIS MOUNTBATTEN: Great-grandson of British monarch Queen Victoria. Naval officer, Viceroy of India 1947. Died in 1979, when the Irish Republican Army set off a bomb on his fishing boat.

RUDOLF NUREYEV: World-famous Russian ballet dancer.

COLE PORTER: American songwriter, famous for show tunes, notably 'Night and Day' made famous when sung by Fred Astaire in the film of the same name.

PRINCESS MARGARET: Sister of British monarch HM Queen Elizabeth II. Noted for attending wild parties during her younger years.

JOHN PROFUMO: The Secretary of State for War when he was involved in a political and sexual scandal in 1963 which has since been referred to as The Profumo Affair.

GEORGE RAFT: American actor of 1940s and 1950s, specialising in gangster roles. Associated with American mafia leaders, front man for mafia interests at The Colony Club, Berkeley Square, London.

PAUL RAYMOND: West End club owner, noted for his Soho Revue Bar and an array of glamour magazines.

MICKEY RICE: Friend of Billy Howard during the latter part of his life.

THE RICHARDSONS: Brothers Eddie and Charlie, head of a notorious South London firm. Jailed for torture shortly before the Krays.

CHARLES RIDGE: Chief Constable of Brighton police. Charged with others that over a ten-year period he accepted bribes. Main defendant in 1957 Brighton Conspiracy Hearing.

DANNY LA RUE: Female impersonator, West End club owner. Top attraction at Winston's Club at the beginning of the 1960s.

DARBY SABINI: Head of Italian firm, prior to Dimes. Wide-ranging interests on the racecourses.

LUKE SANGSTER: Friend and colleague of Michael Howard.

RONNIE SCOTT: Jazz musician, prolific gambler and owner of the world-famous Ronnie Scott's Jazz Club in Soho.

BUGSY SIEGEL: Mafia colleague of Meyer Lansky and responsible for starting the mafia-controlled Flamingo Hotel in Las Vegas (US). Assassinated by the mafia when profits failed to materialise.

TOMMY SMITHSON: Fairground boxer, ran illegal gambling at the dog-tracks and owned a spieler in Soho.

MICKEY SPILLANE: American thriller writer, noted for private detective Mike Hammer series started in the late 1940s, later used as the basis for an American TV series.

VICTOR SPINETTI: British actor, worked in Joan Littlewood's productions and starred in various TV and film roles from 1950s to date.

JACK SPOT (COMER): Jewish gangster, who controlled London's East End and had criminal interests in the West End during 1930s, 1940s and 1950s.

DOROTHY SQUIRES: Welsh-born singer, popular in 1950s and 1960s with songs such as 'Rain Rain Go Away' and 'Say It With Flowers'. At one time married to actor Roger Moore.

STANISLAVSKI: Founder of an acting school in New York (US), proponent of an acting system later to be known as the Stanislavski Method or Method Theatre.

ARTHUR THOMPSON: Head of powerful Glasgow firm.

TOLAINI: Italian family, owners of The Latin Quarter Club, Soho.

THE TWINS: Reggie and Ronnie Kray. See The Krays entry.

UPTON PARK GANG: Gang from area of London with same name, headed at one time by Jack 'Spot' Comer.

HOWARD VOKINS: Chairman of the Bench in the 1957 Brighton Conspiracy Hearing.

JOHNNY WARREN: Also known as Bobby. Part of the Whites' gang.

GEORGE WALKER: Friend of Billy Hill. Developed Brent Walker, a major leisure, hotel and casino operation during the 1980s.

THE WHITES: A gang headed by King's Cross bookmaker Alf White, assisted by his three sons. The gang went up against Spot in 1947 and came off badly.

BARBARA WINDSOR: British actress, starred at Winston's Club. Went on to become identified closely with the *Carry On* films, and more recently the British TV soap *Eastenders*. At one time married to Ronnie Knight and friend to the Kray twins.

VERA YOUNG: Mother of Michael Howard.

ALFREDO ZOMPARELLI: Italian-born protégé of Dimes. Nicknamed Italian Tony. Killed David Knight and was himself shot in revenge killing in Soho in 1974.

Terms Glossary

AWOL: Absent without leave – military term.

BANGED UP: In prison or locked in a cell.

BARON: Powerful prisoner, often based on the baron's ability to supply tobacco or drugs to fellow inmates.

BETTING: Gambling, especially on races.

BILL: Police – Old Bill.

BINS: Eye glasses, spectacles.

BLACK MARIA: Police van, used for transporting prisoners.

BLAG: Rob, steal.

BLOW: Cannabis.

BOBBY: Policeman.

BOYS IN BLUE: Police constables. Any policemen.

BRASS: Prostitute.

BREWSTER SESSIONS: The session at court to grant alcohol licences.

BROWN BREAD: Dead.

BUBBLE: A Greek or Cypriot – rhyming slang bubble and squeak.

BUNG: A bribe.

BUSY: Interfering too much.

BUTLIN'S: Holiday camp – slang for easy life.

CAF: Café, cafe, cafeteria.

CAGE: Staff room for girls working in hostess club.

CASH COW: Business that produces large amounts of cash.

CHAPS: Villains.

CLARET: Blood.

CLOCKED: Seen.

COPPERS: Police.

COUNT (THE): Casino term for cashing up at end of night.

COUNTRYMAN: Operation Countryman. Police corruption investigation carried out by Dorset police, focusing on Metropolitan police in 1978.

COZZERS: Police.

CROAK: Die.

DAILY SKETCH: British newspaper, no longer in print.

DAY PASSPORT: No longer available. Issued on demand from post offices.

DEGENERATE: Usually applied to compulsive gambler (mainly US).

DEMOB SUIT: Cheap suit given to military when they finished service after the Second World War. Also small cash payment made. Derived from demobilisation.

DIPSO: Alcoholic.

EX'S: Expenses.

FACES: Known people in the criminal or police circle – also Chaps.

FAG: Cigarette (UK).

FARO: Card game, betting on sequence of cards.

FEEL HIS COLLAR: Arrest him.

FENCE: Handler or buyer of stolen goods.

FILTH: Police.

FITTED UP: Having false or manufactured evidence used to charge or convict someone.

FORM: Police record. Also applied to horse racing, the racing form being the performance and essential details of each horse in the race.

FRAME (IN THE): Shortlisted, for example, for getting arrested – betting term.

GIVE UP BODIES: Give names (with consent) of those involved in criminal activities to police, in return for favours.

GLASSHOUSE: Military prison.

GO OFF: Happen for example a robbery or fight.

GOUT: Painful medical condition which includes inflammation of joints, usually toe and ankles.

GRAND: One thousand pounds or dollars.

GRASSED UP (TO BE): To have incriminating evidence given to the police about a crime you have committed.

HANDS UP: To accept liability or involvement.

HATTON GARDEN: Area in London noted for gold and jewellery shops.

HIGH ROLLER: Big spender or gambler.

IRA: Irish Republican Army – terrorist group.

JUNKET: Organised gambling tour or trip, paid for by a casino.

KALOOKI: Rummy-style card game, probably of Greek origin.

KNOCKERS: Antique dealers who knock on doors to ask if people have furniture to sell, in the hope of buying something valuable for very little.

KNOWLEDGE: Exam taken by London taxi drivers, to test their knowledge of locations and routes in the capital.

LADIES' FINGERS: Okra – vegetable.

MANOR: Area.

MARK HIS CARD: Let someone know, pass on information, warn.

MEAT-RACK: Metal pavement barrier in Piccadilly, at end of Regent Street, outside the underground station by the Regent Palace Hotel, London. Used by rent boys as a pick-up point.

MET (THE): Metropolitan Police. The Police Force for London.

MILKY: Weak – as in milky tea.

MINICAB: Unlicensed taxi – allowed to pick up customers by telephone order, but not to pick up in street.

MISE EN PLACE: French kitchen term for preparation.

MO: Modus operandi – method of operating, trademark.

MP's: Military police (also MP Member of Parliament)

NICK: Police station/prison, or to steal

NICKED: Arrested or stolen.

NICKER: One pound sterling

NONCE: Child molester.

OLD BILL: Also Bill – police.

OLD FOGIE: Old person.

ONER: One hundred pounds.

ON THEIR TOES: On the run – usually from the police, but also from someone wishing to exact revenge.

PADDIES: Irish.

PALACE (THE): Buckingham Palace, British Monarch's official residence in London.

PENSION (TO BE ON A): To receive on-going payment for name being associated with project or club, or for providing protection.

PIT: Area where gaming tables are located – casino term.

PONY: £25 when referring to money, or rubbish goods (rhyming slang, pony and trap – crap).

PORRIDGE: Time spent in prison, prison sentence.

PROS: Prosecution.

PRUDENTIAL: Traditional life insurance company that collected premiums on a weekly basis, door to door.

PUNTERS: Name applied to gamblers, but now often used more widely to indicate buyers in a market. Often connotations of being slightly gullible.

PUNTO BANCO: Gambling game, variation of Baccarat.

QUID: £1, sometimes called a 'nicker'.

RED CAPS: Military Police – army term.

RED NECKS: People with small-town and chauvinistic attitudes.

RENT – RENT BOY: Young gay male prostitute.

RESULT: To get what you want or better than you expected.

RUBBER HEELS: A10 – police corruption squad.

SANDS (SINATRA AT): Casino in Las Vegas – title of Sinatra record.

SARSAPARILLA: Herbal drink – sometimes alcoholic.

SCRAN: Food.

SCREW: Prison warder.

SCREWING: Breaking into and entering a property without permission.

SHAMPOO: Champagne.

SHILL: House player used to encourage or discourage other punters in a casino.

SKINT: Having no money.

SMUDGES: Fingerprints.

SNAGGING: Listing problems, unfinished or badly done building work.

SOUTHPAW: Boxing term for left-handed.

SP: Information or background (from racing term 'starting price').

SPIV: See Wide Boy.

STRAIGHTENER: A punch or a bribe to wise him up.

SWEENEY (THE): Metropolitan Police Unit dealing with serious crime. From rhyming slang Sweeney Todd.

TANNER: Six old pennies – 6d or sixpence.

THROW IN THE TOWEL: Boxing term – give up.

TIPPED OFF: To have received information about something that is due to happen.

TIR: Transport International Register – a large, heavy truck.

T'PENCE: Two old pennies – 2d.

TUMBLE: Catch on. Understand the situation.

UPPERS (ON ONE'S): Having a hard time or having no money.

VITESSE: Sports car.

WENT OFF: Happened – usually a fight or robbery.

WHACK: Cut or share. (American – kill).

WIDE BOYS: Spivs. Usually refers to men selling things cheap or on the black market, or offering something too good to be true.

WIPE YOUR MOUTH: Finish with something. Forget it. Let it lie.

WISE UP: To understand a situation.

WONGA: Money.

WOODEN TOP: Police constable.

YID: Jew, from Yiddish.

CASH EQUIVALENT: 1d: = less than half a new pence

12d (One shilling): = five new pence

PURCHASING POWER: 3d is approximately equivalent to £1 in today's money

In 1916, the average price of a pint of beer was 3d

In 1999, the average price of a pint of beer was £1.73

In 1952, the average wage was £7.11.00 pw

In 2002, the average wage was £21,000 pa

Average price of a house £250 in 1952

Average price of a house £100,000 in 2002